Native's Guide to New York

other books by Richard Laermer

NATIVE'S GUIDE TO NEW YORK (FIRST, SECOND, AND THIRD EDITIONS)

GAY AND LESBIAN HANDBOOK TO NEW YORK CITY

BARGAIN HUNTING IN GREATER NEW YORK

GET ON WITH IT: THE GAY AND LESBIAN GUIDE TO GETTING ONLINE

Native's Guide

TO

New York

**ADVICE WITH ATTITUDE FOR
PEOPLE WHO LIVE HERE—
AND VISITORS WE LIKE**

◆

Richard Laermer

**Fourth Edition
Completely Revised and Updated**

W. W. NORTON & COMPANY
NEW YORK   LONDON

For information about permission to reproduce selections from this book, write to
Permissions, W. W. Norton & Company, Inc., 500 Fifth Avenue, New York, NY 10110.

The text of this book is composed in Horley Oldstyle
with the display set in Industria + Frutiger Black
Composition by ComCom
Manufacturing by Haddon Craftsmen
Book design by BTD / Mary A. Wirth
Icon art by Mary A. Wirth

LIBRARY OF CONGRESS CATALOGING-IN-PUBLICATION DATA
Laermer, Richard, 1960–
Native's guide to New York : advice with attitude for people who live here—and visitors we
like / Richard Laermer. —4th ed., completely rev. and updated.
    p. cm.
Includes index.
ISBN 0-393-31810-9 (pbk.)
1. New York (N.Y.)—Guidebooks. I. Title.
F128.18.L32   1998
917.47'10443—dc21   97-47585
CIP

W. W. Norton & Company, Inc., 500 Fifth Avenue, New York, N.Y. 10110
http://www.wwnorton.com

W. W. Norton & Company Ltd., 10 Coptic Street, London WC1A 1PU

1 2 3 4 5 6 7 8 9 0

**This fourth edition is dedicated to ex-New Yorkers everywhere.
Come home. All is forgiven.**

—RICHARD LAERMER, THE '90S

Acknowledgments

Thanks to Ellen, Jessie, Jonah, and Karen for helping ensure we actually finished this. And to Bob Richter for keeping the office afloat while I was writing. Whenever that was. Also to the same players: Suki John, Ilene Diamond, Jonathan Herzog, Morgenstern/Metcalf, Grandma, Lou and Gloria, the Columbia Business School, which I remember fondly (yeah . . .), and Natalie.

Thanks also to:

- Alane Mason for having the foresight to continue. Don Rifkin saved the day. And Lisa Swayne! And Bruce Karp.

- Hillary Clipner for keeping the Native's Forum alive.

- And of course, Pat Clifford (X) who helped me with a lot of information.

- Thanks to Donna Black, David Culbertson, Kim Jones, Kelli Souply, and those other people at CompuServe who ushered a difficult sys-op through an even more difficult project ("Smoky Basement"?).

- And to the folks at Native's Guide To New York On CompuServe who aided in providing ideas . . . and so much more. Oh, I forgot to say thanks to CompuServe for providing the impetus for that.

- And Rich Holmstrom for no known reason.

- And to Ric Matamoros for the memories *(really)*.

- To Steve Bradley. Thanks.

And finally, many thanks to those who provided photographs:

- The Empire State Building, courtesy of David Whitworth.
- Garibaldi's statue, courtesy of Rich Santalesa (c/o www.richnet.org).
- The croissant makers in the window, courtesy of the author.
- The Gucci bag on the wastebasket, courtesy of Brien Foy.
- And the montage, courtesy of Susan Chan and Hillary Clipner.

Noo Yawk . . .
Just the way I pictured it
Skyscrapers and everything!

—STEVIE WONDER, "INNERVISIONS,"
LIVING FOR THE CITY, THE '70S

. . . BROADWAY at night was breathtaking: the towering skyscrapers are covered with brightly colored illuminated signs that blink and change with the most unheard-of, marvelous rhythms. Streams of blues and greens and yellows and reds changing and leaping into the sky, higher than the moon, blinking on and off with the names of banks and hotels and automobiles and film companies. The motley crowd of bright sweaters and bold scarves rising and falling in five or six different streams, the horns of the cars together with the shouting and the music from the radios, and brightly-lit airplanes passing overhead with ads for hats, clothes, and toothpaste, changing their letters and playing trumpets and bells. It is a magnificent, moving spectacle put on by the boldest, most modern city in the world.

—FEDERICO GARCIA LORCA, A LETTER WRITTEN HOME,
NEW YORK, THE '20S

Codicil(s)

NOTE TO READERS:

Don't say we "should have put this in." In New York on any given night—allegedly—there are 3,285 places to eat; 431 places to dance; 140 places to see some sort of show . . . the list goes on. It's all subjective. Besides, this is a fourth edition so things have been taken OUT! Meanwhile, I checked and rechecked the phone numbers, but places move and DO go out of business (particularly with usurious landlords).

And also, note that all area codes are 212 unless otherwise noted; there's a rumor that sometime in 1998 a NEW Manhattan code of 646 for new numbers will come into existence.

More change notes: You will notice e-mail addresses/Web site URLs are listed in this edition. Sometimes, yes, these change; usually a forwarding address will appear on your browser if the Web server's amended. If this is not the case, smack 'em.

And for those who care:

I request some help. I want to make the next edition, which will probably roll off the presses in a few years, perfect or more so. My e-mail address is: nativeguy@yeahwhatever.com. Or write to me at W. W. Norton, address on the copyright page in the front.

Contents

Food

Nighttime

Appendices and Stuff

Key to Icon Art

   RICHARD'S FAVORITES

   OLD, BUT DO IT ANYWAY (JUST ONCE!)

   TRUE TOURIST ATTRACTIONS

   ENDANGERED SPECIES

   TOO TRENDY TO TAKE SERIOUSLY

Introduction—City of Innumerable Possibilities: Some Tips For the Ones Who Know

Propelled onto the street one recent summer night, I went looking for something to do. But what? I thought about it for a long moment.

As a reporter whose main subject is New York, my slate was pretty filled with ideas of intriguing things to do. First I thought maybe a long subway ride out to Brighton Beach, Brooklyn, for a gigantic Russian meal at the Odessa (718-332-3223). Nah, it was already 9:00 P.M.—no way could I eat that late.*

Then it hit me: It was a Tuesday in the middle of the summer. I could go sit in on a special chamber music concert at the Washington Square Music Festival (for information about concerts, call 431-1088). Yeah. I headed into the Village.

A giant Greek coffee shop had all its lights on, yet there were no customers inside. I looked at the sign in the window: Food. Music. DJ. Beer. Wine. Live Entertainment. Liquor. Appetizers. Falafel.

Whoah. It was too much to take in. Nobody who goes out for an evening wants to deal with such variety. In this town, we go out for a reason. We

---

* In 1989, when I first wrote *Native's Guide*, eating that late was easy. Guidebook writers are not as immortal as you think!

want somewhere to talk, maybe we'll eat a little, find some entertainment in a club or on the streets. But all-in-one? That's a shopping mall mentality that rarely works in New York City.

So it was no wonder that, when I looked at the window a week later, the signs at the coffee shop were gone. The owners had seen the problem. Now the window read simply: Falafel. Beer. Cheap.

I remembered one night in a similar coffee shop, when a friend from out of town asked me to express my feelings for the city. Except for a brief sabbatical called adolescence in New Jersey, I had never left this place, and I can't bear to do so. My life's blood and state of mind are in the home city of New York.

For people who don't live here, that doesn't say anything. Everyone always wonders why? Why not another city, a town that is just as active? Well, that question is hard to answer. You either love New York with a blind, passionate love, or you don't. But here are some stabs at responding to it:

New York changes its likes and dislikes often. This city changes at such an incredible pace that not even people whose job is to keep up can do so. Fast living courses through the blood of true New Yorkers (as opposed to the untrue ones, who just get what they need here and move on). Yet many would-be-fast-livers who've called New York home for years do not use this city to anywhere near its potential.

It's a challenge to keep in touch with what's in. I like to think I do it. One never knows!

So I got into a subway and without warning, I acted like a New Yorker: I had a sudden urge to go way uptown, where the music's always good.

(Let's talk about the underground. Subways, since last edition, are so-o much easier to use; every station has a slider for the Metro Card—an absolutely brainless way to use the subways. Instead of waiting on line you just buy the darn thing and—voilà!—you can actually take buses, something that always seemed so ridiculous; I mean, who has exact change *ever*. Besides, while I'm being parenthetical, a Gold Metro Card costs the same as a regular and allows for free transfers within two hours. Go, ask, use.)

Since I was enjoying my card-induced subway ride, I went all the way to

Harlem and had a drink.* During conversations at this place (in biz since the 1940s), nearly everyone commented that they loved local places like this (Lenox Lounge); it's just darned impossible to find out where such things are.

It's easier to be taken to an event, or read about it afterward.

How do I stay informed? I write everything down, get on every list, hope the mail's not junk. What's up with residents/visitors who won't buy a 49-cent memo pad?

If you take the time to remember something you will discover that loyalty has paybacks: A decent clerk or store manager or restaurant owner will never feel you have taken him or her for granted. Get serious! Keep the notebook with you, jot down the names and addresses of places that you like. It's so easy, you will think you're cheating.

And why do we live here if not to take advantage of all the things we happen upon, right?

I look at this place as a big concrete slab with adventure around every turn. There isn't too much green, though if you read this guide carefully you'll discover green or blossoming places where you won't believe you're in New York. But most of the city is concrete-stable—it's always there, and unless you're clumsy, it will never slip you up. Speaking of stable, have you been to Claremont?† This is the last of Manhattan's once horse-filled stables. Lessons are not expensive and you can ride a horse along beautiful Frederick Law Olmstead bridle paths. But be fast, or you'll find many riding spots gone forever—endangered species, you know. (And I discovered Chelsea Piers [Pier 59, North River], an expensive downtown newcomer that touts sports, sports, sports, will now host indoor horse riding.)

Again, loyalty.

New Yorkers move quickly. The city is filled with high structures, not many small ones (though the tiniest are a blast to locate). Huge buildings are powerful sights that emit energy, which dwellers seem to thrive on. I often

---

* The drink was at the Lenox Lounge, 288 Lenox at 125th Street, an old-fashioned though newfangled art deco lounge with jazz and a great crowd (427-0253). "Harlem Swings with Jazz" here.

† 175 West 89th Street, 724-5100, quite a place for horse lovers.

wonder if the amount of frenzy here is directly proportional to the huge structures we live amid.

New York is one of the greatest cities. New York is not London, which is prettier. It's not Philadelphia, where U.S. history stares at you from every corner. Nor is it Detroit, with its sometimes bustling industry. It's not as culturally "in" as Paris. And it isn't as ethnically entrenched as Miami. Each of the other cities has traits that deserve respect, but what stands out in this city is the sum of those qualities feeding off each other. Paris, Hong Kong, and Buenos Aires all *want to be* New York!

The city is an island unto itself, plus several boroughs of superlatives. People sit around and yawn and say they're bored, but I don't buy it. To understand a great city, you have to live it. To live it, you have to use it. I am sure you are one who says they are aware of everything—"leave me alone, why should I use a guidebook?" is the cry of the know-it-all.

So, tell me, what about those canals inside the Canal Street train station? These are the fabulous art pieces installed in 1997 so that people won't forget how water-ific the subway station is . . . not. The artist who installed them commented in typical New York fashion: "Hey it's Canal Street!"

Often the problem isn't that the city is boring, but that you're in a boring state of mind. How, I wonder, could anyone get bored when this New York is the most active *verb* in the world. (John F. Kennedy said it best: "Most cities are nouns, New York's a verb.") In New York even the laws are changing—we're able to wear a bathing suit publicly and it's not a misdemeanor. (I kid you not.)

Last word on being boring—which, by the way, is a sin—and then I'll stop boring you: I always feel like a broken record when I say this, but if you work, go home, and see a film on the weekend, you'll definitely be bored with New York.

You may have seen the ad for New York culture in subways: the words— "If this is all there is, go live in Pittsburgh"—and the visual was a no-brand video and a few Chinese food containers!

As the record skips, I tell people to stop waiting on long lines for Jim Carrey movies and see what else is going on. There are a surprising number of events that, more than anywhere else in the world, can stimulate the stubbornest of tastebuds. *Flashdance* was a fantasy!

This *Native's Guide* is for those who already live here, and for the brave who at least are willing to give it a shot, for the long or the short haul. Rather than point out the essence of things that are already popular attractions, I wanted to find the unhyped great events, places, and activities, and bring together knowledge of lots of events from longtime residents.

So that summer night on my way back downtown to my original destination, I heard the music from nearby Washington Square, but before I got there, I suspected that I hadn't really answered the question about my love for New York. I started thinking about DOING this book yet again.

Too much thinkin' can make you antsy. I stood there and thought, hmm. I was rubbing my chin remembering the fab shave I'd had that day at The Art Of Shaving.* There you can get your whisks done professionally or buy all kinds of fancy stuff for beards. What better way for a man to pamper himself . . . it's the guy version of a Day Of Beauty!

These sections will offer more to do than anyone could possibly imagine. You'll never be without something to do. We have daytime and nighttime adventures, and food ideas for a lifetime.

For years, I'd been writing about the latest, greatest, newest, trendiest. I'd been keeping a journal of the places in the city that receive no hype. I call myself the unofficial publicist for all the other New York sites: the ones that get no ink in the *New York Times* or the back pages of *New York* magazine. Believe me, there are many who can't afford publicity!

During my research I was thrilled to finally get to meet some of the people I had been hearing about, to talk to them about their work. I met a theologian who is one of the great Jewish leaders of the area—and he's funny, too; a professor who spends his life studying the presidency; an executive who exists to pursue chamber music; a character who aligns street musicians for shows; a similar character who organizes a show for the semi-talented; and a dozen leaders of great institutions and small burgeoning companies. New Yorkers are impeccable sources!

After each meeting, I would think about the amazing wealth of information I had just received. And then I'd edit it down to a tiny entry so that I could use it in this book. If you feel like being interactive, check out Na-

---

* Art Of Shaving, which is at 373 Madison Avenue (986-2905). Also at 141 East 62nd Street (317-8436). Hours are Monday–Friday, 9:30 A.M.–6:30 P.M.; Saturdays, 10:00 A.M.–5:00 P.M. (ah, but closed Sundays).

tive's Guide, currently on-line at CompuServe (see special sidebars and added "extras" throughout the book for the scoop on what people continue to say).

The night I was prompted onto the streets, I tried to get to my destination. What a shame, I thought as I moved along, that the Museum of the American Piano* isn't open late. I considered several possibilities. A club. That new bookstore. A look at some architecture. Of course, I could go to a movie. (But my favorite movie theaters, such as Theater 80 St. Marks in the East Village, are closed; I usually settle for the Screening Room.†)

Instead of the Washington Square Festival, I wound up listening to a guy who resembled the Addams Family's hairy "Cousin Itt" scream impromptu rock poetry at P.S. 122.** Instead of fully getting into it, I was taking feverish notes. I was wondering, "Did he have to make reservations to read, or was it spontaneous?"

Maybe you're wondering what happened at Washington Square. By the time I finally swung by there, with all this deliberation, the event was over.

In this town, mac, you had best be quick.

---

* 21 West 58th Street, 246-4646. It is for real.

† 54 Varick Street, where you can eat, and while you eat the waitress brings your movie tickets, and then you scramble into small seats and watch eccentrically chosen pics. Call 334-2100.

** Performance Space 122: art, music, dance, theater, 477-5288. It's where Whoopi and Eric Bogosian got their start; Danny Hoch, a featured player on HBO nowadays, is reason to come here now. Also, Eddie Izzard pre-Broadway.

Daytime

GARIBALDI

1807 — 1882

1

Daytime Date Attractions: Oddities and Just Plain Stuff Like Falling in Love

GOLF-LOVE

There are thirteen golf courses in Queens, the Bronx, Brooklyn, and Staten Island that charge $10–$20, depending on the course and the day. The city owns them, but they are run by private concessions. The parks department has golf clinics and private driving ranges, such as **TURTLE COVE** (City Island Road, Bronx, 718-885-2646; fax 718-885-9331) in the Bronx's Orchard Beach, that charge $4.50–$7 per box. For serious golf enthusiasts, the **AMERICAN GOLF RESERVATION LINE** (718-255-4653) is a great way to reserve tee times for groups. There are also the courses in **CLEARVIEW** (20212 Willets Point Boulevard, Bayside, Queens, 718-229-2570; fax 718-631-7681), **DYCKER** in Brooklyn (86th and 7th Avenue, 718-836-9722; fax 718-836-4063), **PELHAM** in the Bronx (718-885-1258), and **SILVER LAKE** in Staten Island (915 Victory Boulevard, 718-447-5686; fax 718-273-7927).

TEA TIME FOR LUVAHS

New York offers a host of spots that make you feel special during the afternoon hours followed by extra-special romantic teas. At the world's "greatest" bar (their words, surely) at the World Trade Center (107th floor,

938-1111; http://www.windowsontheworld.com), you will find, first of all that it's open, and second of all, it is not as expensive as you might think. Go at sunset; being up so high, perhaps above the clouds in a sky splotchy with pink and gold and orange, is almost mystical. Wine school is being offered up there, too, which is engaging, considering the place is not the most festive of late. Same number.

T SALON EMPORIUM

11 East 20th Street between Broadway and Fifth Avenue, 358-0506

This is a neat place to drink. Formerly located in the basement of the downtown Guggenheim Museum, T Salon has moved to a larger location to serve its many types of tea and its dishes made with tea. The selection of tea and tea accessories is large; this is truly a place for tea lovers. A little too "frilly"—but great for casual meets. Coffee? They frown on it.

TEA AND SYMPATHY

108 Greenwich Avenue between 12th and 13th Streets, 807-8329

Stop in this lovely spot for some tea and scones. Tea and Sympathy offers a wide (and delicious) selection of teas and snacks. Many New Yorkers, wishing to pay respects in a memorial to Princess Diana, came for a while for some tea, and the wait staff decorated the room with lilies in tabletop vases . . . in honor of Di.

DANAL

90 East 10th Street, 982-6930

This is a great place for Afternoon Tea. The menu includes sandwiches, scones, and various desserts all baked daily on the premises. Tea is prix fixe at $14, and reservations are required. They accept reservations for seating between 4:00 P.M. and 4:30 P.M. (though, of course, patrons may sit beyond 4:30 P.M.). A few years back, tea was served four afternoons a week; unfortunately, tea times are now restricted to Friday and Saturday only. Danal also serves lunch and dinner. In the winter, it's French country bistro food (stews, soups, roast, etc.) and in the summer, it's California cuisine (salsas, vegetables, salads, grilled foods, etc.). Reservations are required for dinner. Hours are Tuesday–Sunday, 10:00 A.M.–10:00 P.M. Enjoy yourself in the garden when weather permits. Beer and wine are available.

THE OMNI AT BERKSHIRE PLACE
21 East 52nd Street, 753-5800; fax 754-5018

The Omni sets aside most of its lobby, "The Atrium," as a civilized cocktail lounge where you can enjoy afternoon tea, cocktails, an assortment of sandwiches and pastries, and a harpist who provides soft, low-key, lovely music. Also at the Omni, in the Rendezvous Bar, you will find cocktails, lunch, and more.

THE PENINSULA
700 Fifth Avenue at 55th Street, 247-2200; fax 903-3949
(reopening November due to renovations)

This was formerly the Gotham, one of midtown's oldest hotels. The new owners have upgraded it from a tourist attraction to an elegant, but friendly place for meetings and/or trysts. A lovely Afternoon Tea is served daily from 2:30 P.M. to 5:00 P.M. in the grandish Gotham Lounge. The menu includes a set of finger sandwiches, scones, pastries, cakes, and tea or coffee for $20 a person.

Alternately, cocktails are served at the Pen-Top Bar, on the roof. During the summer, you can enjoy the warmth outdoors, but in the winter, you can stay warm inside a greenhouse room. The roof offers a smashing view of Fifth Avenue, particularly of Trump Tower.

RIHGA ROYAL HOTEL
151 West 54th Street, 307-5000; fax 765-6530; e-mail: rihga@ix.netcom.com

This hotel has the Halcyon Room, in which you will also find an "afternoon tea" menu featuring a selection of tea sandwiches, scones, cookies, and coffee or tea for only a few dollars each. RIHGA is currently working on a Web site that gives more information about the hotel and the Halcyon Room.

BEST MARKETING AND EFFORT TO GET
PEOPLE AWAY FROM THE COMPUTER

—Or: The best coffee bar in a marketing sense—killing the competition with an innovative, non-Starbucksian approach to life: Beer Music Wine is a 24-hour café (we call it the BMW fondly, after a friendly auto we know): "Up all night," with microbrewed beer, lite on the attitude, and plenty of beer, music, and wine; "SMOKERS WELCOME"; and . . . call them at all hours at 229-1807. Located at Seventh Avenue between 21st and 22nd Streets. At night it's the only activity for miles and miles.

SMALL TALK LIKE LOVE

Small talk on a date? Try the **AMERICAN MUSEUM OF NATURAL HISTORY** (Central Park West and West 79th Street, 769-5100; fax 769-5006; http://www.amnh.org), open till 9:00 P.M. on Wednesday, Friday, and Saturday. Or try the **METROPOLITAN MUSEUM** (Fifth Avenue and 82nd Street, 535-7710, fax 472-2764; http://www.metmuseum.org), open late on Friday and Saturday. Or how about the **MUSEUM OF MODERN ART (MOMA)** (53rd Street between Fifth and Sixth Avenues, 708-9480, fax 333-1104; http://www.moma.org), also open late on weekends? The rooftop of MOMA offers a beautiful view of Central Park. Purchase a cocktail at the bar, sit on one of the benches with your date, and remember if you're nervous to breathe deeply, because the brain needs oxygen (breathing is often forgotten on a nervous first date).

A DRINK PERCHANCE TO DREAM

THE ALGONQUIN
59 West 44th Street, 840-6800; fax 944-1449

The hotel that New York's mid-century literati made famous, the Algonquin, retains its dowdy and respectable air. Despite the venerable reputation, it is nonetheless one of the most comfortable and welcoming sites in midtown. The chairs in the lobby are mismatched and drinks are served any way you like.

CAFÉ DES ARTISTES
1 West 67th Street between Columbus Avenue and Central Park West, 877-3500; fax 877-7754

A romantic lunch? One of the prettiest places to go is this café, whose original lush murals by Howard Chandler Christy have recently been restored. The food is not great though, so be prepared for a momentous setting with not many memorable edibles.

Still, we must value the Café des Artistes because it's one of the few spaces in New York where you will feel as though you have stepped from our city into the City of Light. Though regulars will tell you that the French menu is filled with culinary buzzwords that are unnecessarily tough to comprehend, Artistes' polite, friendly staff makes up for such pretensions.

ENDOMORPHINE-ITES ALERT: PHOEBE'S CHOCOLATE CAKE
359 Bowery, 473-9008

Since 1969, this watering hole has battled all others to remain the most popular and least pretentious East Village haunt for the theater and music crowds. People go back for Chocolate Decadence, an amazing dessert of slow, rich death whose only rival in New York is David's Chocolate Mousse Cake, created by a Connecticut-based man who is not the cookie monster. Find this at the yup-town markets **ZABAR'S** (2245 Broadway, 787-2000; fax 580-4477) and most branches of **FAIRWAY** (595-1888; fax 595-9843).

In a date situation, all you need is the chemical found in chocolate—phenylethylamine—to get something, well, started.

PLACES TO MAKE LOVE IN PURE DAYLIGHT

FREEDOM PLACE
End of West 66th Street at West End Avenue

New York's Lovers' Lane! Freedom, a little drive built for romantics, is at the westernmost end of West 66th Street, where you must make a right in order to keep driving. This handle-shaped strip is rarely traveled. Best of all, it looms over the Hudson River, with the Henry Hudson Parkway a notch above.

There are spotlights at night—Freedom's situated behind a hospital— bright enough so that you feel safe but not so bright that you feel uncomfortable. Completing the picture, the overshadowing Santa Monica apartments at the foot of this four-block oasis make this spot feel like a boulevard in a small town.

GONDOLA RIDE IN CENTRAL PARK
Parks Department Info Line: 800-201-PARK

Central Park offers many attractive outings for the romantic, but hardly any as fabulous as the boat that was imported from Venice, piece by piece.

The gondoliers have been trained by experts from Italy, and their poling is magnificent to watch. Take wine or champagne on this $30, half-hour outing and be prepared to imbibe during a long wait that can last up to an hour. Yet the ride is perfect—one of those rare experiences when you stop and think, "Where am I again?"

PADDLEBOATS, PROSPECT PARK
718-965-8999

Many people who visit the boats at Lull Water in Brooklyn's Prospect Park are skeptical at first. Then they get into the swing of things and discover that these paddleboats are heaven indeed.

Some 200 small crafts are available during spring, summer, and fall; they are a perfect antidote for that period when the city's concrete steams. After a send-off in Lull Water, you head out into the sixty-acre human-made Prospect Lake, which is skirted by lawns, shady trees, and perfect spots for picnicking.

DA FERRY

What can beat a trip across murky waters with a lady-in-waiting in attendance? Bring a bag lunch and sit at the front of the Staten Island Ferry, and you'll get a great view of the Statue of Liberty. (A ferry ride at night also has a romantic view of the statue.) There is something truly cinematic about cutting through New York Harbor on the night ferry.

During the day, throngs of commuters at the rush-hours (6:00 A.M.–9:30 A.M., 4:30–7:00 P.M.) make this a difficult journey. It's twenty minutes each way, and only beer is served. (Some ferries even have pay phones on board!) Once you get to the Island, find a park or the giant lighthouse, or in nice weather, find a perch on the bow and pop open a bottle of bubbly. (Information: 718-390-5253.)

Might I suggest a hike along an official Staten Island Walk (718-667-6042), encompassing some twenty-eight miles of circular trails in the Greenbelt (their word for park). It's once a month—call for more info. And wear your sneakers because unlike Manhattan this island has a lot of unmarked twists and turns . . . and cows, too.

One of the most picturesque cottages in the five boroughs is the Alice Austen House in Staten Island, an eighteenth century farmhouse with exhibits of Austen's photos and a garden with a panoramic view of New York Harbor.

SIDEBAR SPECIAL What Is a Real New Yorker?

For years I have been running this forum for CompuServe. You know, the information service that basically gives people an opportunity to learn something while they contribute lots of their own facts. Real fun facts.

My forum is Native's Guide to New York (a shameless plug for my long-known-and-requested book [namely, this one]). I decided to ask all the people who wandered into my New York forum, "What is a native New Yorker?" We started by getting things like—well, like this—across the screen:

> The other night I was taking my dog for her 10 P.M. walk in the grassy median that splits Riverside Drive. I got into a conversation with another dog-walker who had relocated from Los Angeles a few years ago and the subject of just how long you had to live here to be considered a New Yorker came up. I found myself defining a New Yorker as someone who had been born here,

though I realize that's a strict interpretation. Obviously, someone born here is a "native" New Yorker; but when you dig further, you run the risk of falling into the "Native American" trap: If I was born here, am I a native American? Or are the American Indians the only Native Americans?

Slowly, I realized that people were a little offended by the idea of the native thing and I rephrased it: We ran a thread (messages that are threaded together) that began by asking people, "What is a New Yorker?" Here—more or less—is how the conversation ran. A New Yorker:

• Never stands on line, for anything, even the bank.
• Knows she can cross the street leisurely when the Walk/Don't Walk signs are flashing "Don't Walk," and can scamper across when the signs bear a solid "Don't Walk."
• Knows the "Close Door" buttons in elevators really do nothing; pronounces "Houston Street" properly; calls Manhattan "the city"; calls the subway "the train"; and knows what TriBeCa stands for.
• Can spot a tourist a mile away.
• May never get a driver's license (and won't miss it).
• Knows the true meaning of "hurry up and wait."
• Has never been to the Statue of Liberty or the World Trade Center observation deck.
• Can take an argument about pizza seriously.
• Knows what end of the subway to get on so he'll end up at the stairs when he exits and/or knows what door won't open so he can lean on it.
• Says "New York" when out-of-staters ask where he's from. (Only upstaters expect someone to say "New York City.")
• Can get the *Village Voice* early—even now that it's free.

To add your own two cents, go to NYNY in the Native Forum on CompuServe, or send e-mail to me at NativeGuy@yeahwhatever.com. Eyes on your own work. Okay?

EXTRA: VOLUNTEER WORK

The two charities where friends of mine have met the most people have involved AIDS-related work and museums/institutions. For the latter I recommend calling the Fraunces Tavern Museum, way downtown, in the small space that remembers George Washington, since they have a small, mixed volunteer staff of articulate, informed helpers . . . who seem to like each other! Call 425-1778. (They also have a restaurant upstairs where people go a-wassailing . . . and volunteers get to know one another way better.)

GOD'S LOVE WE DELIVER (294-8100) is the place that provides meals to homebound or bedridden people with AIDS. Volunteers are used throughout the organization, in food preparation, delivery, office work, data entry, working at benefits, or sitting on committees. This is a way to get involved in the community—and help provide luscious and nutritious food. Volunteers I've spoken to say they are making a direct and positive contribution to the lives of very sick PWAs. And it's a nice group.

GAY MEN'S HEALTH CRISIS GREETING CARDS PROGRAM (for all "denominations"; 807-6655, in the fall) is an easy way to support one of the most important and well-thought of institutions in our city. This is the time of year (fall/early winter) where you give money to the largest AIDS charity group in town and it mails a seasonal greeting card to whomever you like, mentioning that this came about by a contribution to GMHC.

There are a million ways to contribute to this place. You can help with fund-raising, in organizing events, or just take part in one of the major events sponsored by GMHC annually—the Walk-A-Thons and Dance-A-Thon that raise millions. During these events, you meet a lot of people who are doing just what you're doing—helping out. And of course, after the work is done, the rest is up to you . . .

BIDE-A-WEE (410 East 38th Street, administration 532-6395, shelter 532-4455, fax 532-4210) is an animal shelter specifically for homeless cats and dogs. They offer adoption services and full clinic services for the public. They also have dog training and bereavement counseling. They always need volunteers for dog walking, cat care, grooming, pet therapy (you must have a friendly, gentle cat or dog), humane education, and special events. Free neutering in July and August. Shelter hours are 10:00 A.M.–6:00 P.M. every day. Their services fall into the utilitarian category, rather than hip and up-beat. However, it is a great way to meet people in the city. Marguerite Howard, a woman who not only volunteers there but handles their public and media relations, has met Bill Cosby, Carol Burnett, Warren Eckstein, Walter Cronkite, Julio Iglesias, Sarah Ferguson, and Jerry Orbach among many other personalities through the organization.

Lastly, but most importantly for all readers, is the idea of bringing an-other into the fold: Help fellow New Yorkers with their reading and writing skills at **LITERACY PARTNERS** (30 East 33rd Street, Sixth floor, 725-9200; fax 725-0414). They recruit, train, and supervise volunteers who teach reading and writing to adults in small groups at their tutoring centers, which are lo-cated in midtown and Harlem. Literacy Week is in April and has included "An Evening of Readings" by celebrity authors at Lincoln Center. (And re-member that Be Nice To Editors And Writers Month is September!)

MORE IDEAS FOR PLACES TO VOLUNTEER:
- Ronald McDonald House, 405 East 73rd Street, New York, NY 10021, 639-0100
- Henry Street Settlement, 265 Henry Street, New York, NY 10002, 766-9200
- Evelyn Lauder Breast Center of Memorial-Sloan Kettering Cancer Center, 205 East 64th Street, New York, NY 10021, 639-5200
- Harvard AIDS Institute, c/o Harvard Club of New York City, 27 West 44th Street, New York, NY 10036, 840-6600
- AIDS Care Center of New York Hospital–Cornell Medical Center, 525 East 68th Street, New York, NY 10021, 746-5454
- New York Metropolitan Museum, Fifth Avenue and 82nd Street, New York, NY 10028, 535-7710
- United Way, 99 Park Avenue, New York, NY 10016, 973-3800
- Salvation Army, 120 West 14th Street, New York, NY 10011, 337-7200
- Hale House, 300 Manhattan Avenue, New York, NY 10027, 663-0700

Interested in volunteering, but not sure where you would be most help-ful? Call the Mayor's Voluntary Action Center (49–51 Chambers Street, 788-7550). The center will set up an interview with you, and refer you to several groups from a database of over 2,500 volunteer organizations. The only requirement to volunteer: you must be at least 14 years old. And ready to do something!

EXTRA: LITTLE PARKS AND LITTLE PLAZAS

Pocket parks are tiny green places that sprout up mysteriously. For example, both sides of 105th Street in Central Park are unusual. On the West Side (see Chapter 7) is a well laid-out running track; on the East Side is the **CONSERVATORY GARDEN,** the only formal garden in the park. There is an authentic Shakespearean garden in this park's center designed by Thomas Price, and a secret garden in the back called South Garden, which names southern states on the concrete floor.

Over on the right is an informal box, an open space high atop the greenery, perfect for dancing if you bring a portable cassette player. Open at 8:00 A.M., closed at sundown.

Noted for its music in summertime, **DAMROSCH PARK** (West 65th Street and Broadway, in the heart of Lincoln Center) is a park that was built to make Lincoln Center theater beautiful—and concert-goers feel glad they splurged for tickets. In the morning, there are only trees, benches, and roving people. (Two evenings a week in the summer, you have a choice of free entertainment from New York's only classical music station, WQXR, which brings live radio broadcasts of Lincoln Center Out-of-Doors.)

Designed just above street level, the park is surprisingly quiet when you consider that three major avenues converge below. Get your bagel and cappuccino at Lincoln Square Coffee Shop, across the street, and enjoy the peace and sunshine.

The Parisian's dream, New Yorker style, is an odd-shaped park built inside the plaza and along the side of the **MCGRAW-HILL** building (West 49th Street between Sixth and Seventh Avenues). First, buy a meal at the street-level Umbrella Room—that is, at a hot dog stand. Then travel downstairs and sit on a stone bench. See the fountain? Look inside and watch the seasonal Pool of Planets, nine spheres that represent the planets in their relation to the sun—the gold line in the center.

Back on street level you will note that the park extends along 48th Street. Early in the summer mornings, this part is teeming with executives enjoying the sunbathers' paradise.

Nature-loving groups in need of a private pocket park should acquire a permit from the Asphalt Green (where you can swim indoors in an Olympic-size pool for about $10) to take a boat to the 4½ acre **MILL ROCK IS-LAND** (off East River at East 95th Street). During the Revolutionary War it was a military base, and it's now an abandoned, barren wasteland. No plumbing or any conveniences like snack stands, but it does get you away from it all. Used mostly for kids' leadership training and Outward Bound programs. But definitely worthy of "state-parkhood." The flora-filled island, which is mostly weeds and brush, can be spotted if you drive along the FDR Drive at 95th Street.

PALEY PARK (3 East 53rd Street) is an area near the Museum of Television and Radio, a stopover for executives on the way from the gym to the office Danish cart. It's a place to find solace among the suite.

This park was a 1957 gift from CBS chairman Bill Paley to his neighbors. It now features a wall of flowing water, stone ashtrays, a refreshment stand, and a relaxing breeze. If the space is too crowded, be sure to go next door, underneath 520 Madison, and find the cool, chair-laden hideaway.

Two others in the area: On Madison & 56th is the IBM garden, with its high ceilings, chairs, tables, bamboos, trees—a great place for a chat. . . . And **GREENACRE PARK** at 221 East 51st Street with its granite walls, soothing waterfalls, tables, chairs, and refreshments.

RECTOR PARK (outside Liberty Court at Rector Place in Battery City) gives Jersey fans the chance to gaze out over the Hudson and note, behind the Statue, factory sites along the opposite shore (find the giant Colgate tube). This was built only recently, after population boomed in Battery City. It has large sculptures, flower beds in the summer, stone benches, and shrubbery designs. The sculpture area is called Real World Garden.

Located on Rector Place, far west of Rector Street, this park feels much like Miami. Look up, and you will see why: High-rise condominiums are everywhere!

Along the side of Rector now stands a fabulous walkway that serves as a jogging path all the way to 14th Street and beyond. A great nature run and a gorgeous way to drop pounds.

Next to the World Financial Center, **ROCKEFELLER PARK** (the other side of Battery Park) is hands-down one of the most interesting parks because of the sloping grass and great views. On Tuesday nights in the summer you can enjoy free concerts.

For kids the well-padded swing-and-climb area comes complete with sandbox, swings, climbing walls, and a circular seesaw. Information about concerts and other park events at 267-9700.

The view of the 59th Street Bridge from **SUTTON SQUARE** (Sutton Place and 58th Street) is an authentic New York scene. The small park has a replica of the boar, "Il Porcellino," that stands in the Straw Market of Florence. In order to fully appreciate this vista, watch the children frolicking, the couples sitting close together, and the young artists reading poetry on chipped park benches.

The romantic element in pocket parks is the freedom: No one charges you for the time you spend. In this, one of New York's most policed pocket parks, they don't even allow vendors. More romance: This is where Diane Keaton and Woody Allen had their first date in *Manhattan,* parodied in nearly every jokey movie script since.

Sometimes the words "built for the community" truly fit. One of the most beautiful parks in the city is **WASHINGTON MARKET PARK** (at Greenwich and Chambers Streets) on the grounds of the Borough of Manhattan Community College. It was built for residents of Tribeca, who take care of the grounds and garden.

This park boasts a splendiferous view of the Hudson River and many grand buildings of the burgeoning area, plus a special attraction: a sculptured dollhouse veranda perfect for speech making, dancing, and peering out over the endless grass.

CHAPTER 2

Shopping Tips, a Q & A (Including Flea Markets And Other Specials)

These pages comprise hard-earned pieces of information from years spent shopping. I have taught many classes on this subject, so I feel equipped to share some of the questions would-be bargain hunters have asked me, in hopes that they are your questions, too.

Q: CAN I TRUST SIDEWALK SALESPEOPLE?

A: Approach these vendors with suspicion—but don't ignore them. Sometimes you will discover that people simply enjoy vending on the street. But more likely than not, they do it because they can't afford a store, or have lost the lease on a shop.

The good thing is, street sellers hawk merchandise that you can touch: it's the what-you-see-is-what-you-get school of vending. But never buy anything shrink-wrapped because vendors have learned how to take old stuff and rewrap it to make it look brand new.

Q: HOW COME CHAIN STORES POST PRICES THAT VARY WIDELY FROM BRANCH TO BRANCH?

A: When shopping, remember to use whatever sense of neighborhood you have. For example, a Woolworth's on the Upper East Side was more expensive to meet the demands of a higher rent than the 14th Street Woolworth's. On West 23rd Street, where Woolworth's had been located since before the area was gentrified, the rent was much cheaper, which has an effect on the prices inside the store. Operating costs are cheaper, therefore retail prices are cheaper. (FYI: Woolworth's is closed but we miss it.)

Q: YOU TALK ABOUT CHAIN STORES A LOT; PLEASE TELL ME WHY YOU THINK THEY'RE DECEIVING.

A: First, chain stores usually sell merchandise at regular price—a little below "list price." Chain boutiques often look like they are discount outlets; they're not. For women, the Conway chain on East 34th Street is the exception to the rule. Most important, chain store names are deceiving. For example, Sock Express and New York Sock Mart sound alike and even look similar. However, Express sells $7 pairs of athletic white socks while the "Sock Man" in the East Village (529-0300, 27 St. Marks Place) offers two pairs for the same price.

Q: FASHION, WHERE ARE YOU?

A: Mind these fashion notes: Artful fashion is everywhere, but you have to be on the lookout for it. Make friends with the sales help at fine stores; they will more likely take a phone call from you, they may clue you in about private sales, and they may even put something aside for you. Go, look, come back. Clerks like careful shoppers. . . . Try to have an idea of what you're looking for; then the salesperson will be willing to help for as long as you need. The best advice: buy off-season merchandise as much as you can.

Q: WHY ALL THIS TALK ABOUT SEASONS?

A: Understanding seasons is essential for the bargain hunter. The seasons in the fashion world are known as Spring, Fall, Transition, and Holiday. Window appearances aside, Spring starts right after real-time spring begins, and the rest of the seasons follow suit. (All except Holiday, which begins in late Fall.) But don't shop at the beginning or in the middle of a season. Wait until the end, when people are trying to clear the racks at high speed! And that's the best time to visit a department store.

Q: WHAT'S THE BEST MONTH TO GO SHOPPING?

A: August—or anytime in late summer.

Q: THE WORST IS DECEMBER, RIGHT?

A: Not necessarily. (Though, to be frank, you'd be smart if you attempted to get your Christmas shopping out of the way during the pre-Christmas sale days in November. Or better yet, shop for gifts in March when sales on winter items occur.) December is a madhouse, true, but there *are* blissful late afternoons before hordes of shoppers descend onto the streets. At about 3:00 P.M. on any December weekday, wander into any store and peacefully enjoy various last-minute "shopping bonuses" to help you save money.

Q: HOW IS IT YOU COMPARE SHOPPING IN DEPARTMENT STORES TO SHOPPING IN SUPERMARKETS?

A: Shopping at a department store should be seen in the same manner as shopping at a supermarket. When you go into a supermarket, never buy what's straight ahead of your eye: those are the high-end, heavily advertised products. Instead, if you look down or up, you will see bargain products or the no-name brands.

Likewise, at a department store you should never buy the clothing right off the aisle, because that's the most accessible merchandise and it's usually the very expensive stocks. If you wander through to the back, you will see bins and off-rack items that at one time stood in that privileged position of the aisle, and now their prices have dropped considerably. (There are close-outs in nearly every section of a department store!)

Q: WHAT ABOUT BIN-SHOPPING?

A: Bins are places where clothing and other merchandise is folded and not hung up. In many instances, this is your lucky place to shop. Things taken off hangers are placed in bins and are cheaper. You'll have to do some ironing.

Q: WHAT DOES THE TERM "PREVIOUS MARKDOWN" MEAN?

A: Often you'll see a line in a sales circular or advertisement that says, "There have been previous markdowns." All that means is this is a unique promotion but that, yes, you might have seen a better price at that store on that item at an earlier date.

Q: HOW CAN I AVOID BEING TAKEN ADVANTAGE OF?

A: Simply, never appear desperate. And, again, take your time.

Q: WHAT'S THE MOST USED NAME IN RETAIL?

A: For some reason, a different store with the moniker "Vogue" pops up at regular intervals. Who knows, maybe store owners think that the public is gullible enough to imagine that *Vogue* magazine runs the shop.

Q: PUBLIC BATHROOMS ARE A PROBLEM—ANY SUGGESTIONS?

A: Except for grungy bathrooms in the subways, no. But I have one friend who is always out and about; her trick is to say to a restaurant or café owner, "If I ask you nicely, can I use your bathroom?" No one has ever turned down that straightforward approach! P.S. Watch Guiliani put in public bathrooms during his last term.

Q: WHAT ABOUT SHOPPING ON CANAL STREET?

A: Canal, one of New York's two-way shopping thoroughfares, is a legendary street; earlier in the century, many of the city's brothels were located on these blocks, from the Hudson River to Chinatown!

If you compare the old Canal Street to the new, not much has really changed. Now, though, it's overflowing with junk shops and very unfriendly vendors. (The electronic stores along Canal have unfriendly service and bargains galore.)

Q: WHY DO MANY PEOPLE CONSIDER BARGAIN HUNTING RUDE, UNNECESSARY, OR A COMPLETE WASTE OF TIME?

A: Those people haven't learned one thing my family instilled in me: that money is pretty much irretrievable. To me, taking the time to hunt out a bargain is always worthwhile, especially when you can be proud of what you bought, and proud of how little money was doled out.

Q: WHAT'S "WHIM SHOPPING"?

A: Whim shopping is buying on impulse. Some people call this "spec shopping" (as in, speculate) because, though you buy it, you aren't sure it's right for you. Often whim shoppers find themselves rationalizing a good buy with the fact that it is a good bargain. If this is an inexpensive item, fine. But bargain hunters, beware, this could be your nemesis.

Q: WHAT WILL I FIND AT THE TRAVELING GREENMARKETS THAT'S TRULY CHEAP?

A: Wine, bread, muffins, flowers, some apples (some are expensive but delicious), and more. Call 556-0990 to see where these outdoor markets are on any given week. (Now they even do seasonal "theme" weeks.)

Q: I SAW A STORE AT 49TH STREET AND SEVENTH AVENUE THAT WAS ACTUALLY CALLED "CLOSEOUT!" WHAT WAS THAT ALL ABOUT?

A: Just like those outfits that constantly advertise "Going out of Business" (GOOB), these are stores that want you to believe they are turning over stock every day. The difference between closeout shops and GOOB operations is that often closeouts are really getting rid of tons of merchandise at outlandishly low prices. The GOOB boutiques are 100 percent gimmick.

Q: ARE THERE NEIGHBORHOODS I SHOULD AVOID?

A: No. But I will qualify my views on midtown Manhattan, since I do talk about it a lot. This isn't the safest area to shop in, particularly with all the newly added neon. Be extra careful. Don't be flamboyant with your cash. Don't shop alone. Don't give out your credit card number (someone could use it to charge things over the telephone) and if you use a card, be sure to get your carbons back. Don't ever volunteer personal information on a credit card slip—a 1989 New York law states you do not have to give a phone number or address when charging. And don't make it known that you don't regularly shop in the neighborhood.

Q: WHAT'S THE BENEFIT OF GETTING CHUMMY WITH CLERKS?

A: Particularly in the districts, you should encourage a friendly sales clerk. This way, in areas where everyone sells something you're interested in, you will be privy to insiders' information: who's moved in, who's moved out, who's closing their stock, who's disreputable. Also, when you're friendly you are treated like a friend. And friends don't want you to waste your money, right?

Q: YOU TALK ABOUT WAREHOUSE SALES; WHAT'S THE BEST ONE?

A: It happens a few times a year, when **BARNEY'S**, the pricey men's and women's store new based on the Upper East Side, still has a warehouse at 243 West 17th Street (593-7800) with a semi-annual sale. During this week-long event, dressed-up folks line up for blocks to see Barney's normal prices become almost affordable.

Q: WHAT'S THE SECRET OF MAILING LISTS? AND WHY DO YOU TALK ABOUT THEM SO OFTEN IN <u>NATIVE'S GUIDE TO NEW YORK</u>?

A: Just like with going-out establishments, you must be on lists to get things. Ask twice if you must, but just make sure you're on the mailing list of the stores that intrigue you. You get invited to private sales, you find out about "sneak previews" before the public, and you get wonderful coupons in the mail.

Q: IS THERE A SNEAKY WAY TO FIND OUT IN ADVANCE ABOUT THE BIG SAMPLE SALES HELD IN MIDTOWN?

A: Call Accurate Distribution Network, which prints and distributes leaflets and flyers. Ask 'em (766-1900).

Q: DO "WHOLESALE ONLY" SHOPS STILL EXIST?

A: At one time it was an advantage for an establishment to limit itself to wholesale; wholesalers could avoid heavy tax burdens. So even today, a vendor will often refuse to sell retail if he hasn't discovered the 1990s-instituted tax advantages of selling to everyone. But in most cases—particularly in shops from West 23rd to West 29th Streets just off Broadway—you will find that "wholesale only" places will sell to individuals who ask them, "Please?"

Q: HOW CAN I KNOW WHICH MAIL ORDER OR CATALOG HOUSES TO TRUST?

A: Only buy from people whom you can get in touch with quickly. That is, make sure they have an 800 or some other phone number with which you can check up on them. Try to get the office number instead of a customer service number.

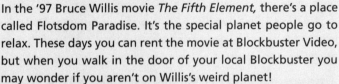

SIDEBAR SPECIAL Greet This—How Blockbuster Has Ruined Friendliness

In the '97 Bruce Willis movie *The Fifth Element,* there's a place called Flotsdom Paradise. It's the special planet people go to relax. These days you can rent the movie at Blockbuster Video, but when you walk in the door of your local Blockbuster you may wonder if you aren't on Willis's weird planet!

I sure did the last time I visited the video rental megachain. Blockbuster has a new policy to make customers feel special. They are not accomplishing this by reducing prices or offering three rentals for the price of one. Oh no no! That would cost money.

Instead, Blockbuster is offering friendly service . . . really friendly service. According to the company, that means a clerk greets you right when you walk through the door, and Blockbuster employees treat you like family while you're there.

I got a taste of this warm fuzziness when I hit the check-out line with my tape selections one evening (*101 Dalmatians* and *Fatal Attraction,* because I'm a Glenn Close freak). As I was leaving, the clerk at the register said, "Enjoy your tapes, Richard," and my skin crawled.

I write these books and I couldn't help wonder: How come this nice bit? What's in it for them? Do they think I am going to rent more videos because my "friend" helped me? Come on, there's only so many hours to couch-potato in the day, and anyway, it's not like I'd trust some video clerk to help me choose between *Porky's* or *Airplane 3* (or, to help me choose between *The Last Metro* and *A Man For All Seasons*).

And . . . and . . . how dare Blockbuster employees call me Richard!

This is the video store that New Yorkers go to; they have made it a habit to get rid of the locals and in many cases have thrown out another darn good video store. Blockbuster is also the largest chain of its kind in the world. They have very strict policies on the videos they carry, and require that all videos in Blockbuster have "PG"-rated labels (meaning they don't want any S-E-X on their shelves.)

So, with that in mind, I got into fighting mode and I called the company. The representative I spoke to explained that Blockbuster was just trying to make customers feel "at home." Now, me, I consider my home to be a place with a couch and a TV, not stacks of videos and a smiling Stepford clerk who knows me by name.

The first name gimmick is merely an excuse for someone not to give you the good customer service you deserve as the number one customer. If a waiter says to a customer, "Hello, my name is Todd," he thinks that once the friendly thing starts going you would never say, "Look, Todd, I don't care what your first name is, I just want my soup hot and sometime before my next meal!"

When I called Blockbuster I asked if they would at least consider dropping the phony personal friend part of the greeting. The response: "We really can't. It's something that has been decided from above. It's our policy . . . Richard."

Now I go to Alan's Alley and Video Blitz, the alternatives. Forget that Blockbuster claims to be offering "independent films—easier to find than fund"; in reality, Blockbuster's own brand of censorship was but the second-to-last straw. The friendliness of Blockbuster employees is over the top. From now on I'll be sitting in my living room, watching ads for impersonal Pay-Per-View.

Q: HOW CAN I BE SURE NOT TO GET RIPPED OFF VIA MAIL ORDER?

A: Remember to inspect all merchandise for general defects and the accuracy of the order the very minute the package arrives. Before you pay in full, follow these rules for shopping by mail: Make sure they tell you how long it will take to get to you, ask how valuable or vulnerable merchandise will be shipped, and insure those valuables.

Q: IS THERE ONE PIECE OF DEFINITIVE ADVICE YOU CAN GIVE TO THE BARGAIN HUNTER?

A: Never hurry your selection. Go slow. You can go back for it, and if you can't, it probably was not meant to be yours.

Q: THERE MUST BE ANOTHER PIECE OF ADVICE YOU'VE LEFT OUT.

A: If you want something and aren't sure if the price is right, ask the vendor if he is "sure" that's the going rate on the item. You'd be surprised how many sellers will drop the price a little to get you to buy. Note well: it's always a buyer's market.

Q: IF YOU HAD ONE PLACE TO SHOP IN, WHICH WOULD IT BE?

A: I'd have to choose two: Since I shop a lot for clothing and CDs, find me at Manhattan's **CENTURY 21** (22 Cortlandt Street, 227-9092) where I can find outerwear, underwear, face cream, toothpaste, socks, and much more; and find me at any branch of **DISC-O-RAMA,** which can be found at 186 West 4th Street between Sixth Avenue and Christopher Street (206-8417) and 40 Union Square East (260-8616). All stores sell almost all available new releases at $9.99 and sell the oldies at a discount. (The used ones surface without scratches for, oh, maybe $8.)

WHERE YOU CAN FIND BARGAINS IN AN UNORTHODOX MANNER

BROADWAY IN SOHO

This used to be all factories and wholesale outlets. In the early '80s, most opened their doors to the public, making this neighborhood savings headquarters for the adventurous. You can find lingerie, shoes, sheets and pillowcases, and other bargains and closeouts at mainly Hispanic-owned factory warehouses. Yes, the Tarot readers are still here, but unlike the rest of Soho, only a few stores are fashionably expensive.

Best bets: **FASHION HATS INC.,** a rare breed that sells Easter and Christmas specials. Or **SOHO SURPLUS,** a trendy army-navy store with last year's price tags. Right above Houston is **NATIONAL WHOLESALE LIQUIDATORS,** an aesthetically pleasing junk shop—stationery, kitchenware, even paintings.

CHAMBERS STREET

There are several areas around town that are known as "transitional blocks." This neck of Chambers Street is soon to become co-op heaven; meanwhile, it's an area that landlords have allowed to be used for low-rent stores.

That's incredible news for the consumer. You can go into so-called warehouse stores that sell anything they can find, sometimes at below cost. Proprietors have no overhead and usually buy in bulk. So go—buy books, linens, jewelry, slightly damaged clothing, chocolate, and hardware. Best to remember: Chambers may soon be a memory. And at press time, there were many stores still open and clamoring for your hard-earned dollar, by selling items at rock-bottom prices.

NASSAU STREET

During the week, around lunchtime, the streets behind Lower Manhattan's Park Row overflow with people who, by most accounts, are quintessential shoppers. You will find cameras, electronic equipment, pharmacies, fashions, boutiques, "shoetricians," health food and vitamin shops, cheap and fast food, costume jewelry, shoes, and many street vendors.

Best bet: hawkers with handouts, which you should take. Around here, take seriously the unadvertised specials that shout "Big Sale" in big lettering.

Also found on Nassau, an original **PUSHCART JOB LOT,** selling remainders from overcrowded delivery trucks.

ORCHARD STREET

The Orchard Street market can be used in two ways. On a Sunday, many of the waves of vendors that clutter the street scream prices and advertise sincere specials.

The flip side is that Orchard merchants know they are a tourist attraction, so many of them take advantage of that in an unbusinesslike way. Without posting prices, some will first see what you are willing to pay, and often make a pretty penny through your ignorance. *Caveat emptor.*

Best shopping: several **FORMAN'S** ladies' clothing shops, **LACE-UP** shoes, **PAN AM MENSWEAR,** and **MENDEL WEISS** lingerie, where there's some fun for everyone.

WEST 8TH STREET

Although they have no proof, residents swear Imelda Marcos was born on West 8th Street, where there are over fifteen reputable and *inexpensive* shoe stores. It is difficult to find good women's shoes at a reasonable rate anywhere else. Here are **VILLAGE COBBLER, SWEPT AWAY, SWEET FEET,** and **PAULA SHOES.**

Stay away from the gimmicky spots, with names like **RITZ** and **PLAZA ON 8TH,** which are attempting to capitalize on the street's newfound fame. Best bet: pit stores against each other, because many carry the exact same stock. New video stores have popped up on 8th. **TLA** stocks everything! (Eighth Street between Sixth and Fifth Avenues.)

WARREN AND CHURCH STREETS

Warren is an especially good "transition" street, with two women's clothing outlets called **DAMAGES,** and a variety of women's kick-around shoe stores. See the **FOUNTAIN PEN HOSPITAL** for a great selection of stationery goods and stores that include a pet shop, a plant shop, and a shop for quality briefcases.

Best bet: the only soul food for miles—**HAM HEAVEN.** Your shopping expedition will then be complete as you turn onto Church Street and find stores with leather bags, vitamins and coffee, Irish books, and electric razors.

WEST 14TH STREET

If you can put up with hawkers who have no shame—they sit on scarves in the middle of the sidewalk and use bullhorns—you can buy from several reputable dealers on West 14th Street. Since the Union Square area was cleaned up (by residents, not the Zeckendorf company), consumers can do very well there. Limit your shopping to household necessaries, such as towels, kitchen goods, even microwaves. Many stores offer 14-day, cash-back guarantees. (PS: A **VIRGIN MEGASTORE** will open in 1998.)

Strewn throughout the block between Fifth and Sixth Avenues are small appliances and chain shoe stores. Best to remember: On this block, products cost less than at those same stores' other city locations.

Next door to the failed Herald Center tower, where stores' prices are now lower that the original stores', is the **ABRAHAM & STRAUSS (A&S) PLAZA,** (Manhattan Mall) which, thanks to the devaluation of the department store concept, was fast becoming a **STERN'S!!** This complex, across from Macy's, which owns Stern's, includes some 120 stores. Despite the posh surroundings, some are bargain shops. Across the street from Macy's is *the* place to shop for a gift: every department features regular closeouts without the benefit of ads or public notices.

But the shopping bonanza is on the street itself. You can find anything on West 34th if you go store to store. Women do best here—there are two **CONWAY**s between Seventh and Eighth Avenues, plus gaudy leather places, jewelry stores, and the new "clique-clothing" boutiques. Here you and your friends can mix and match—and purchase—coordinated outfits.

Street shopping hint for West 14th and West 34th: On the street, you are certain to get the best prices for trendy perfumes and knockoff Polo shirts. You will, however, get *ripped off* if you buy appliances off the street, such as phones and answering machines. Sellers use shrink-wrap, and junk goods appear to be new. Lead yourself not into temptation.

EXTRA: BUYING ON THE PHONE/GIFTS/RUSH SHOPPING

Best gift is junk food—but classy stuff only. Rush down to **ECONOMY CANDY MARKET** at 108 Rivington (254-1531) and eat Jujus, buy big suckers . . . feel good.

HOWDY DO (72 East 7th Street, phone/fax 979-1618; e-mail: Howdy72@aol.com) offers a complete selection of '60s, '70s and '80s television memorabilia as well as an eclectic mix of pop culture. Their merchandise includes goodies from "Charlie's Angels," "The Bionic Woman," *E.T.,* "The Six Million Dollar Man," and also, Snoopy, Dawn, Liddle Kiddles, Kroft, Celebrity Dolls, The "Gay Billy" Doll, and much more. They also buy and sell dolls and collectibles. And they're very nice.

J.J. HAT CENTER (310 Fifth Avenue, 239-4368, 800-622-1911; fax 971-0406) is New York's oldest and largest hat shop. It has over 15,000 caps and hats in stock for men and ladies—that is, dress, casual, western hats in all major brands including Borsalino, Biltmore, Kangol, and Stetson. All sizes, fun to shop, and they'll special order too!

I saw some terrific Indian headdresses . . . Many Broadway plays, movies, and TV shows outfit their actors here; famous hat wearers they tell me have shopped at J.J. include Aaron Neville, Elton John, Rod Stewart, and J. Monk, Jr. (I have no idea either.) Call for a 32-page catalog, if hats are your thing. Open Monday–Saturday, 8:45 A.M.–5:45 P.M. Open Thursday, 8:45 A.M.–7:00 P.M.

GAME SHOW (474 Sixth Avenue, 633-6328; 1240 Lexington Avenue, 472-8011): It was only a matter of time, I thought back in '89, when a store filled with adult, political, and sexual board games would come on the scene and make people *forget* "Wheel Of Fortune" for a change. It happened that year—and by now many of these pastimes (board games that contain seriously ilicit topics) have become the successful brainchild of two very well-meaning entrepreneurs. My favorites in a store meant for the politically incorrect CHILD in all of us, are "Thou Shalt Not Cheat Unless Thou Canst Get Away with It" and "How to Be a Broadway Producer," which did not make my friend Jon one. (Though he plays it all the time—and well.)

There are games for kids—"Anti-Trust Monopoly" (not invented by former Prez Jimmy Carter)—and a bunch of sexual attractions, because these are the nineties, right? Open seven days.

LITTLE RICKIE (49½ First Avenue, corner of First Avenue and 3rd Street, 505-6467) is best described in the words of the manager: "It's like no other store." The merchandise ranges from toys for kids and adults to T-shirts to Elvis memorabilia to folk art. The store even has a working black-and-white photo booth, something you rarely see anymore. Shopping at this store is a great, yet slightly bizarre experience. Hours are Monday–Saturday, 11:00 A.M.–8:00 P.M.; Sunday, 12:00 P.M.–7:00 P.M.

CLAYTON HATS (161 Essex Street, 477-1363): "It's not a Stetson, it's a Clayton" is Clayton Paterson's motto—and rightfully so. Once you see one of his designs on a baseball cap or jacket back, you will forget all other hats and tattoo-style emblems. Clayton and his partner, Elsa, design hats that, at $70–$130 each, are unique culture, serious art. Anything you can imagine—a cross, skull, and crossbones combo, a thorny tulip—is clearly emblazoned on a washable hat.

Look at their past work, and see all of the famous people that own Clayton hats (such as the Pet Shop Boys and local gang members). In many cases, Clayton and Elsa claim they found out after the fact. These two also exhibit their personal artwork that consists of scraps found on the Lower East Side. (Clayton is president of the Tattoo Society of New York—$35 yearly for meetings and literature regarding this important body art.) Open daily, 11:00 A.M.–5:00 P.M.

UNIQUE TABLEWARE (340 East 6th Street, near First Avenue, 533-8252) sells closeouts of name brand items from gifts to housewares. The store takes credit card orders over the phone, for your convenience. Hours are Tuesday–Sunday, 3:00 P.M.–11:00 P.M.

BUYING SECOND HAND

Thrift shops are excellent places to find great bargains. **HOUSING WORKS** (202 East 77th Street, 772-8461) has been renovated, and proceeds benefit PWAs. It has other locations at 306 Columbus Avenue (579-7566) and 143 West 17th Street (366-0820). Other great thrift shops: **CANCER CARE SHOP** (1480 Third Avenue, 879-9868), and the **SPENCE-CHAPIN THRIFT SHOP** (1850 Second Avenue, 426-7643; 1430 Third Avenue, 737-8448). It can take some work, but bargains can be found. At times, new clothing is donated by stores.

Unlike thrift stores, who are operated by charities, consignment shops help rich ladies sell their stuff. Having said that, there are two on Madison Avenue worth trying: **ENCORE** (1132 Madison, 879-2850) and **MICHAEL'S** (1041 Madison Avenue, 737-7273). These consignment shops are more high-end in brand and price—used Chanel suits, for instance—but people do say good things about them.

3

Quiet Places for Meditation

BROTHERHOOD SYNAGOGUE BIBLICAL GARDEN
28 Gramercy Park South off Third Avenue, 674-5750; fax 505-6707
The former Quaker Friends' Meetinghouse on Gramercy Park is one of the quietest temples in New York. Now a Reform Jewish synagogue, this children's after-school community center is quite noisy during the day, but after 4 P.M. offers an overwhelming sense of peace. Spend a solace-filled hour in the outdoor gardens with such tropical plants as oleander, pistachio, and date palm, and see the synagogue's thoughtful monument to Holocaust victims.

Ask a porter to take you to the cellar, where you can view one of the tunnels of the abolitionist underground railroad.

CATHEDRAL OF ST. JOHN THE DIVINE
West 112th Street and Amsterdam Avenue, 316-7540; fax 932-7348
The largest gothic cathedral in the world is also one of a few places where you are guaranteed (a) a seat; (b) total peace with no hecklers; and (c) an open house where someone will smile.

St. John's is most well-known for the Blessing of the Animals, which takes place on Saint Francis Day, the first Sunday of October. With creatures great and small including everything from pythons to mice, the annual event draws some 6,000 people and over 7,000 animals. The Philharmonic plays a free concert in the cathedral annually on Memorial Day, which is one of ten large concerts every year. The church also holds art shows, tributes to the ill and less fortunate, exhibits of news events, and an extraordinary "peace fountain." At St. John's, groups and couples sit in silence observing awesome ceilings and the art of a place so inspiring that an avenue was named for it.

THE CLOISTERS' GARDENS
Fort Tryon Park, West 190th Street, 923-3700; fax 795-3640

Nowhere else in Manhattan will you feel less like you are in the city. Part of the Metropolitan Museum system, the imported Cloisters came piece by piece from France to resemble a variety of monks' habitats of old Europe. In the cloister gardens—a quadrangle enclosed by a roofed or vaulted passage—you can imagine the quiet introspection of the life of a man of prayer.

In environments like this, the spring was especially beautiful. See that spring beauty year-round in the herb garden, with its impressive array of 250 imported plants and a fragrance that wafts throughout the museum. The beds are arranged around a fifteenth-century Venetian wellhead and are framed by views of the George Washington Bridge and the Hudson River.

While you're there, go see the "sex bed," which is a bed of plants devoted to aphrodisiacs. Closed Mondays and New Year's Day.

THE ENGLISH-SPEAKING UNION
16 East 69th Street between Fifth and Madison Avenues, 879-6800; fax 772-2886

For $70 a year, or a free one-time use, you can visit a quiet spot on the Upper East Side that will have you rubbing elbows with British royalty in the library, or listening to anglophiles discussing the monarch in the townhouse's tea room. This concept came about when Prince Albert and friends decided that Brits around the world didn't have proper places to congregate. Now there is an ESU in every major U.S. city and in eighty-five countries around the world. Every one has issues of *Punch* inside.

Plus there are more than 8,000 volumes relating to the Commonwealth. First rate, old chap.

CRYSTAL GARDENS
21 Greenwich Avenue near Sixth Avenue and 10th Street, 727-0692
While the store is very knowledgeable about gems and alternative healing methods, people often come in just to hang out because, they say, "the energy is so good." I go for the smell. Plus: personalized advice about crystals, flower essences, metaphysical gifts, tools, and other New Age supplies can be found here. Open Sunday–Thursday, 12:00 P.M.–8:00 P.M.; Friday and Saturday, 12:00 P.M.–9:00 P.M.

HUDSON VIEW GARDENS
116 Pinehurst Avenue, West 183rd–West 184th Streets
A replica of a private English country land in the midst of a bustling section of town can be found only after climbing many steps. It's so far above the usual city noises that you will think you've entered a Hospital Quiet Zone. Here are what seem to be the cottages of a medieval English town, all covered with moss and vines. There is no ball playing, eating, shouting, etc. Since it's a private area, residents can, if they wish, ask you to leave.

As you go out, note the designs on the manholes (fancy eagles) that exude a British sense of street tidiness.

MUSEUM OF MODERN ART GARDENS
11 West 53rd Street between Fifth and Sixth Avenues, 708-9480
Here is authentic quiet, where people sit during the four seasons and meditate on art. Look at sculptures by Picasso and Scott Burton, and a weeping willow that seems to stand guard. Then muse on how all this midtown space was left for plants and air.

In summer, a free Summergarden concert series invites famous and obscure musicians to entertain the crowds every Friday and Saturday from 6:00 P.M.–10:00 P.M. Although this is noisy, you can come to the museum early, sit in the garden, and wait.

Changing the subject a little: A room recommended by friends over at the Metropolitan, the Nu rad-Din Room, is decorated in the style of a Syrian home during the Ottoman period. It features marble floors, stained glass windows, and quite beautiful, high, ornamental ceilings. See the Metropolitan Museum's special room below.

NEW YORK PUBLIC LIBRARY, BERG COLLECTION
Fifth Avenue and 42nd Street, 930-0803

If you enter the library and go to Room 320, you will think you have stumbled upon an English manor library. In this room you will discover first editions and original manuscripts only to be found in the New York Library's Berg Collection of Literature.

Luckily, writers don't have to be New York City natives for their works to qualify for a place at the Berg. Authors range from Hawthorne to Keats to Twain to Poe to Shelley. Feast your eyes on some of the most important handwriting ever—and be at peace with your surroundings. Also, check out the Arents Collection, devoted to the "study of tobacco."

PROSPECT PARK'S LONG MEADOW AND WOODS
Enter in Park Slope at Boat House, east of ball fields

This area of tranquillity is found right outside the business district of Park Slope. When you walk into the park at Lincoln Road and Ocean Avenue, you will note paths that lead to a wooded area that seems more New York State than New York City.

This meadow was designed with the Adirondacks in mind: It features the same craggy, imperfect, winding fields. See also Boulder Bridge, built entirely from rocks. Warning: It's not advisable to visit this area at night.

MAIN READING ROOM OF SCHOMBURG CENTER
515 Malcolm X Boulevard, 491-2200

On Thursday–Saturday, 10:00 A.M.–6:00 P.M., sit inside an African drum in their octagonal reading room. The room is built to resemble that traditional instrument and is filled with a collection of history and literature from several regions.

THE GARDENS OF ST. LUKES IN THE FIELDS
487 Hudson Street

Wind your way through a labyrinth of shrubs and flowers, and as in many of the vest-pocket parks in the book, pause, snooze, and read on a shaded bench! Do this Monday–Friday from 7:00 A.M. to 7:00 P.M.; weekends from 7:00 A.M. to 5:00 P.M.

Ah, simplicity.

NEW YORK ZENDO SHOBO-JI—ZEN STUDY PROGRAM
223 East 67th Street, 861-3333

This is a traditional Japanese meditation hall, with floor cushions, burning incense, and a small stone garden for meditation on Thursday evening. Visitors can attend an introductory meditation class for $10; after that you can gain weekday access for $40 a month.

IRIS AND B. GERALD CANTOR ROOF OF THE METROPOLITAN MUSEUM
Fifth Avenue and 82nd Street

Some sixty-five feet above the ground, atop the museum's Wallace Wing, you can visit an open-air sculpture garden that offers a spectacular view of Central Park and the whole Manhattan skyline! The roof is open on Sunday and Tuesday–Thursday, 9:30 A.M.–5:15 P.M.; Friday and Saturday hours are 9:30 A.M.–8:45 P.M.

Also, a brief mention of the **JEFFREY CHILDS MEMORIAL GARDEN**, at **GAY MEN'S HEALTH CRISIS (GMHC)**, the People With AIDS health group, which has an informal roof garden with the most amazing horticultural treats—the herbs are used in the kitchen of GMHC! Located at 119 West 24th Street, it is not generally open to the public but if you ask nicely at the front door they may let you go in and peek. Also, if you are a volunteer at the organization (337-1238), you get to use the garden as a pretty cool place to eat lunch! (Note: This closed at press time.)

VAN CORTLANDT PARK AND HOUSE MUSEUM
242nd Street and Broadway, The Bronx

This one is open Tuesday–Friday, 10:00 A.M.–3:00 P.M.; Saturday and Sunday, 11:00 A.M.–4:00 P.M. For $2, skip the mansion and hit the park's fabulous colonial herb garden. A very pretty place but only during weekdays when the crowds are no longer thronging. Wander around for a dose of eighteenth century history as if the same civility existed today.

JAMAICA BAY WILDLIFE REFUGE
Broad Channel Queens (Take the A train to Broad Channel Station)
One of a few surprises to "hard-core" New Yorkers, this place is a bird watcher's paradise: 10,000 acres of woodpeckers, herons, and lots of other wildlife. (Some of that includes toads and bats!) Open 9:00 A.M.–5:00 P.M.

LAST NOTE: UN PEACE GARDEN
First Avenue and 45th Street
Open weekdays, weekends, and holidays, 9:00–5:00 P.M.: just come to watch the hand-holding, and see the roses, sculpture gardens, and self-important diplomats.

SIDEBAR SPECIAL The Most Quiet Places Period

THE BELL TOWER, in the Riverside Church (490 Riverside Drive at 120th Street) is definitely one of the quietest places ever to exist in New York. No car horns, no loud traffic, no sirens, no shouting—in fact, it is very difficult to believe, when inside the Bell Tower, that you haven't left New York.

THE CONSERVATORY GARDEN (105th Street and Fifth Avenue) may be the best-kept secret in Manhattan. As mentioned in the sidebar "Little Parks and Little Plazas" in Chapter 1, there is an authentic Shakespearean garden designed by Thomas Price, and a secret garden called the South Garden.

While the **DIA CENTER ROOFTOP** (548 West 22nd Street between 10th and 11th Avenues) may not sit on the city's tallest building, it does offer a remote roosting place for safety and solitude above the mean streets. One of the city's best quiet places (of the city's interior public spaces) is inside the **EQUITABLE ATRIUM,** where they've hidden a gift of solitude: a forty-foot, semi-circular marble settee (787 Seventh Avenue between 51st and 52nd Streets). At the **FORD FOUNDATION BUILDING** (320 East 43rd Street between First and Second Avenues) the air is dense with the earthy scent of bursting horticulture, a kind of intoxicating chlorophyll panacea guaranteed to calm the most hyperactive minds.

Bathed in sunlight streaming through several floor-to-ceiling windows, and tastefully furnished with colorfully upholstered reading chairs, the **POETS HOUSE** (72 Spring Street between Crosby and Lafayette Streets, second floor) is more a cozy living room than a stuffy library. At the **RUSSIAN AND TURKISH BATHS** (268 East 10th Street, between First and Second Avenues), once you recover from the initial fear of having all your body fluids boil out your ears, you begin to appreciate the palpable feeling of tension melt.

Here's the dirt: one of the most pristine yet peculiar sanctuaries in New York is the **NEW YORK EARTH ROOM** (141 Wooster Street; one block south of Houston Street), a Soho loft filled with 280,000 pounds of topsoil. Finally, the **WATER STREET PLAZA** (55 Water Street at Old Slip Road), an enormous brick plaza, is an open space that's all yours.

EXTRA: CHURCHES AND SYNAGOGUES TOO "PUBLIC" TO FORGET

The **CHURCH OF THE TRANSFIGURATION** (1 East 29th Street, 684-6770) is an unlikely place, settled in the midst of Murray Hill's tallest buildings; it even has a small, ancient well in the garden. Inside are three separate areas for prayer. And the Episcopal Little Church offers a wide assortment of extracurricular activities as they relate to the changing times of religion.

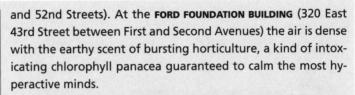 **FIRST CORINTHIAN BAPTIST CHURCH** (1912 Seventh Avenue, 864-9526), once the Regent Vaudeville Theater of Harlem, presents fine trained and untrained voices that resonate with spirit. They are led by Pastor Thomas McKinzie who admits that he acquired the vaudevillian space because it lends "an air of theatricality" to the services. The thirty-member choir is a great early show.

The 1913 theater remains the same, including an extended balcony. Some 500 regulars and bystanders participate in an uplifting and sporadically religious experience. Non-hymn singers are duly welcomed, says the Reverend McKinzie. (They do ask for a $3 donation.)

Located in the theater district at 239 West 49th Street (489-1340), **ST. MALACHY'S CHURCH,** "The Actor's Chapel of New York,"™ is a happy church (of sorts) that caters to the acting community with special thespian services and a feeling of home that is important to actors. Just about every Catholic on Broadway attends services, which are usually on Saturdays at 5:00 P.M. and Sundays at 9:00 A.M. and 11:00 A.M. (the choir performs at the 11:00 A.M. mass only). Many famous types have been mourned here—so says their press material.

A Gothic Church for Episcopalians, **GRACE CHURCH** (802 Broadway, 254-2000), is an 1846 monument (by Renwood, builder of St. Patrick's Cathedral) offering a full organ service that is ultimately serious and formal. Considered to be an important attraction in New York, the Sunday services are welcoming to outsiders. The day's Bible passages are posted, and a 14-person choir follows the pastor's every word. Sunday services are at 9:00 A.M. and 11:00 A.M.

The Gothic trimmings of the church are haunting. Tours are held at 12:15 P.M. on Sundays. On a fun, historic note: In 1864, P. T. Barnum's celebrated midget, Tom Thumb, proudly took a bride here before 12,000 spectators and a press bonanza.

DIGNITY NEW YORK (218 West 11th Street, 620-0369) is an organization which offers spiritual support to lesbians and gay Catholics and runs an AIDS Ministry. This is a fellowship community of lesbian and gay Roman Catholics. Main activity is eucharistic liturgy and social, held on Sunday evenings at 7:30 P.M. at St. John's Episcopal Church. Also, for reference, Dignity Brooklyn (718-769-3447), holds a liturgy in members' homes every third Saturday of each month, after which a potluck dinner is served. Call for schedule.

In addition to being a midtown neighborhood church with open services all week long, **LAMB'S MANHATTAN CHURCH OF THE NAZARENE** (130 West 44th Street, 575-0300), is a group that pursues health and other community issues, including a hot meal program, food pantry, clothing, counseling, job training, tutoring, and health care for the needy. They also hold soul-lifting gospel services and house an Off-Broadway theater. The building, designed by Stanford White, has had many uses. It's a historical landmark well worth visiting.

ST. BARTHOLOMEW'S EPISCOPAL CHURCH (109 East 50th Street, 751-1616) offers a multitude of special programs and services, such as a bulletin board of apartment listings, a terrific amateur theater group, a schedule of classes that would put some colleges to shame, and a City Club that sponsors athletic events and weekend adventures for singles. But don't forget that this first and foremost is a church with diverse prayer services.

The neighborhood and St. Bart's work together in a "Community Ministry" for feeding, clothing, and sheltering the homeless. This is not like soup kitchens run by many churches; caring parishioners lend support by "hosting," or staying overnight with the guests. People can come and see the place daily from 8:00 A.M.–6:00 P.M. Services are held Sundays at 8:00, 9:00, and 11:00 A.M.

Plush furnishings and a jazz ensemble that changes weekly doesn't sound like church to you? Minister John Gensel supervises at the popular **ST. PETER'S LUTHERAN CHURCH** (619 Lexington Avenue, 935-2200), where congregants lead the service. The Reverend Gensel believes in the call of the bass, and always ensures that music is first on the bill. On closer inspection, you will see that parishioners of this Evangelical Lutheran church come for the music, which helps create a most relaxed churchgoing experience.

Of course, if you need to be reminded of where you are, a partially ecumenical service about peace and responsibility occurs during band breaks. Peacefulness is shattered, though, if you look up at the windows—that's Citicorp Plaza right outside.

WEST-PARK PRESBYTERIAN CHURCH (165 West 86th Street, 362-4890) acknowledged its growing Spanish-speaking congregation of Puerto Ricans, Dominicans, Salvadorans, and Chileans by combining an English and Spanish service on the first Sunday of each month. Hymns are sung alternately in English and Spanish, and the Scripture and meditations also bounce between both languages. The pastor reports that Latin congregants are pleased, because although they speak modest amounts of English for daily use, the regular services are difficult. Afterward, participants of different cultures huddle at the coffee hour.

It's been 150 years, but New York's oldest continuing Jewish worship house still stands at the same spot where its congregants prayed during the Civil War. There is a sense of history in everything that occurs at the **CENTRAL SYNAGOGUE** (123 East 55th Street, 838-5122), although the rabbi's sermons seem to concentrate on modern spirituality. The 122-foot domed sanctuary is impressive, yet simple. Though there is a choir that accentuates much of the service, there is no sense of grandeur here; it's really a family atmosphere. Central displays religious art in its lobby, as well. Saturday services are at 10:30 A.M.

CONGREGATION BETH SIMCHAT TORAH (57 Bethune Street, 929-9498) is a Reform synagogue for lesbians and gays. There is a weekly Shabbat Service where everyone is welcome and dress is informal. Tickets are not needed, and services are held on all holidays. Yom Kippur service (late September, thereabouts) is especially touching; held at the Jacob Javits Center, the room overlooks the Hudson and conducts the evening's "Sunset Service" under the pale sunlight. Events throughout the week include Feminist Forum, workshops and classes on topics such as coming out to your family and having children. The congregation participates in important community events such as the Gay Pride March (and annual Jewish events such as the Israel Day Parade) and publishes a monthly newsletter and calendar. Friday services are usually held around 8:30 P.M., but sometimes earlier. Rabbi Sharon Kleinbaum is a beloved speaker with a "cultish" following. (No Jewish/non-Jew marriages, though.)

A community center for Upper West Side Jews, the **STEPHEN WISE FREE SYNAGOGUE** (30 West 68th Street, 877-4050), boasts a large, dedicated congregation of local families who work on the two chapels' upkeep and hold small Saturday services in the round. Among the special events are modern plays about the holidays, outreach programs for the poor, a women's studies group, and a popular weekly music service.

The place is packed on Friday nights for the 6:00 P.M. service—at most city temples Saturdays are far less popular—and so it's on Friday that Stephen Wise uses its looming synagogue. The rabbi gives zesty, vignette-filled sermons without any element of preachiness.

Easy and unpretentious, rarely crowded, and with no membership requirements, the **VILLAGE TEMPLE** (33 East 12th Street, 674-2340) is a neighborhood space where families and singles comfortably pray, and have done so for generations. Village's unusual adult education sessions offer Hebrew, Jewish history, and courses such as "Blessings and Their Roles in Everyday Spirituality." On Fridays, there are singing lessons. If you choose to pay dues, you will be added to the temple's mailing list. Services are Saturday at 10:30 A.M., and the first Friday of every month at 7:30 P.M. High holiday services are held at Cooper Union in the East Village.

Down in the financial district, the **WALL STREET SYNAGOGUE** (47 Beekman Street, 227-7543 for the office, or 227-7800 for schedule) Orthodox temple holds daily services (8:10 A.M.) packed with 20-year members and newcomer executives who work in the area. Rabbi Joseph Hager, a Jewish leader for over twenty-five years, presides at Lower Manhattan's only temple, which boasts a wooden replica of New York's first prayer house on its roof. Mill Lane Synagogue, from 1654, is now used only on Succoth and Purim, but can be seen for the asking.

Lunch hour services (1:30 P.M.), lasting about twenty minutes, are attended by over 100 local worshipers. (On holidays, only members can attend.) Rabbi Hager hosts relevant speakers, and lectures on area-related topics, such as "Judaism and Technology."

Sabbath and weekend services: Friday, 4:50 P.M.; Saturday, 9:00 A.M. and 4:45 P.M.; and Sunday, 4:50 P.M.

4

Museums, Libraries, and Open Homes

AUNT LEN'S DOLL EMPORIUM

Note: This Harlem mainstay has been sold and will reportedly reopen in 1998 (281-4143, for further information).

Lenon Holder Hoyte was a feisty woman with a mission: She moved umpteen hundred dolls to a larger home than her brownstone overshadowing Hamilton Mansion, before the dolls ran her out. Aunt Len's home atop the museum is a testimony to her affinity. Dolls make the staircase unusable, and favorites line the walls.

The place is no kid's stop: it's for adults who want to see how far a collector can get carried away. Aunt Len was our town's doll aficionado from 1960 until her death in the early 1990s, having garnered private collections of irreplaceable and fixable junk.

If you have ever owned a doll, you must see Len's paraphernalia, featuring clothing trunks, hair braiders, dollhouse appliances, and petunias for the garden. Some of her dolls are toys: windup walking elephants, music boxes, and former TV stars (Sonny and Cher) that really talk. Len was, as she herself said, "a real legend."

ALTERNATIVE MUSEUM
594 Broadway, 966-4444; Fax 226-2158

Back in the 1970s when Soho was all about unusual visual art, Alternative was the area's leader. Today it is plunging ahead with even newer visions, such as the exhibit of a few years back titled "Americans," in which an artist aligned ethnic photos with each group's best known slurs. Simultaneously, this gallery ran the "Baby 'M' case" whose creator ranted offscreen, and where they featured a ladder leaning against a shiny black floor.

Alternative produces work with a statement, whether it's religious, political, or purely artistic. One artist "exposed" pop culture by painting pop objects (such as Walkman headphones) pure white. Open Tuesday–Saturday from October through May. Hours are 11:00 A.M.–6:00 P.M.

EL MUSEO DEL BARRIO
1230 Fifth Avenue, 831-7272

The people of El Barrio—the area just above 100th Street on the East Side—call themselves *vecinos* (neighbors). The Hispanic art and dance and film and video and theater center was formed to help people learn about this often persecuted and misunderstood group. Besides local art exhibits, "Writers At El Museo" supports artists, while guest curator programs explore specific careers.

The museum also features a panel discussion every month on themes of racial and social class during several tumultuous periods. They also note, during such dialogues, the divergent views on New York's Hispanic culture. Open Wednesday–Sunday, 11:00 A.M.–5:00 P.M.

MUSEUM OF THE CITY OF NEW YORK
1220 Fifth Avenue, 534-1672

I've always wanted to use this cliché. . . . If you're like me you'll love this place. City of New York is a time-honored way to understand New York's past and present via large-scope photos, glass-enclosed landscapes, multimedia, an opulent silver collection, and creative views of the past. The Costume Collection is a look at the moodiness of fashion while the Theater

Collection contains a wide array of sensational stage paraphernalia. But of course, adults want the Toy Collection!

Singular exhibits in the past included "City Play," examining how New Yorkers frolicked in past decades, and a special show on how this city became the country's communications capital. A regular presentation, "The Big Apple," is a glitzy history trip via video, film, filmstrips (yeah, just like in high school), and taped music. Open Wednesday–Saturday, 10:00 A.M.–5:00 P.M.; Sunday, 1:00 P.M.–5:00 P.M.; closed Monday and Tuesday.

NEW MUSEUM OF CONTEMPORARY ART
583 Broadway at Prince Street, 219-1355

This always-new museum is committed to exploring nontraditional ideas and experimental works of art. The exhibition schedule frequently includes shows of a political nature. They have a comprehensive schedule of lectures, films, and gallery talks, which complement their exhibition schedule. Hours are Wednesday, Thursday, Friday, and Sunday, 12:00 P.M.–6:00 P.M.; Saturday, 12:00 P.M.–8:00 P.M. Sorry, closed on Monday and Tuesday. Admission is: adults $5; seniors, artists, and students, $3; 18 and under free; Thursday, 6:00 P.M.–8:00 P.M. is free. Call for recorded information.

When meandering around Soho, please note the window outside the museum for a floating exhibit of sexually aware art. Sometimes, it is quite explicit, such as the Prostitutes of New York/Gran Fury piece on safe sex and how the American mainstream is afraid to discuss it. In 1987, New Museum's window made a powerful and quite prolonged statement when it featured busts of several top world leaders with that person's most prominent statement on the AIDS crisis. Underneath former President Reagan was nothing.

NEW YORK CITY TRANSIT MUSEUM
Abandoned subway station at Boerum Place and Schermerhorn Street, 718-243-3060. Note: The museum is scheduled to move to City Hall (in addition) Subway Station in 1998.

Some may badmouth New York's subway system but it is the world's largest. At the New York Transit Museum you'll learn about the history of this monstrous wonder down under and its relationship to the growth and development of New York. In the summer, they offer many activities and tours inside and outside the museum. Inside there is a series of free workshops for children. Outside, you will go exploring some neighborhoods in New York's five boroughs while learning about a variety of related topics and issues. Examples include the Brooklyn at Work tour series or a bridge and neighborhood tour at either end of the city. Every year, around the third Saturday of November, the Museum sells fire boxes, original brass operator handles, El signals, uniforms, and a subway car! Other yearly events include tours of the shuttered, chandeliered City Hall Station yearly. During the winter, when it's too chilly for exploring, check out the lectures and other events being held at the museum.

From 1936 to 1946 this was a shuttle subway stop. In 1976, the Transit Authority opened the station to the public. And that's enough of a reason to come and see it. This is a prime example of a place worth being on their mailing list. Prices for walking tours vary between $10 and $25. The museum hours are: Tuesday–Friday, 10:00 A.M.–4:00 P.M.; and Saturday–Sunday, 12:00 P.M.–5:00 P.M. Admission is $3 for adults and $1 for children and seniors.

Incidentally, Warsaw has an 11-stop subway that was in the works for decades. They waited seventy years for the train!

POLICE ACADEMY MUSEUM
235 East 20th Street, Second floor, 477-9753

Learn the history of combat between criminal and cop—in an austere setting of jackknives, pistols, whips, handcuffs, and facsimiles of the SWAT team bomb patrol. The Police Academy Museum does give you a sense of pride about New York's Finest, especially after you peek at what they're up against. The historical element is boring, but the merchandise (such as drug bins and a counterfeit section) is certainly exciting.

The exhibit yields an understanding of the city's, and possibly the world's, toughest and least-appreciated jobs. Open Monday–Friday, 8:00 A.M.–4:00 P.M., but call first for an appointment. Admission is free. (And if this excites you, might I note the *national* Police Museum in Miami as a vacation destination.)

GARIBALDI-MEUCCI MUSEUM

420 Tompkins Avenue, Rosebank, Staten Island, 718-442-1608

In 1956, the Order Sons of Italy opened a free museum dedicated to Antonio Meucci, who many believe is the person who invented the telephone, the second-most precious American device.

Story goes, he heard a scream travel over a wire in 1849 and he filed a provisional patent some five years before Alexander Graham Bell. (The museum deftly does not present Bell's side of this oft-told story.) The tale of Meucci is an amazing one to follow and a great excuse to visit Staten Island. The museum is tiny and somewhat wistfully romantic. Open daily, except Monday, 1:00 P.M.–5:00 P.M.

Q: WHAT'S THE MOST PRECIOUS U.S. COMMODITY?

A: Read on.

MUSEUM OF TELEVISION AND RADIO

25 West 52nd Street, 621-6600; http://www.mtr.org

Recently expanded to twice its size, here is home for serious couch potatoes, with over 7,000 favorite television shows from three decades. And why, it's home to every American who has lived during these decades, when television became the only national pastime we had.

Now, I'm not knocking the glorious tube, but in this place you can really tell how bad our infatuation with television has become, compared to how bad it once was: In addition to private watching areas, you have regular salutes to big legends in the business, from the late and honored writer Dennis Potter *(The Singing Detective),* to Lucy, Monty Python, and even Larry Gelbart of "M*A*S*H" fame. What's new is heaven for radio nuts, combing the airwaves for FDR chats, Burns and Allen, "War of the Worlds," Fred Allen . . . and a host of seminars on radio topics throughout the year.

Open Tuesday–Sunday, 12:00 P.M.–6:00 P.M., the museum (one of two—the other is in Los Angeles) caters to young'uns with its "Rock-and-Roll and Radio" series and to older fans with public affairs programming and the dying art of documentaries. See a showcase of commercials. There are weekend children programs too.

Admission is $6, $4 students and seniors, 13 and under $3, with membership offered also. "We have Elvis's TV appearances from 1956 to his death in 1977, including docs and dramatizations," an excitable staff person told me.

FORBES MAGAZINE GALLERIES

62 Fifth Avenue at West 12th Street, 206-5548

Open for free to the public Tuesday, Wednesday, Friday, and Saturday, 10:00 A.M.–4:00 P.M., the Forbes galleries are filled with all kinds of trivia and history, and have quite a selection of trophies. Malcolm Forbes, the late publisher and editor-in-chief of *Forbes,* had a great sense of humor and an uncanny collection of toy boats and soldiers, which he loved to share. Check out the collection of genuine Fabergé eggs from the last czars of Russia—a rare collection. See some of the oldest Monopoly sets in existence. These galleries present an interesting and eclectic collection. Malcolm was a character.

JACQUES MARCHAIS TIBETAN MUSEUM

338 Lighthouse Avenue, Staten Island, 718-987-3500; fax 718-351-0402

Although it is far from the Staten Island Ferry terminal, this is one of New York's great wonders and worth the trip. An inexpensive day with Tibetan art in a small house and garden just might turn you into a fan of the stringent and dedicated Tibetan way of living. The museum was begun forty-five years ago by Mrs. Jacques Marchais, a Staten Island woman who was fascinated by Tibet's masks and dolls, and she left a legacy enough to fill three houses (alas, there's only one). But you can find tours, lectures, and classes on topics ranging from Tibetan family rituals to origami. Exhibits change quite often.

While listening to the music in the garden, you can actually sit on the wooden sculptures. The museum is atop a steep cliff and boasts a fantastic view of suburban fields. You may become superstitious when you learn what the Tibetan saying, OM MANI PADME, means. Open Wednesday–Sunday 1:00 P.M.–5:00 P.M., from April to November; Wednesday–Friday (same hours) during winter months. A great place to meditate.

MUSEUM AT FIT—FASHION INSTITUTE OF TECHNOLOGY
Seventh Avenue at 27th Street, 217-5970

For fashion aficionados, this gallery is open Tuesday through Friday and focuses on issues relevant to fashion and its satellite industries. Admission is free and some of the avant-garde work (*Chairs* was the title of one singular exhibit) is bizarre and worthy.

INTREPID SEA-AIR-SPACE MUSEUM
Pier 86, West 46th Street between 12th and 13th Avenues, 957-7055

A cool 900-foot aircraft carrier, the museum houses and exhibits World War II history, and stuff from the modern navy; there are also exhibits on space exploration, the deep sea, and early aviation.

The *Intrepid* was NASA's prime recovery vessel that retrieved astronaut Scott Carpenter and his Mercury capsule in 1962. It was designated as the official Navy and Marine Corps Bicentennial Exposition Vessel in 1975 and has been docked here since. Yet maritime paraphernalia is all tourists care about on this ship. Open Wednesday–Sunday, 10:00 A.M.–5:00 P.M.

By the way, sometimes, at night, it's a disco!

NEW YORK CITY FIRE MUSEUM
278 Spring Street, between Hudson and Varick, 691-1303; fax 924-0430

Suggested admission: $4 for adults, $2 for seniors and students, $1 for children under 12. Open Tuesday through Sunday, 10:00 A.M.–4:00 P.M. (office hours 9:00 A.M.–5:00 P.M.).

This three-floor museum houses one of the most comprehensive collections of fire-related art and artifacts from the eighteenth century to the present, including beautifully preserved hand- and horse-drawn and motorized pieces of apparatus. The Commissioner's Room, in the top tier of the building, is available for meetings and catered events. For the little tykes, junior firefighters ages 4 through 8 can have a birthday celebration, right here, with a visit from a New York City firefighter.

This is an odd place for a lecture; nevertheless this museum honors our men in red, and, for architecture buffs, is located in an abandoned Beaux Arts firehouse dating from 1904. It offers exhibits on vehicles, tools, and the art of firefighting. One concerns the city's most notorious fire, the Greene

Street Triangle Shirtwaist fire of 1911, the event which prompted modern building codes.

Lectures are both serious and offbeat. They include "The Juvenile Fire-setter—A National Problem," about youthful pyromaniacs; "History of the New York City Fire Department"; and something we can learn from, "Fire Protection in Japan." Coffee is served—hot. But, of course.

LOWER EAST SIDE TENEMENT MUSEUM
90 Orchard Street, 431-0233

Hours: Tuesday–Friday, 12:00 P.M.–5:00 P.M.; Saturday and Sunday, 11:00 A.M.–5:00 P.M. Closed Mondays. Tours of tenement: Tuesday–Friday, 1:00 P.M.–3:00 P.M.; Saturday and Sunday, slotted times between 11:00 A.M.–4:15 P.M. The anything-but-charming Tenement Museum was chartered in 1988, seeking to promote tolerance by teaching the history of the various settlement experiences on the Lower East Side of New York. The museum is housed in a pre–Old Law tenement building (which is listed on the National Register of Historic Places). There are a few exhibits (for example: peddlers, photos of the Lower East Side from the turn of the century, a scale model of the tenement, and humans demonstrating the lives of tenement-dwellers in 1870 and 1915). There are also slide and video shows. Best time to go is on Sundays, when they offer various walking tours ($8 for adults, $6 for seniors and students) throughout the day, as well as the slide show. An excellent place to go before starting out on an exploration of the Lower East Side is their bookstore, which sells various historical materials about this area.

The real museum is as follows: Designers have placed actors in rooms above the ground floor who play roles of turn-of-the-century families (Irish, German, Jewish, Italian) suffering through their daily, cramped, impoverished routine. You are the observer. Not meant to be fun, exactly, this is a "site specific" way for you to understand exactly what Lower East Side residents lived through in the early 1900s. And a way for you to leave cherishing New York's culture even more.

THE HALL OF FAME FOR GREAT AMERICANS, ON THE CAMPUS OF BRONX COMMUNITY COLLEGE OF THE CITY OF NEW YORK
University Avenue and West 181st Street, 718-289-5161, fax 718-289-6014

Open seven days a week from 10:00 A.M. to 5:00 P.M.; free admission. Have you ever wondered why New York City does not have an acclaimed wax museum? (It has *one* in Harlem; see Harlem Days, Chapter 5.) Here in the Big Apple, we prefer a more permanent medium. Up in the boondocks of the Bronx stands a decrepit, but poignant hall featuring ninety-eight bronze busts in which to meditate on America's past. This monument to 1900 is truly one of the strangest finds around: Abraham Lincoln, Alexander Graham Bell, Booker T. Washington, the Wright brothers, George Washington Carver, and other contributors to our society are poised on pedestals, surrounded by weeds, on the grounds behind BCC's Gould Library.

Ninety-minute tours begin with a video introduction in the rotunda of the landmark Gould Memorial Library, designed by Stanford White. Guides provide American history, an informed view of classical architecture, and a fine arts learning experience for school children, family, and adults. The free exhibit stands in an area that once served as a Revolutionary War fort. An official says the hall's existence is endangered because "yearly attendance, which was once 50,000, is about a tenth of that now." Quite endangered—so go!

AMERICAN MUSEUM OF NATURAL HISTORY
West 79th Street and Central Park West, 769-5100; fax 769-5006; http://www.amnh.org

If you've lived in New York all your life, you've been to this museum at least once; it is a favorite for school trips! At the Museum of Natural History you can learn about dinosaurs (a renovated floor has been devoted to the topic, and it is by far the most popular exhibit there), whales, diamonds, water irrigation in Africa, and almost any other topic imaginable. Catch a movie at the IMAX theater there, or go to the planetarium and learn how stars are created. You will never be bored at this museum, but if you don't like large crowds and lots of tourists, you may be annoyed. Go on a weekday, when the museum is quieter and there isn't a long line for the dinosaur floor. Oh, and definitely do check out the lifesize plastic whale hanging from the two-story high ceiling in the mammal section.

METROPOLITAN MUSEUM OF ART
1000 Fifth Avenue at 82nd Street, 535-7710; fax 535-3879;
http://www.metmuseum.org

There are over 2 million pieces of art in the collections of the Metropolitan Museum, featuring great artists like Degas, Monet, Cezanne . . . the list goes on, and they are all names you know well. Down the long hallways of the Met you can view art from all different periods around the world. There is a great section of musical instruments from different ages and countries as well. Again, this is a museum that will always be very crowded, especially with tourists, and as natives to New York you probably don't need it pointed out to you. But, like the Museum of Natural History, it highly deserves mention.

ABIGAIL ADAMS SMITH MUSEUM
421 East 61st Street, 838-6878

Mrs. Smith, the daughter of John Adams, shared her life with her alternately rich and destitute husband, Col. William Stephens Smith. Their estate was a country farm in the 1700s; now it's flanked by monstrous hospital buildings. Smith's house is gone, too, but her stables are one of New York's few intact eighteenth-century buildings. For $2, the stables tour offers views of letters from George Washington and a frilly dress Smith made during those lean years.

Here's the wonderful part: From late winter until early fall, the Smiths' backyard—a magnificent three-tiered beauty—comes alive with crocuses, daisies, and moss. Ye olde American backyard is maintained by the Colonial Dames of America. Find "1779" crudely sculpted in brick under the stables' upper-left-hand window. Closed on Saturdays.

MAIDENFORM MUSEUM
(Location moving at press time; call first, 856-8909)

My new favorite place to visit, the Maidenform (Bra) Museum, which is located at the True Form Intimate Apparel building, is an advertising tribute to the brassiere—*but read on first:* You can go only after making an appointment with "the marketing director" at the above number. Called a "unique educational resource for those interested in the history of fashion and advertising," I must say, I once dreamed about a museum like this.

HISTORY PROJECT

CHINATOWN HISTORY MUSEUM
70 Mulberry Street, 619-4785
This has reopened with complete community documentation to inform residents and visitors exactly how Chinatown came about. Now a museum—it used to be a gallery—this place promotes area history and art. Its archives project includes clippings, store signs, immigration papers, laundry irons, and letters that date from the late 1800s. This project demonstrates the hardships of organizing a community; the Chinese call it "showing a tree's roots." Those profiled in the project made history and shaped the future. Open weekdays, 10:00 A.M.–6:00 P.M.; walking tours available.

BETTMANN ARCHIVE
902 Broadway, 777-6200
How do 25 million images sound? These include movie stills, theater stills, jazz-era photos, and scientific artifacts relating to such subjects as fine art, TV and general entertainment, religion, current and ancient news, and obscure American history, all of which can be found at this fancy media center for the journalistic brethren and sistren. Bettmann charges for research, but not for casual browsing.

Bettmann Newsphotos, available by appointment, gives hardcore mediaphiles a peek at historic clippings. Open Monday–Friday, 9:00 A.M.–8:30 P.M. By the way, this was recently purchased by Microsoft, so expect to see all these images on the Web.

CENTER FOR THE STUDY OF THE PRESIDENCY
208 East 75th Street, 249-1200
The presidency is a favorite trivia subject in this country. Perhaps that's why Gordon Hoxie, the former chancellor of Long Island University, started this home for presidential research in 1971, six years after he took over President Eisenhower's Library of Presidential Papers. (Ike had writ-

ten a paper, "Why You Should Study the Presidency," and Hoxie seconded the motion.)

Hoxie is an infallible source on the subject and has been a confidant of several presidents. His library has over 3,000 volumes on most everything that concerns our past and present leaders, and he recently opened a new floor complete with two spacious reading rooms. Open Monday–Friday, 9:00 A.M.–5:00 P.M.

COLUMBIA UNIVERSITY EAST ASIAN INSTITUTE AND CHINA INSTITUTE
East Asian Institute: College Walk, 116th Street and Broadway in Kent Hall, 854-4318
China Institute: 125 East 65 Street, 744-8181

Since the China Institute's library does not open its doors to the public, the next best thing for Asian studies is the East Asian Institute's fascinating collection of material from China, Japan, and Korea at the C.V. Starr East Asian Library. Hidden off a path near Low Library, this is the only Columbia media center that you can enter without a Columbia ID. Open Monday–Thursday, 9:00 A.M.–7:00 P.M., Friday 9:00 A.M.–5:00 P.M., Saturday 12:00 P.M.–7:00 P.M.

China buffs, take heart: The China Institute does allow scholars with specific needs to use its overcrowded library. Open Monday–Friday, 9:00 A.M.–5:00 P.M. And the public is invited to a regular spring and fall season of lectures and classes on a variety of topics.

 **THE HISPANIC SOCIETY OF AMERICA**
613 West 155th Street, 926-2234

Hours: Tuesday–Saturday, 10:00 A.M.–4:30 P.M.; Sunday, 1:00 P.M.–4:00 P.M. Closed New Year's Day; February 12 and 22; Good Friday; Easter; May 30; July 4; Thanksgiving Day; and December 24, 25, and 31. Admission is free. Archer M. Huntington founded the society with the objective of establishing a center for the advancement of the study of the arts and culture of Hispanic peoples of the Iberian Peninsula. They have an "unrivaled" collection relating to Spanish culture, including a print collection that dates back from the fifteenth century, with special works by Ribera, Fortuny, and Goya.

MERCANTILE LIBRARY/MECHANICS INSTITUTE

Mercantile: 17 East 47th Street, 755-6710; fax 758-1387

Mechanics: 20 West 44th Street, 840-7648

Pay a few dollars and join the Writer's Studio at the Mercantile Library, where authors can get quiet work done. Or just come in and enjoy this literary center in the heart of midtown. It houses over 200,000 volumes and 30 current periodicals (not all mechanics related), and has been in existence for over 176 years. The library presents sixty programs of public interest, including films and seminars. Open weekdays, 9:00 A.M.–5:00 P.M. Regular users must pay membership fees.

If working with your hands is your thing, try the Mechanics Institute, a not-for-profit technical school that, while not as hushed as Mercantile, does have a fully-stocked library that describes every nut and screw. The same ilk loiter in both media centers.

SIDEBAR SPECIAL West Village Literary Homes

Ruth and Eileen McKenney had their famous fights—that eventually became the basis of the stories "My Sister Eileen" and the musical *Wonderful Town*—at 14 Gay Street. Louisa May Alcott wrote *Little Women* at 130 Macdougal Street. O. Henry's poignant story "The Last Leaf" was inspired by the gate at 10 Grove Street. He met with his muse at 49 East 9th Street, too. Hart Crane moped in a room at 45 Grove Street. In the boisterous piano bar MARIE'S CRISES (59 Grove), Tom Paine allegedly scribbled *Common Sense*.

Eighty-two Washington Place was home to Willa Cather and to Richard Wright—though not, of course, at the same time. James Fenimore Cooper once rented 145 Bleecker Street. Eighty-three West 3rd Street was the site of a raucous club where Edgar Allan Poe sat and created "The Raven." Seventy-five and a half Bedford Street was Edna St. Vincent Millay's home, and it's the thinnest—and ugliest—structure in the Village.

MERCHANT'S HOUSE MUSEUM
29 East 4th Street, 777-1089; fax 777-1104

This 1780 structure in the East Village has withstood a number of neigh-borhood changes. With ninety percent of the Tredwell family's original be-longings on view, the best part of the old place is that you can touch things.

Most historic homes are replicas, but this one truthfully displays four stories of bona fide nineteenth-century living. Compare the velvety, origi-nal carpeting to the cheap, new padding of our day; note the rooms de-signed with two doors on each side—one just for show—to achieve a sense of balance. See how an upper-middle-class family spent their spare time back then. Then look at old books, period clothing, and the uncramped ser-vants' quarters upstairs—and make sure to visit the Tredwell's majestic garden. Everything's intact. Open Sunday–Thursday, 1:00 P.M.–4:00 P.M.

MORRIS-JUMEL MANSION
65 Jumel Terrace (West 162nd Street), 923-8008

This impressive homestead was where the mysterious Eliza Jumel played mistress, hostess, or wife to such men as Aaron Burr, and where George Washington reportedly slept in his own room. The Morris-Jumel mansion is supposed to be haunted; as the legend has it, several people died there mysteriously. An official swears that Madame Jumel hangs out in the man-sion's office typewriter.

The house is a series of dichotomies: The Jumel estate stands a few blocks from a desolate area, yet it's surrounded by well-kept streets. The structure itself is in disrepair, yet the furniture is gorgeous, original masterpieces. A Washington-era trunk made from tree bark (that's how the trunk got its name) is on the second floor.

In the 1800s, when Washington Heights was largely Haitian, residents reportedly exorcised the house. According to the above-mentioned official, the ghosts have returned. Open Wednesday–Sunday, 10:00 A.M.–4:00 P.M.

NEW YORK GENEALOGICAL SOCIETY
c/o Library at 122 East 58th Street, 755-8532

If you are unsure as to how Brooke Shields and the Marquis de Sade man-aged to be distant cousins, go check their genealogical charts. This library, founded in 1869, is an offshoot of the *New York Genealogical Society Record*, one of the nation's leading magazines on genealogy. Inside the library's quiet study center are manuscripts of church records from several states. Family Bibles are also fun to browse through (it seems so nosy).

Over 66,500 volumes of literature on family histories are housed here, many of which can aid those seeking New York state history. More than 8,600 additional volumes are on microfilm. Anyone can visit and attend the occasional public lectures on charting the past. Open Tuesday–Saturday, 9:30 A.M.–5:00 P.M., $15 per day.

PATENTS DIVISION OF THE NEW YORK PUBLIC LIBRARY
188 Madison Avenue, 592-7000

If you read the "Patents" column in Monday's *Times* or *Newsday*, you might discover an interest in old and new inventions. Our public library has a Newspaper Project and a Patent Section where you can view, on microfilm, every concept on file at the Washington Patent Office. This peaceful space is housed in an old library building and staffed by knowledgeable, almost fanatical, patent experts. See the many crazy ideas that have been certified, and note how many were never manufactured.

Read the library's walls for the Inventor of the Week ("First Flying Saucer") and see the latest information on dangers to inventors' rights. It's for the highly imaginative. Open Monday, Friday, and Saturday, 10:00 A.M.–6:00 P.M.; Wednesday and Thursday, 11:00 A.M.–7:00 P.M.

HISTORIC RICHMOND TOWN
441 Clarke Avenue, Staten Island, 718-351-1611; fax 718-351-6057

Hours: Wednesday–Sunday, 1:00 P.M.–5:00 P.M.; extended hours in July and August. Admission: $4 for adults, $2.50 for seniors and children 6–18. Children under 6 free. The quaint, historic Richmondtown restoration may not be the most scintillating exhibit in town, but where else can you see such great art in an antique setting . . . and in winter months, *wassailing!**

This is the only historic village in New York, with 27 buildings, some dating back to the seventeenth century, on 100 acres. It includes the oldest school house still standing in the United States, the Voorlezer, which was built in 1696. Founded in 1690 by the Dutch, the village was established as a historic community in 1958. (It's changed very little since.) Special events

* Songs are sung, tales are told, people get drunk.

include Christmas events throughout the month of December, a concert series each Saturday between January and April in their candle-lit tavern, and the Richmond County Fair, the largest on Staten Island.

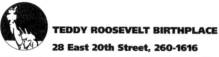

TEDDY ROOSEVELT BIRTHPLACE
28 East 20th Street, 260-1616

The only president born in New York City lived a childhood full of adventures. And we can relive them at his Gramercy Park birthplace for only $1. The tour guide will take you on a three-story trip with unmatched energy and a rare ability to put everything about young Teddy's life into a modern perspective.

Learn which exploit named the Teddy Bear; how "T. D." grew his bulk after a sickly childhood; why Teddy's mother was always dolled up around the house; and what pose New York Police Chief Roosevelt actually affected on San Juan Hill. Please speak softly, and do visit a lower-level collection of memorabilia commemorating the man that political cartoonists never tired of. Hours are 9:00 A.M.–5:00 P.M. Chamber music on Saturday and Sunday. Closed Monday and Tuesday.

ZIONIST ARCHIVES AND LIBRARY
110 East 59th Street, 339-6000

Speak to Ester Togman to discover more about this repository for books, pamphlets, periodicals, and other archival material regarding Israel, Zionism, and such topics as Jewish life in the Diaspora. The staff is helpful to those who wish to check facts or find information, much of which is readily available, just by calling. Xerox machines are standing by.

This fine place to expand a fledgling interest is the largest center for Zionist studies in the West. Open Monday–Friday, 10:00 A.M.–5:00 P.M.

MUSEUM OF JEWISH HERITAGE: A LIVING MEMORIAL TO THE HOLOCAUST
1 Battery Park Plaza, 968-1800

First proposed in 1982 by then-Mayor Ed Koch, the much-anticipated "Holocaust Museum" finally opened in September 1997. Located in the center of Battery Park, the six-sided museum stands as a living memorial to the victims of the holocaust. This is a personal monument to millions of relevant citizens and visitors in New York, and its purpose is to tell the tales of individual survivors, their grace and courage. The museum achieves its goal through its poignant exhibits—over 13,000 personal items donated or loaned by families and survivors. Rather than go through the historical implications of this dreaded period, the Living Memorial allows survivors and their families to speak through artifacts.

The museum is three floors—the first floor is devoted to Jewish culture throughout Europe before the Holocaust, the second floor focuses on the Holocaust, and the third showcases Jewish culture after the Holocaust and World War II. The museum offers its visitors not only a link to the past, but a message of hope for the future. Quite an accomplishment for New York.

A FEW EXTRAS

NEWSEUM NY (580 Madison Avenue, 317-7596; www.newseum.com), funded by the Freedom Forum, is a museum devoted to media, journalism, and the First Amendment. Programs here include exhibits, films, roundtables, and guest speakers on topics such as books on the media, and the families of past presidents. Open six days a week, Monday through Saturday, 10:00 A.M. to 5:30 P.M.

Check out the **SKYSCRAPER MUSEUM** (44 Wall Street, 968-1961; fax 677-7325), featuring exhibits and slide shows on some of New York's most famous towering architectural accomplishments, including the original Woolworth Building and AT&T headquarters. This is new on the museum scene in Manhattan and is a must-see for all who appreciate the New York skyline. Admission is free; hours are Monday–Saturday, noon till 6:00 P.M. "Wow—big buildings!"

The **ART DIRECTOR'S CLUB** (250 Park Avenue South, 674-0500; www.adcny.com) is a nonprofit organization of creatives from a variety of industries that holds regular exhibitions, symposiums, and workshops in several art disciplines, with the goal of getting more students interested in these fields. The gallery is open Monday through Friday, 10:00 A.M. to 6:00 P.M. A museum-quality exhibit hall.

AARON BURR FOUGHT DUELS HERE

Burr made a name for himself by chartering the Manhattan Savings Bank through dubious business dealings. At age seventy-eight he married former prostitute Eliza Jumel—it was convenient for her politically and for him financially. Burr's constant public disputes with politician Alexander Hamilton culminated in a famous duel along the Jersey banks of the Hudson in 1804; the hilly area is now Boulevard East in Weehawken, New Jersey. A plaque at 82 Jane Street marks where Hamilton died of his wounds.

It's said that Burr still haunts the restaurant **ONE IF BY LAND, TWO IF BY SEA** (17 Barrow Street, 228-0822) because he inhabited the house now occupied by the eatery. Lest you hear otherwise, the ghosts don't affect the food quality!

BUILDING NO MORE

Nobody knows exactly how this happened, but here's a version: Sometime in the late 1840s an organization studying the then-modern material of cast iron decided to take apart a gigantic (for its time) structure in the area known as Washington Market. These brick decapitators left the building in pieces under the Brooklyn Bridge—in a makeshift parking lot for horses. It was just overnight, they thought, but that night the building was stolen from the lot! The cops were furious, and the owners had to find a new place to experiment on. File this under "early bummer."

Postscript: Police did eventually recapture most of that cast-iron marvel. Soon after, it was placed in a different lot, where it was stolen again. At that point, police termed the whole thing a joke. Imagine how today's *New York Post* would handle such a crime.

SECOND AVENUE AND EAST 13TH STREET

This was New York's most celebrated crime spot for years: On October 5, 1912, Big Jack Zelig's body was thrown over by a conductor who got angry because, according to media reports, he felt the lout was "ride mooching."

The killer was no slouch. He had posted his rates and methods in several pubs. "Slash on Cheek with Knife: $10. Shot to the Leg: $25. Throwing a Bomb: $15." Sure, that was big money, but he charged still more for murder—$100.

THE DAKOTA

On December 8, people gather at this august apartment building and at Strawberry Fields in Central Park to remember John Lennon, who was shot outside the building's entrance on that date in 1980. In the crowd you'll see the large, diverse, and almost fanatical following of the ex-Beatle.

The Dakota was always a forceful and ominous presence on the Upper West Side. Before 1980 it was famous as the home of Lauren Bacall and the set of the haunted hallways in *Rosemary's Baby.* But the Lennon killing will undoubtedly remain its most powerful association.

LEGS DIAMOND'S DANCE WITH DEATH

Jack Diamond was a real '20s gangster—not some character invented by singer Peter Allen. On the corner of East 110th Street and Fifth Avenue, he was shot by Bill Dwyer, a bootlegger who was sick of Legs's show business mentality. (Diamond wasn't in show business, but he certainly was affected.)

Diamond did not die here. A year later, at the HOTEL MONTI-CELLO (35 West 64th Street), the cold-hearted killer who boasted of his deeds survived a holster-full. In 1931—finally— he met his maker in Albany, while in a compromising position with a "friend." Some years later, killer Irving Bitz was accused of the heinous crime when he was already in prison. Bitz got out much later and was mysteriously rubbed out . . .

100 MOTT STREET

This was the site of **MIKE KERRIGAN'S SALOON,** where kid crook Johnny Dobb planned big heists with the famous River Pirates. In the early part of this century, they attempted the now-legendary Manhattan Bank Robbery. It was three years in the making and a total mess-up for Johnny and the gang.

At the station he was asked, "Hey, Johnny, why did you plan a robbery so close to the precinct?" His infamous reply: "The nearer the church, the closer to God."

LOWER MANHATTAN NOTES

Gramercy Park is a private area used only by residents whose apartments or hotel rooms face the park. It's also the site of a 1911 murder that made an imprint on Lower Manhattan like none other. Well-known novelist David Graham Philips wrote a steamy book that society patron Fitzhugh Coyle Goldsborough was convinced had maligned his sister. Goldsborough shot Philips in the park at noon, when the area was overcrowded with sunbathers.

Another memorable address: a vegetable store at 12 Pell Street in Chinatown was once the Chatham Club, where young singing sensation and novice waiter Irving Berlin complained about the criminal element—and was fired as his reward.

IS IT A CRIME?

In 1945, a detective busted a woman at a West Side hotel because she had allowed a soldier into the premises. A plain-clothes cop had found the twosome in a state of undress. She said, "But officer, this man is my husband!" and the punch line is—he was! Both spouses sued the hotel. His case was thrown out on the grounds that he was an unregistered guest, but hers won them a minor fortune.

Take a look at West 52nd Street in midtown and imagine each contemporary outpost of wealth as a speakeasy or gin joint during Prohibition, when "Swing Lane," as it was then known, had nothing but narrow taverns. Leon and Eddie's, 33 West 52nd Street, remained a swank hangout through the '50s, and a reminder of those thrilling and dangerous times.

A VILLAGE SHOPKEEPER'S LEGACY
Since the attack in mid-1989 on a female jogger in Central Park, there's been a stigma attached to the 102nd Street thorough-fare, where the victim was running.

New York has supported her in much the same way that cit-izens mourned Roberta Sari Kaplan in 1983. Kaplan, a gregar-ious person whose life was dedicated to her customers, was senselessly murdered by a robber in Arabella's, her jewelry store at 135 West 3rd Street, and the entire West Village was enraged. At the site near the northeast corner of Sixth Avenue, you can still see political graffiti and a tiny cardboard memor-ial plaque. ("Purple Onion," the unlit neon sign above it until late 1997, referred to a shop from the 1960s.) The stunned landlord has only recently cleaned and attempted to rent out the space. Someone regularly puts flowers on Arabella's store-front. And there are reportedly no suspects or leads in the Ka-plan case.

EXTRA: WHAT TO DO WHEN YOU WANT TO TOUR

Here are some tour companies that never charge too much and almost al-ways take you where you wanna go:

How to have a sensational time in Harlem: **HARLEM YOUR WAY!** ($15–$75, 690-1687) allows your group to pick from several choices. **HARLEM SPIRITU-ALS** ($33, 757-0425) has a gospel tour on Sundays that is available in several languages.

How did New York get that sleek art deco architecture of the 1920s? The

ART DECO SOCIETY OF NEW YORK ($8–$12, 679-3326) will answer that question and take you on a tour of the city's most impressive areas.

Cheap tours of backstage Broadway and other theaters are offered through **BACKSTAGE ON BROADWAY** ($7, 575-8065). The tours are often led by celebrities, or someone who would like to be.

Yes, it takes more than practice to perform at **CARNEGIE HALL,** but here's a hint: after taking a tour (903-9769), if the stage is unused, you can go up on the apron and sing! Cost: only about $6. The Rose Museum inside Carnegie Hall is open Monday–Sunday, 11:00 A.M. to 4:30 P.M. (closed Wednesday), for a free historical exhibit of the great building. Look out for anniversary exhibitions, such as the one devoted to George Gershwin (September 1998). Open Monday, Tuesday, Thursday, and Friday for tours.

On the first Saturday of June, learn everything you would or would not need to know about James Dean's life by taking the free **JAMES DEAN ANNUAL WALKING TOUR** (244-8426). Not kidding.

Not entirely advised, the **DOORWAY TO DESIGN TOUR** ($20–$25 for half-day extravaganzas, 221-1111) is a tour of furniture showrooms and antique and other dealers, though nobody can tell me what tour-meister Sheila Sperber has as credentials. Great idea though.

THE PERFORMING ARTS LIBRARY (870-1630) is the best media center for those with an interest in arts. Hint: see the vast collection of dance and theater on tape, viewed at your leisure. Also stay for a free tour on Thursdays.

Tours of places like the Algonquin Hotel (Tour and Tea at the Algonquin), the D&D Building (Design Showrooms Tour), the Apollo Theater (Evening at Apollo), Soho (the Sights series), and even artists in downtown lofts (Tribeca Trio) are given through the **CENTER FOR ADULT LEARNING AT THE 92ND STREET YM-YWHA** (996-1100). That and more. All prearranged.

BIG ONION WALKING TOURS (439-1090) has taken the baton from the folks of Governor's Island who used to ship people over to see the little island that once housed the British Army and which now displays plenty of history. Prices vary. Call Big Onion for information on their many tours of New York. Not to be confused with the semi-serious Onion Web site (www.theonion.com) for media junkies!

Sid Horenstein is not a nut but a natural history consultant who knows about fossils found in the walls of New York and other obscure places. Call him at home for the **SID HORENSTEIN FOSSIL TOUR** (569-5351). Prices from $8–$15.

For general information on all **URBAN PARK RANGERS TOURS** call these numbers:

Manhattan—772-0210;

Bronx—718-430-1832;

Brooklyn—718-438-0100;

Queens—718-846-2731;

Staten Island—718-816-9192.

Park rangers present a large selection of always-free tours: birds, crafts, living history, and hikes to places you've never even heard of. A hardly used idea for families. (Discover edible fruits in Inwood Park!)

Marcus Mosiah Garvey, the first African-American activist ever to get mainstream attention, left quite a legacy uptown. See his world through the Schomburg Center's brochure (found at the library), or just start at the first of thirty Garvey-related sites outside the library at Lenox Avenue and West 135th Street. Call 491-2200, ext. 214 for information on the free **"UP, YOU MIGHTY RACE" SELF-GUIDED TOUR.**

HERITAGE TRAIL TOUR

Go see the plaque in the Wall Street subway station near the 4, 5, and 6 lines and you will see the first of many maps built with American Express funding and in honor of the 1976 bicentennial celebrations. The maps will show you a free, self-guided tour—the **HERITAGE TRAIL TOUR.**

34TH STREET TOUR

Information: Hosted by the 34th Street Partnership, 868-0521

The 34th Street Partnership hosts the **34TH STREET TOUR** (868-0521). The tours meet at the tourist booth inside Penn Station at the Amtrak level, southern rotunda. The booth is open Monday–Friday, 8:30 A.M.–5:30 P.M.; Saturday and Sunday, 9:00 A.M.–6:00 P.M.

Free walking tours of the neighborhood take place every Thursday at

12:30 P.M. from the Fifth Avenue entrance of the Empire State Building. Also, a free walking tour of historic Penn Station leaves on the fourth Monday of every month from the booth at Penn.

ALLIANCE FOR DOWNTOWN NEW YORK holds an annual five-hour tour of old corporate buildings like the AT&T headquarters, Standard Oil, Woolworth, and historic sites like the Custom House, Trinity Church, and City Hall. The tour starts at Bowling Green at noon. (Call 566-6700; 786-1308). Dates for this change, so to say what date is uniquely useless.

The **NEW YORK CITY MOUNTED POLICE STABLES TOUR** (239-9352) is an equestrian adventure with a half-hour tour of horse patrol cars; Q & A for kids of all ages. These tours are generally for groups and have to be reserved at least one week in advance, but they tell me they will take individuals too.

Joyce Gold is the owner, operator, and tour guide of **JOYCE GOLD HISTORY TOURS OF NEW YORK** (141 West 17th Street, 242-5762; fax 242-6374; http://www.nyctours.com; e-mail: nyctours@aol.com). These are comprehensive historical tours of New York. She has read over 1,000 books in her research of Manhattan's history. The public tours are held on most weekends from March through November, and are $12 a person. She also holds private tours, with rates depending on tour and group size. Gold's expertise is also put to use when she talks about Manhattan history once a year on the *Queen Elizabeth II* Atlantic Crossing.

The **ADVENTURE ON A SHOESTRING** (300 West 53rd Street, 265-2663) touring company has been giving tours of New York for over thirty-four years! With experience like that, it's difficult to believe that all the various tours this company offers only cost $5 per person. Their slogan: "Exploring the world within our reach . . . within our means." Tours are generally ninety minutes in length, and have expanded to cover areas of Queens, such as Astoria. Many tours include discussions with members of the community being toured. Tours are based on themes, and tours with ethnic themes will usually end in front of an ethnic restaurant (not included in tour fare). What a way to end a tour! Tours take place all months of the year, rain or shine.

Designed for both natives and tourists, the **MUNICIPAL ART SOCIETY OF NEW YORK** offers the **DISCOVER NEW YORK** tour program (457 Madison Avenue, 935-3960; fax 753-1816). Tours on architectural and historical aspects of New York, with area tours including Soho, Union Square, Harlem, and Wall

Street. The Society also offers a weekly tour of Grand Central Terminal every Wednesday at 12:30 P.M. for free!

The Museum of the City of New York (MCNY) offers a variety of **NEW YORK ON FOOT** tours that usually don't require reservations (1220 Fifth Avenue, 534-1672). Tours include East Harlem, the Bowery (as a part of their New York on Stage program), Gay and Lesbian New York, Times Square, Queens Gets Married Bus Tour (a tour of ethnic areas in Queens and the effects of marriage on these areas), Historic Harlem, and Artists and the City. What better experts than museum historians to create tours of the area?

CHAPTER

5

Art and Inspiration Points

STARK GALLERY

113 Crosby Street, 925-4484; fax 274-9525

The Stark Gallery shows reductive abstraction and conceptual work. No lectures, no events, save an annual benefit for changing causes. Open Tuesday–Friday, 10:00 A.M.–5:00 P.M.; Saturday, 11:00 A.M.–6:00 P.M.; closed on Sunday. They mount nine exhibits a year from September to June, and are best known for their collections of contemporary European and American Art. "Contemporary International Art," is the slogan of the gallery.

WHITE COLUMNS

154 Christopher Street, 924-4212; fax 645-4764; e-mail: whitecolumns@compuserve.com

Founded in 1969, this not-for-profit gallery (open to the public ten months of the year at no cost) is the oldest alternative art space. Its mandate is to represent the best work being done by New York's emerging and under-supported artists. An ongoing program of culturally diverse exhibitions mixes political assemblages with picturesque artworks. The gimmick is whiteness: white rooms, white architectural design, white floors, and matching promotional brochures. The space is ever-changing and it claims to aspire to represent meaningful works, not what area artists dub "fun art."

The gallery's season is from September to May. Open Wednesday–Sunday, 12:00 P.M.–6:00 P.M. Leave a message for an appointment at the space.

BRONX RIVER ART CENTER AND GALLERY
1087 Tremont Avenue, Bronx, 718-589-5819

Deep in the southeast Bronx, a fabulous neighborhood most people wouldn't think of going into unless they absolutely had to, is a brave artist named Noah Jemison. Noah took a building on the shore of a filthy river, worked with local government and stoic residents, and turned four floors into an artistic diamond in a fairly rough part of town. Jemison succeeded in housing the most vivid works of several community artists in his first-floor gallery.

Upstairs is a photography center. A special attribute of the gallery is the sculpture garden, dirty and graffiti-covered, located by the river. During summer, behind the gallery, a fenced area houses complete sculpture shows. Open Monday, Tuesday, Thursday, and Friday, 3:00 P.M.–6:00 P.M.

CITY HALL PARK SCULPTURES
Park Row and Broadway

During the spring and summer (sometimes, I should add) and right behind the steps of our beloved City Hall, you will find the best collection of outdoor sculptures I can recommend.

Organized by the New York State Cultural Affairs Division, these art pieces include bird signs that seem oddly out of place. (Once they tried to make you aware of non-New York birds by placing cute signs reading, for instance, "NEW YORK: YOUR HOST TODAY IS *CARDINAL.*") Strange meshes of stuff—art and history—intermingle in this important exhibit. You can see it all in a single lunch hour. In winter, well, heck it's a nice park anyway.

KITCHEN CENTER FOR VIDEO, MUSIC, AND DANCE
512 West 19th Street, 255-5793

Performance artists say if you watch what the ages-old Kitchen does, you will be ahead of the trends. The first place to house video and performance art, the Kitchen has always said its purpose is "to encourage the development of contemporary, high-risk art." The Kitchen has introduced into the mainstream such bygones of the 1980s as Eric Bogosian and Ann Magnuson, the latter of whom maintained a sense of dignity by going back to perform there and other places like it. They were both once serious oddities in this "downtown scene" that unfortunately for us, no longer exists.

Today, the Kitchen is a skinny Chelsea fixture (no sink) filled with small theaters; a video viewing room and an exhibition space are also among them, but my favorite is the two-hundred seat "black box" where one person shows are performed. Wonder of wonder, why would anyone love to see a person get up there and make a total fool of himself in the dark? Open Tuesday–Sunday. Hours vary.

ISAMU NOGUCHI GARDEN MUSEUM
32–37 Vernon Boulevard, Long Island City, 718-721-1932

The building has a funny shape, and it's situated on a sidewalk curved to make the octagonal structure look natural. Out in Long Island City (near the N train stop), the late designer set out to "conserve the artistic environment" by building a theater, a garden, an outdoor lighting scheme, and a fancy setup for unusual pieces that allows an artist's vision to come forth without crowding. The museum of Isamu Noguchi is a rarity that gives visitors enough space to ponder the sculpture's message.

Although it seems improbable that such a beautiful place would sit in the midst of factories and warehouses, Noguchi was truly a pioneer in an area that has now become an art circuit. Open Wednesday, Saturday, and Sunday; April thru November, from 11:00 A.M. to 6:00 P.M. At 2:00 P.M. there are free gallery tours. On Saturday and Sunday, you can take a shuttle bus from Park Avenue and 70th Street for $5, round-trip, or go by tram and bus via Roosevelt Island for $4.

RED SPOT OUTDOOR SLIDE SHOW
Spring Street and Broadway

It's an odd concept at the very least: A man named Red Spot performs outside with a slide show Saturday nights in the dead of winter. This occurs at Spring Street and Broadway. (There's no phone number—what, are you kidding?) They advertise, "Freeze your butts off" to catch him at 9:00 P.M., all seasons. This is a perfect representation of the combined efforts of the artist Spot, the New York State Council on the Arts, and the Lower East Side Print Shop.

The title of an earlier show was "The Quite Serious Art Show." With his show, Spot often simulcasts music on some daring radio station (FM of course, dahling). Some people go to unheard-of lengths to promote art. Dedication is his credo.

Last note on Spot: Franklin Street subway station (the 1 and 9 subways) is offering a tribute to the various works he has displayed, for the price of admission, a $1.50 token.

LA MAMA LA GALLERIA
6 East 1st Street, 505-2476

La Mama ETC, also in the theater chapter, was the place for avant-garde theater until recently when they started looking into money making. Thankfully, their nearby gallery still, as always, believes in the outrageous stuff; if their exhibits of recent times are indications, the credo is here to stay. Their additional gallery, Second Class, is a former garage that is a work of art in itself that creates things totally unique and oblique.

There are new visual art exhibits every three weeks, a Friday evening poets series, and new music concerts almost every weekend. It's a lot of new. Open Thursday through Sunday, 1:00 P.M.–6:00 P.M.

ARTMAKERS
Information: 718-832-1951

An immovable feast of sorts found in the work of a nonprofit group of muralists who produce surreal pieces, political statements, and group and solo inspirations. Artmakers think underground art (no capital letters on those words) serves a purpose: They want art lovers who will not generally visit a gallery to see their work. See Manhattan examples of Artmakers at the Broadway-Lafayette subway station; Ninth Street and Avenue C; and the wall along West 142nd Street between Amsterdam Avenue and Hamilton Place. For other, less publicized locations, keep your eyes open. That's part of being in New York. Note: don't think "a coupla kids" did that wall by a park! A decade or so ago, Bob Dylan drove by a painted wall in Harlem, saw it, loved it, and put it on the cover of his 1989 album, "Oh Mercy," now especially hard to find (try http://www.cdnow.com). It's a gorgeous painting—the music's unlaudable.

At the **BROOKLYN BOTANIC GARDEN** (1000 Washington Avenue, Flatbush, 718-622-4433; fax 718-622-7839; e-mail: publicaffairsoffice@bbg.org; http://www.bbg.org), you'll find fifty-two luscious acres of gardens including Japanese Hill and Pond, Rose, Local Flora, Osborne Formal, Herb, and Shakespeare. The grounds are very well maintained and very lovely. There's a conservatory with three pavilions, known for the best bonsai collection in the United States. Join the walking tours at 1:00 P.M. on Saturdays and Sundays, or if you want to learn a little, you might try the special topic walks and lectures (i.e., see the azaleas and then hear a lecture). The Annual Cherry Blossom Festival is wildly popular. Oh, and don't forget to visit the Garden Shop and Terrace Café. The Garden is just adjacent to the Brooklyn Museum and Prospect Park, and admission is free! Hours are: Summer, Tuesday–Friday, 8:00 A.M.–6:00 P.M.; Saturday and Sunday, 10:00 A.M.–6:00 P.M.; and October–March, Tuesday–Friday, 8:00 A.M.–4:30 P.M.; Saturday and Sunday, 10:00 A.M.–4:30 P.M.

The Plant Information Service will help you with home plant problems (same as above). Call Tuesday–Friday from 1:00 to 2:30 P.M. Or write Plant Information (Help! My Azaleas Are Not Happy!), 1000 Washington Avenue, Brooklyn, NY 11255. Fees: Standard adult admission (ages 17 and over) is $3; $1.50 for adults over 65 and students with valid ID; $.50 for children 6 to 16; and children 5 and under, school groups, Community Pass holders and Garden Members are free.

Enter the 108-year-old lobby and you will immediately discover why the clichéd **CHELSEA HOTEL** (222 West 23rd Street, 243-3700) has intrigued so many literary, musical, and cinematic luminaries, such as O. Henry, William Burroughs, Pete Hamill, Joni Mitchell, Arthur Miller, and Milos Forman, all of whom lived relatively peaceful existences here as they created art, made friends and contacts, and then moved uptown.

Infamous as the locale where Sid Vicious killed Nancy Spungen, the Chelsea is filled with crazed stories about the downtown world; it stands as a monument to an artists' movement that lingers. A plaque commemorates the structure's importance. Now an art gallery (negligible as to the quality) stands inside the structure, for your gazing pleasure. As does the memory of Sid and Nancy.

Terrorist acts may seem like a recent development, but realistically they date back at least as far as 1920. That's when a bomb left in a pushcart went off in front of the site where J. P. Morgan built his bank, **23 WALL STREET.** The type of dispute is familiar to New Yorkers: Citizens passionately felt the area should remain residential; Morgan said their wishes could be ignored because he was so rich. (Shades of Mr. Burns on "The Simpsons.") This statement, covered in the press, angered a terrorist—possibly a group—who scarred the building and killed 140 people.

See the mark the bombing left under the fourth window on the Wall Street side. And next time you see a headline and think our innocence as a country is gone, recall that history repeats itself.

In 1694, water actually roared along the eastern edge of **PEARL STREET AT YE OLDE EDGE OF MANHATTAN.** Go to the corner of Pearl and Wall Streets and look out—now there are more than three blocks that have been added to the island. In the late 1600s, New York's original Dutch owners discovered landfill and sold off plots of water to merchants, who had to build their establishments on expensive stone retainers of soil, architectural debris, and trash.

Pearl Street is thusly named not because pearls lined the shore, but because Pushcart Pearl fenced wares (and took bets) from a mobile veggie cart. Walk west to the Barclay Building and read about Pearl Street's first merchants in a window exhibit that recounts how people once refused to settle on the West Side because the Hudson got too icy in the winter.

Some things never go out of style. One of the most charming and almost forgotten monuments is the **MILLER LADIES** on the side of the 1552 Broadway building. It's the site of the once cherished I. Miller shoe store, which in 1929, only a week before the stock market crashed, thanked its loyal theatrical customers with a tribute to four famous ladies of the performing arts. The monuments are still on the brick building, which has miraculously withstood the ravages of time and the neighborhood. Mary Pickford was chosen for her achievement in film; Marilyn Miller is the musical comedy stand-in; Ethel Barrymore represents drama; and Rosa Ponselle has opera duties.

ART AND INSPIRATION POINTS

According to the Arts Commission and the Municipal Art Society (both organizations are paid homage elsewhere in this volume) Pickford is playing Little Lord Fauntleroy; Miller is Sunny; Barrymore, Ophelia; and Ponselle is good old Norma (*Sunset Boulevard*)!

The **WINERY OF THE SCHAPIRO FAMILY** (126 Rivington Street, 674-4404) is the only true bonded winery on Manhattan Island. The wine takes six months to age after the grapes are crushed, all of which is conducted under a rabbi's strict supervision. Visit Schapiro's on Sundays, 11:00 A.M.–5:00 P.M., and see the building's famous inscription, "So thick you can just cut it with a knife." Then taste the real thing. Grape juice for children, pure Concord for the rest.

This is not your average field trip. At Schapiro's you can watch the youngest of the Schapiros, teenage Jonathan, at his family business, intently drawing wine for the Sabbath. "Eighty-three years and still in the cellar" is their slogan. Not fancy, but oy, is it kosher!

Built in 1811, the **CASTLE CLINTON** (Battery Park at the southernmost tip) was a fort after the British attacked the American frigate *Chesapeake* during the War of 1812; afterward it was a U.S. military headquarters. In 1824, it became a garden resort with concerts, fireworks, and lots of shows. It also had a huge bar! In the 1840s it was roofed over and opera was presented there. For twenty-five years it served as a contemporary theater. Then, the "Castle Garden" became an immigration landing depot; the New York Aquarium; now, a national monument with history and trivia lining its hallowed halls. Open 9:00 A.M.–5:00 P.M. No relation to the prez.

A LASTING INSPIRATIONAL POINT

A couple of years ago, a young man named Lee Schy produced dozens of raw pieces, called Lee's—fables of a life now ended. Lee told of gay and lesbian life in New York in the early '90s. The ones on the street are fading but are still evident: Titles such as "Exhilarated Family Independence" and "Extended Family Fable" can be found on walls of old buildings and fences and the like, in Chelsea, the East Village and Soho, with inscriptions that are at times bizarre and always touching. Notes are magic-markered onto photocopied pictures. His fame lasted a few minutes—though fame was not his game.

The theater that has stood here off and on since 1934 has a seasonal Wednesday night talent gig ($10–$18) at 7:30 P.M. that beats most other shows in town. At the **APOLLO THEATER TALENT NIGHT** (253 West 125th Street, 749-5838), you can see young people "doing" Aretha Franklin or Luther Vandross, often very well.

The show, however, is the audience; it's a totally infectious gathering that is never afraid to show some emotion. (Do not confuse the Wednesday gathering with the schmaltzy Hollywood version shown on NBC; the televised version is all pomp and glitz.) If the consumers in the no-holds-barred version love the entertainment, they cheer and stomp. If they hate the crooner, boy, do they let him know. This crowd can make an amateur sorry he picked up the application form!

Ralph Cooper ran the show from the '30s until he died a few years ago. Since then, the show has been picked up by his son. Give credit to Cooper and son who both successfully mimic every pop icon's gimmick from Durante's schnozz to Jackson's moonwalk. The Cooper talent is half the show; the other half is that "Gong Show" mentality.

One of Harlem's untouched treasures, **MARCUS GARVEY PARK'S** four-block radius is filled with fauna, rocks, and, oddly enough, a large watchtower building that serves no apparent purpose (East 120th–124th Streets at Madison Avenue). Right off East 122nd Street, you can climb up rocks to get a gander at the three-tier, cast-iron structure. It's the only one of its kind left, and it stands as a tribute to the Harlem Heights battle of the Revolutionary War. It looks like a modern Soho sculpture.

For free ranger tours, call the ranger office at 360-2774. See "What to Do When You Want to Tour" on page 89 for information on how to follow what Marcus Garvey believed in, on foot, by yourself. Last mention: Show up here on Father's Day for the annual Skyscraper Bike Race. It's free, challenging, and

ART AND INSPIRATION POINTS

duly endorsed by the U.S. Cycling Foundation for pros and amateurs.

On a pretty day, take a field trip to **TRINITY CHURCH CEMETERY'S GRAVEYARD OF HEROES** (West 153rd–155th Streets between Amsterdam Avenue and Riverside Drive), the island's largest graveyard. You can practice the art of grave-rubbing here, which involves rubbing charcoal onto paper over the stones. Find America's first plaque on West 154th Street and Broadway, which reads, "the heights of the main line of defence in 1776."

If you would rather find more peaceful graves, wander the path and see the famous stones for, among many, Madame Eliza Jumel (see "Crime Scenes" sidebar on page 84) and Clement Clark Moore (who wrote "A Visit From St. Nicholas," *not* " 'Twas the Night Before Christmas").

MARKETS

HARLEM STREET PUBLIC MARKET
Lenox Avenue between West 125th and 126th Streets
LA MARQUETA
East 112th–116th Streets at Park Avenue

These are being fought by the city and will one day be closed. If you are interested, keep this in mind as something to do now.

Merchants on Lenox Avenue constantly override such unnecessary developments as the Commonwealth Mall, a structure that seems strange on a block overflowing with street vendors. You can find some great jewelry buys on this block, but shopping can be hazardous on West 125th Street where cheap junk masquerades as bargains.

On a Saturday at La Marqueta, however, it's a top-notch few blocks for fruit, vegetables, even salsa. For a kick, find the botanica with dozens of different dried herbs and snake oils. Lord only knows what a hardy flea-market-goer might find aroundy here . . .

Few places in the world keep a better record of black history and African-American culture than the **SCHOMBURG CENTER FOR RESEARCH IN BLACK CULTURE** (515 Lenox Avenue at West 135th Street, 491-2200). The Schomburg is a tribute to its people, as an art museum on the first floor attests. There, exhibits on such topics as "The End of an Era [in Haiti]" include political cartoons, magazine clippings, paintings, and devastating photographs.

The treat downstairs is the research material found in computer files, books, original manuscripts, notebooks, and diaries of the famous; also there are unusual artifacts of the black experience. Special collections of art, photography, and film are worth several trips to pore over. Schomburg is also a vital part of the community, sponsoring exhibits and events throughout Harlem and the entire city.

SYLVIA'S RESTAURANT (328 Lenox Avenue at West 126th Street, 996-0660) bills its owner and chef as the "Queen of Soul Food"—and no one argues. If you can get a reservation at this top tourist attraction, you'll find the barbecued ribs dinner is unbeatable, as are the collard greens, wild rice, candied yams, and pickled beets. Ordering your meal can be confusing, because specials change twice a day. Be warned: never bring a vegetarian here! Eat everything, then get a killer peach cobbler for dessert.

In the summer, people from all over the tri-state area line up for blocks to get a whiff of the food and a seat at Sylvia's outdoor patio, a real oddity and treat on Lenox Avenue.

Raven Chanticleer built the **AFRICAN-AMERICAN WAX MUSEUM** (316 West 115th Street, 678-7818) in a basement that by all accounts is totally sensory: music, incense, artwork, and portraits of famous Black women and men. The figures immortalized in wax are the big show. Booker T. Washington, Dr. Martin Luther King, Jr., Josephine Baker, and Nelson Mandela are among the many personalities made by Chanticleer each month.

You must take off your shoes when you enter, a nice touch

that makes the experience whole. $10 for adults, $5 for children. By appointment only.

EXTRA: CULTURAL FREEBIES (OTHER PLACES TO HANG)

 AUDUBON TERRACE
Washington Heights Museum Group, Broadway at West 155th–156th Streets

This ancient spot in Harlem is one of our most picturesque and authentic sights. If this were London, it would be a major landmark. But New Yorkers prefer downtown and rarely take advantage of this attraction because it's too far uptown to be taken seriously. Once the estate of bird lover John James Audubon, the Audubon Terrace hasn't changed much since East Harlem's high life of the 1800s.

The museums on the terrace (Arts and Letters, Hispanic Society, and Numismatic Society) are High Beaux Arts buildings with paved brick courtyards. A sunken group of statues created by the lady who devised Joan of Arc is titled El Cid Campeador. It's a classic—the medieval defender of Spain against the Moors—whose original stands in central Seville.

I imagine in fifty years, some university study group will look at New York history as it relates to tourism. They will shake their heads, wondering why people in the twentieth century didn't take advantage of this great location to visit, study, and get revved up about history and hobby. Then again, the tides may turn in the next ten years and uptown may see a renaissance.

THE MUSEUM OF THE AMERICAN INDIAN, meanwhile, took the hint. They moved to Washington, D.C., but kept a satellite museum downtown. **THE GEORGE GUSTAV HEYE CENTER OF THE NATIONAL MUSEUM OF THE AMERICAN INDIAN** is now located at One Bowling Green near Wall Street (668-6624).

SCHOOL OF VISUAL ARTS
Information: 592-2900

For forty years the Chelsea–Gramercy Park area has housed many SVA complexes: As you enter 30 West 17th Street a man with outstretched arms greets you with a grimace. That's a half-finished cast at the Sculpture Studio, SVA's gigantic 9-year-old warehouse. They are building a window to the public so that passersby can observe work at street level.

Student galleries and year-round shows are held at 209 East 23rd Street (the SVA Museum with guest curators), 141 West 21st Street, 250 Park Avenue South (the Art Directors Club), 214 East 21st Street, 137 Wooster Street, 30 West 17th Street (a sculpture exhibit), and 380 Second Avenue. SVA also has many transient downtown spaces, same as most artists.

GO—READ—BUBBELAH

A live person will tell you about exhibits at all libraries (340-0849), or at the Performing Arts Library (870-1630). Or try www.nypl.org.

OTHER PEOPLE'S BUILDINGS

New York visitors are amazed by the small wonders found in buildings' nooks and crannies. Take the craft exhibit always on display at **MANHATTAN SAVINGS BANK** (385 Madison Avenue at East 47th Street). Or clothing history at the **ILGWU ARCHIVES** (275 Seventh Avenue at West 25th Street; moving soon, so hurry) that indeed boasts news clippings about ladies' garments alongside fascinating garment workers' memorabilia.

Gaze at **TWEED COURTHOUSE** (52 Chambers Street), an 1861 series of balconies and skylights—and a major misappropriation of city money by the infamous Boss Tweed. This structure has been used in many movies for its eerie qualities. Also, see the mass of sculptures above the doorway at **NEW YORK SURROGATES COURT** (31 Chambers Street), an original Hall of Records with an amazing four-story lobby.

POLITICAL FREEBIES

THE VILLAGE INDEPENDENT DEMOCRATIC CLUB (741-2994) hosts Candidates Nights at local auditoriums starting six months before elections. Lawyers help people with landlord dilemmas on Mondays, the same night the VID screens movies with a political bent. **ANSONIA DEMOCRATS** (200 West 72nd Street, 877-2074) holds debates during election season. Candidates make each other bristle—it's fun. Additionally, Ansonia holds monthly meetings to discuss political issues and street campaigns;

voter registration is their big issue. Particularly now, when New Yorkers forgot to vote and got Pataki.

A forum sponsored by **NYU'S POLITICS DEPARTMENT** (988-8500) is overseen by the American Institutions program. This features obscure subjects such as "Liberalism in American Politics: Change or Decline?" at 5:00 P.M. at 100 Washington Square East, Room 703.

Five outdoor sculptures to take in: Picasso's *Sylvette,* 100–110 Bleecker Street; Nevelson's *Shadows and Flags,* William and Liberty Streets; Weller's *Garment Worker,* 555 Seventh Avenue at West 39th Street; Noguchi's *Rhombohedron,* 140 Broadway; his sunken garden, 1 Chase Plaza. An additional structure to ponder is Castoro's *Ethereal Concrete Flasher,* 450 West 43rd Street.

WHERE TO GET A SUNTAN

While getting all this summer culture, you might want a break, or a tan. Try Bell Plaza, Sixth Avenue between West 41st and 42nd Streets; Family Court Park, Hogan Street at Centre and Lafayette Streets; Grand Army Plaza on Fifth Avenue and East 59th Street; Riverside Park, on the Hudson, at West 90th Street (concrete chess tables); the UN's twelve-acre park with rosebushes, 405 East 42nd Street; or St. Vartan's Park at Second Avenue and West 35th Street.

A lovely, uncluttered space without statues and hardly any pigeons is St. Marks Park at Second Avenue and East 10th Street. Bask in the sun while reading memorial plaques that date back to the eighteenth century.

Or you could do muscle beach and hit the piers at about West 10th Street!

LAST FREEBIE FOR THE MOMENT

Get your free franks! I kid you not: Doled out at the General Post Office, which is currently the JAF Building, Eighth Avenue and West 33rd Street—only on Tax Day, April 15* —by Hebrew National, who else? Hot dogs and taxes, that's all you can depend on, kids.

---

* Ed.'s note: A lot of the General Post Office will move to Ninth Avenue to make room for the now-set-to-go Penn Station . . . and Tax Day may move in 1998 to May 16th. The latter is a rumor.

6

Park It

CATCH-N-FETCH IT TOURNAMENT
Information: 777-2297

The rules are simple for this popular event that usually occurs in late June: Master and dog get together and throw a Frisbee. If the dog catches it with all four feet off the ground, he or she gets two points. If the dog touches the ground, one point. Sponsors say, "We get real champion dogs in the tournament." There are prizes, excitement, cheering crowds, and winners who travel to the Florida finals.

The grand prize of this much-anticipated event is a $1,000 bond, and all participants get a T-shirt. Frisbee Field is at West 67th Street and Central Park West.

CRICKET, CROQUET
Information: 408-0204

Cricket is a game with 11 players on each side, two teams ("A" and "B"), a wicket deeper, and bowlers who do speeds of up to 90 miles an hour. The British movie *Hope and Glory* introduced America to spinning "googly-bowlers," a googly being as fast as a pitch goes.* Staten Island has its own

---

* "Googly" was recently made famous in these parts by Jerry Seinfeld's American Express ads set in England.

cricket club, but the most popular place for the veddy British sport is, iron-
ically, the Bronx's Van Cortlandt Park (West 242nd Street and Broadway)
on Saturdays and Sundays. This is an exciting place to watch a match, because the competition often gets heated!

A more refined sport is croquet, imported from Palm Beach by the New
York Croquet League. Six wickets go around the course twice, the optimum
course being a score of 26 or "a little over twice 12." If that's confusing, go
and observe at the New York Croquet League, West 67th Street and Central Park's West Drive. Their May charity benefit is the Hall of Fame
Celebrity Tournament.

MODEL BOATING

The members of the Empire State Model Mariner's Association speak about
their hobby in fanatical detail. They treat their tiny crafts, complete with
miniature outboard motors, deck chairs, cabin cruisers, even passengers, as
if the models were life size, at Central Park Reservoir every Saturday and
Sunday.

On certain summer days you can watch them out on the lake with other
club members, who all have a permit to play. Heading the group in the past
are people who told me, "We're just a bunch of hobbyists who spend their
days off on the water." Well, not exactly on the water. Join them at Conservatory Water, East 72nd Street and Fifth Avenue.

Other locations:
- Bronx's Crotona Park, East 173rd Street and Crotona Park East
- Queens' Bowne Park, 29th Avenue and 155th Street
- Queens' Flushing Meadows—Corona Park, Meadow Lake and Van
Wyck
- Queens' Captain Tilly Memorial Park, Highland Avenue and 165th
Street

PROSPECT PARK SPECIALS
Information: 718-965-8999

Prospect Park in Park Slope is a great afternoon outing. Besides a horseshoe
pitching ground, Prospect has glorious fake horses that once made it the
"carousel capital of the world." Unfortunately, only fifty-six remain intact;

fortunately, a private fund is restoring them, the carousel* has reopened. To keep it whirling, send cash to Prospect Park Alliance, Park Center, 95 Prospect Park West, Brooklyn, NY 11215. They also have real horses. Call their information number for information.

New Prospects is a regular program of drama, comedy, and obscure objects of desire, among them puppets, mask plays (with audience participation), and dance companies. Recently, the groundbreaking Women of the Calabash mixed harmony and third-world percussion instruments with modern tunes.

Every Halloween, Prospect Park hosts a spooky tour of its woods, attended by adult goblins from the neighborhood.

WILDMAN STEVE BRILL'S EAT-THE-PARK TOURS
Write: 143–25 84th Drive, #6C, Jamaica, NY 11435 (send S.A.S.E. for complete schedule), 718-291-6825

At this point, Steve Brill is kind of a cliché. Wildman, as legend and his own masterful press releases tell it, was "caught" eating plants and other growing things in city parks. After his arrest, he appealed to the people of the city, who took an overwhelming interest in Brill. Parks officials noted this and hired him to give tours on edibles in 100 acres of oases within Manhattan, Brooklyn, and the Bronx. Tours are the suggested price of $10, or $5 for kids; no one is turned away due to lack of funds. Remember, he got started on a bench!

He tells me, "I'm famous for having been arrested by undercover agents for eating dandelions in Central Park." For more information, give a shout to Steve's, er, office.

PICNICKING

Picnics are happy occasions throughout Central Park. But special private picnics are held at the forgotten landscape between West 71st and 81st Streets, West Drive, and Central Park West. It lies down low—southwest of the Belvedere castle—so people don't see it. There's a little stream there, too.

People munch over near the city-supervised pool on Great Hill's south-

* There are more carousels in the parks if you or your children are carousel people. Call Public Information for more.

ern slope (West 106th Street) where the swimming hole is actually clean. The most secretive place to picnic is the sole table that someone always puts up at the Levin Playground above East 75th Street. You can see it if you peer into the park from Fifth Avenue.

The Brooklyn Botanic Garden is one of the city's most desirable, and difficult, places to picnic. Food and drink are strictly prohibited, and the guards will keep you from putting a blanket on the grass. But if you become a member you are invited to members-only picnics, as well as quiet summer hours on Wednesday evenings. (Membership is $25.)

If I was *really* into the land of the picnic, I would write away to the city's Parks Department and ask for the listing called the Green Page, with dozens of notions for park-going: Write to: Arsenal, Central Park, New York, NY 10021. Send a SASE.

THIRD-TO-LAST "PARK IT" ENTRY

So-called Quiet Zones allow you to wallow in sunshine without—by law—tape decks or portable CD players. Most popular is Sakura Park by General Grant's Tomb at West 124th and Riverside.

Old-fashioned roller skating is best at Literary Walk, where the statue of Robert Burns stands. Enter at 72nd Street and Fifth Avenue. Skaters are happiest when the park drives are closed, from 7:00 P.M.–6:00 A.M., Friday–Monday.

The Wollman Rink in the park offers in-line skating lessons (unbeatable leg muscle exercise), so call 396-1010. The Lasker Rink, further uptown, at 110th and Lenox (396-0388), though still in the park, costs less, and is quite pretty.

Oh, did you know the park offers horseback riding at Claremont Riding Academy, 175 West 89 Street? Cost is $40. Call 724-5100 for info. This again is the last of the city of Manhattan's stables. There used to be one on every block. Lessons are not expensive, about $35. And you can ride a horse along the beautiful Frederick Law Olmsted bridle paths. If you are in Queens try Lynne's Riding School at 718-261-7679; in the Bronx at Pelham Bay Park, 718-885-0551, and Van Cortlandt Park, at 718-548-4848.

Folk dancing takes place in Central Park on summer Sundays, 2:00–6:00 P.M. at the east shore of Turtle Pond (East 81st Street) in the middle of a ruckus of activity.

Play boccie, a complicated game of skill and timing, at the remaining local team courts at Houston Street and Second Avenue, or the Roosevelt Parkway Courts between Canal and Houston Streets (both on the Lower East Side). There's a boccie league located downtown, too. Call 387-7677. Boccie courts exist in all five boroughs; call 408-0212 for info on who to call.

Really like boccie? The East Side restaurant, **IL VAGABONDO** (351 East 62nd Street, 832-9221), has its own court in its exclusive courtyard! And the food's not bad either.

For lawn bowling, call 360-1311; participants battle each other.

Cross-country skiers can whoosh in Van Cortlandt Park on the Marine Park fitness course, both reached at 408-0204.

For tennis at outdoor courts, call (212) 360-8133 and tell them your borough of choice. They will help you get a permit.

For golf, see the introduction.

PARK INFORMATION NUMBERS

Before 1987, Parks Department events were rarely publicized. Then suddenly the department began an all-out push for people to get to know their green spaces, particularly Central and Battery Park. There are hundreds of big and small events—even a Rodeo School—promoted by the parks people.

You can call a recorded information line (800-834-3832) to find out what events are coming and what's especially good. For particular details, try the public information office (360-8141). There is a seasonal calendar of special events, too (360-8140). For special events being planned far in advance, call 408-0226.

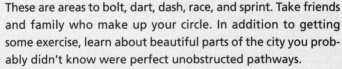

SIDEBAR SPECIAL How to Be Physical in New York

These are areas to bolt, dart, dash, race, and sprint. Take friends and family who make up your circle. In addition to getting some exercise, learn about beautiful parts of the city you probably didn't know were perfect unobstructed pathways.

If you visit **BROOKLYN HEIGHTS PROMENADE** (Pierrepoint and Montague Streets, Brooklyn) in the early hours, you are treated to a breathtaking view of downtown Manhattan. In the morning, the five-block Promenade is far removed from high city decibel levels, which means you can jog along the walkway without noise or traffic.

You get unobstructed views from the World Trade Center right up to the Empire State Building, not to mention the harbor's Statue of Liberty as she awakens. Hint: Go early. From a misty perch, you can spot the nets at Fulton Fish Market, unfurling seafood from ports far and wide.

The **CROMWELL CENTER INDOOR TRACK** (Pier 6, Staten Island, 718-816-6172) is really for aficionados. Traveling to Cromwell is a schlep, but the odyssey is worth it on Tuesday, Wednesday, and Thursday, free days for jogging and sports-walking on an unbanked eight lanes of wood surface. An annual fee entitles you to basketball, weight room, and aerobics classes. (This book spends time talking about Staten Island because most books don't. As a matter of factual evidence, you will find over fifteen reasons to take the Staten Island Ferry in this book.)

For those anxious to test every prime jogging spot in the city, this Staten Island location is not to be missed. Hint: Don't fret—it is close to the ferry terminal.

Glenn Close lived in the **MEAT-PACKING DISTRICT** (Little West 12th Street, off Greenwich Street) in the movie *Fatal Attraction*. While a great deal of this industry has moved out of New York, a few plants remain at the intersection of Little West 12th and Gansevoort Streets, of historic significance—and a jogger's delight.

During Herman Melville's era, this corner was New York's first outdoor farmer's market, divided into ten lanes. Today it is open space, nearly devoid of traffic, and always open to the public. A great hint: dawn is an especially great time to sprint. The meatpackers are just starting to work and the area is not so barren. This is not the safest place at night, but then again, what is?

105 STREET "PRIVATE" CIRCULAR TRACK

105th Street off Central Park West, inside Central Park

At the Great Hill at 105th Street off Central Park West inside the park is the ultimate in private tracks. At the **"PRIVATE" CIRCULAR TRACK** the grounds are soft, but not mushy, a water fountain stands regally on the side, and the track does not go on forever.

It is never crowded because the circular track is hard to find. Enter the park from 103rd Street, and climb up the path until you reach the lavatory house. There you will see the circular track. Hint: After you finish, slowly climb down the rocks, re-living your childhood—and *then* continue your day.

The popular entrance to the park at **90TH STREET AND FIFTH AVENUE** has a cinder track that goes around the reservoir for 1.7 miles (inferior, when you consider that Brooklyn's Prospect Park, goes twice that—see below). A favorite jogging spot, al-though when you think about it, most everything above 72nd Street on either side of Central Park is filled with runners.

Hint: If you run the entire length of the park and its varied and happenstance lanes, you will have jogged fifty-eight miles of paths. Not bad!

PROSPECT PARK'S INNER PATH AND BUTTERFLY HILL

Enter At Boat House, on east side of Lull Water, Park Slope, Brooklyn

A scenic run is available at **PROSPECT PARK'S INNER PATH AND BUT-TERFLY HILL.** Start with one steep hill and then you're off—with the 3.5 miles of completely reserved jogging space that is Prospect Park. This park is the widest unoccupied space in the five boroughs, which means getting lost is pretty easy . . .

The road for runners never closes and is specifically marked "Runners." The loop of the path does go the entire length of this spot, located in perfect Park Slope, where people go before they leave New York for Portland, Oregon. (Rumor has it that Park Slopers recycle more than most New Yorkers.) The meadow for butterflies to roam in seems like a forest gone out of control It is a safe romping ground. HINT: In summer, you'll see amazing flowers and some beautiful flying creatures!

If you have not been to TOMPKINS SQUARE PARK (East 7th–10th Streets off Avenue A) in the last five years, it's time to go and see what's up. Tompkins Square has undergone a complete and total renovation after 1991's abrupt closing. Zigzagging paths remind me of London's parks. The new park offers joggers, as always, benches and playgrounds and public bathrooms.

The old park was a home for the homeless and much grandstanding on soap boxes. The new greenery and children's mini-park are classy additions. HINT: Even with the beauty of this new space, don't crowd anyone, as tempers flare readily since that troubled summer night when riots made this a mess. As a reminder, bring children here—even kids who don't jog!

WASHINGTON SQUARE PARK
West Fourth Street–Washington Place, off Sixth Avenue

In the summertime, you must be careful to avoid types who would probably sell you everything they own, and everything on you. But you can run in WASHINGTON SQUARE PARK (West 4th Street, one block east of Sixth Avenue, call 360-1492 for info on special events) along the outskirts from sunup to sundown. This was once a potter's field graveyard for con artists in the eighteenth century. Historically, Washington Square was a target of famed city planner Robert Moses, who had planned to build a downtown highway right over this land. The project would have destroyed Soho as we know it today and was stopped by the discovery of that graveyard underneath—it is illegal to build over cemeteries!

Knowing all that, look around the park and be amused. The large Washington Arch is a marble structure built by Stanford White in 1892. Around that area find jugglers, dancers, and comics—quite the scene. Greet an entertainer, nod to an elderly reader. Listen to the offers of "Smoke, smoke" and begin to jog. Hint: Stay off the grass. Village dogs are individualists.

Want to do more than just jog? Try Central Park's fields, great for baseball, softball, football, rugby, and soccer. Played on the fields at the Great Lawn, North Meadow, and Heckscher Playground, sports require permits from the park. Call 408-0209.

ROLLERBLADING can be done in most parks, but the road west of Sheep Meadow near 69th Street is designed for rollerskating and rollerblading. Skates can be rented at **WOLLMAN RINK**. Call 396-1010 for hours and prices.

Ice skating can be done at Wollman and Lasker Memorial rinks, both in Central Park. Ice hockey is played at Lasker Rink every Saturday and Sunday morning between 7:30–9:00 A.M. For $4 per person, anyone can join in the game. Mini-golf lovers, try Donald Trump's 9-hole course, Gotham Golf, located at the Wollman Rink in the summertime. Its holes are designed after New York landmarks like the Statue of Liberty, Trump Tower, and the Plaza Hotel. (Gee, do you think it really is owned by Donald?)

Rowboats can be rented for $6 an hour in Central Park, but nothing tops the gondola rides available (see Chapter 1).

What can you do in the parks in the winter? Sledding, of course! There are hills throughout Central Park, popular for sledding with kids and adult kids alike. Most-used are Pilgrim Hill by 72nd Street and Fifth Avenue, and Cedar Hill near Belvedere Castle.

Tennis is available at twenty-six clay courts, and four all-weather courts. They are located at the west side of the park at 95th street. To play in the summer you need a permit. To obtain permit applications and info, call 360-3456. Basketball is available through the Parks Department at courts throughout the city. Call 408-0209 for court locations. No permits or reservations required.

ROTATION POINT PRODUCTIONS, INC.—FLYING DISC (FRISBEE)
PROMOTIONS
406 East 9th Street, Suite 8, phone/fax 777-2297
Offering frisbee workshops and sports event productions. Their disc club is called the "New York Flying Disc Institute" (NYFDI). They have produced a New York dog disc tournament and the 1997 Eastern National Freestyle Flying Disc Championships. The most exciting event was Drastic Plastic '96 featuring the Freestyle Disc World championships in Central Park.

AND OF COURSE, POOL!

AMSTERDAM BILLIARD CLUB
344 Amsterdam Avenue at 77th Street, 496–8180
Open 11:00 A.M.–3:00 A.M. (4:00 A.M. on weekends). Lessons available, rates vary depending on date and time.

THE BILLIARD CLUB
220 West 19th Street between Seventh and Eighth Avenues, 206-7665
Open Sunday–Thursday, 10:00 A.M. till "whenever"; Friday, 11:00 A.M.–3:30 A.M., Saturday, 1:00 P.M.–3:30 A.M. $5 an hour, $10 an hour after 7:00 P.M. Two floors of a converted warehouse with thirty-three tables.

BROWNSTONE BILLIARDS
308 Flatbush Avenue at Seventh Avenue, Brooklyn, 718-857-5555
Open Sunday–Thursday, 12:00 P.M.–1:00 A.M.; Friday and Saturday, 12:00 P.M.–4:00 A.M. Thirty-two tables, six ping-pong tables, air hockey tables, and video games. Always $3.95 per hour for pool. Pool classes every Wednesday at 8:00 P.M., but you must reserve.

CHELSEA BILLIARDS

54 West 21st Street and 5th Avenue, 989-0096

Has forty-four pool tables, four antique snooker tables, and two billiard tables. The hall is two floors of an old converted printing plant. Open 24 hours. Rates are $6 per hour from 9:00 A.M.–5:00 P.M., and $8 per hour from 5:00 P.M.–9:00 A.M.

Note: See other, more rowdy pool spaces in/around chapter 19.

AND FOR OTHER ENTHUSIASTS

METROPOLIS FENCING SCHOOL (45 West 21st Street between Fifth and Sixth Avenues, second floor, 463-8044) offers a wide variety of courses and workshops in fencing, from beginner to advanced competition. Foil sessions are $20 for three one-hour sessions. Advanced foil, sabre, or epee classes are $25 for three one-hour sessions.

Bowl till your heart's content at the Chelsea Piers Bowling Alley (Pier 62, West 23rd Street and the Hudson River, 835-2695). They have 40 lanes and are open 24 hours on Friday and Saturday; open 9:00 A.M. to 2:00 A.M. on all other days, and they have a full service restaurant and bar inside. Cost is $6 per person per game, shoes not included. Warning: Unless you go at night, you will find yourself in the midst of lots of childrens' birthday parties.

More bowling alleys: Bowlmor Lanes in the Village (255-8188) and Leisure Time in the Port Authority Terminal (Eighth Avenue and 40th Street, 268-6909).

LAST HINT AND MOVE ON

Many people who are both visitors and residents of the city love the color green and particularly how much of it there is in the city's parks. So why not volunteer at one of the local parks or the big one in the center. Call 408-0214 and speak to a volunteer coordinator. While you are having a good time, you might meet people for social (i.e., friendship or dating) or networking purposes. One obvious plus to becoming a volunteer is you know you will have something in common with the people you meet.

Food

CHAPTER

7

Eating before Noon*

ALGONQUIN HOTEL'S ROSE ROOM

59 West 44th Street, 840-6800

In the 1920s, the Algonquin Hotel's Rose Room served as a meeting place where publishers, editors, and many of the elite came seven days a week to have a relaxing—albeit costly—cappuccino. This is midtown's most civilized café. A pianist in the nearby Oak Room and musicians who play in the hotel's lobby send melodies aloft constantly. Be warned: Service is slow, and with the revamped and much plusher Algonquin come newer prices. Breakfast starts at around $10 for a continental meal, the à la carte service can run up to $20.

THE PALM COURT AND THE EDWARDIAN ROOM

Plaza Hotel, 768 Fifth Avenue, 546-5310

The Palm Court is a delicious way to start your morning, particularly if you are the kind that enjoys dashing into an exclusive hotel and breakfasting in the lobby.

---

* In these chapters, fax numbers are included where applicable. Fax for hours, directions, menu requests—and the all-important delivery details.

EATING BEFORE NOON

119

Mornings are exciting at the newly redesigned Plaza—all that scurrying about—and there is a general feeling of elegance as they serve meals that, although expensive, are lovely to look at. "The Central Park" features chilled juices, eggs Benedict, and tea or coffee—for a luxurious, eyebrow-raising $15.50.

The remarkable thing about breakfast in the equally expensive Edwardian Room is that it is closed off from lobby traffic. In the Palm Court, patrons might get irritated by curiosity seekers who wander in to gawk at the Court as an attraction. At the Edwardian, the tables are secluded and widely spaced to afford privacy. And their luncheons are superb, three-course affairs. At a recent outing, when asked for the check and some more coffee, the waiter responded with a classy, "I'll let you enjoy your coffee first."

Don't look for Trump; he sold out.

ROYALTON HOTEL
44 West 44th Street, 869-4400; fax 944-1419

Oh, posh. The Royalton, the most-plush scheme from the late Steve Rubell and the current Ian Schrager (of Studio 54 fame) is not a disco, but it might as well be. Enter this old dowager of a hotel (on a street famous for transient hotels) and discover an art deco, strangely colored gigantic hall. The same people who brought you this palace have since done likewise at the Paramount Hotel (235 West 46th Street). And they are going hogwire in Miami Beach too.

In the restaurant "44" (944-8844), breakfast is served elegantly from 7:00 to 10:00 A.M. In the lobby, patrons lounge about on couches, chairs, banquettes. Though the selections in both are very expensive, the menus do help you calculate how much you'll weigh after you eat. ("American with French influence" is their take on post-morning food, I should add.)

THE "21" BREAKFAST CLUB
21 West 52nd Street, 582-7200; fax 586-5065

The "21" Club is a beautiful spot in the evenings, when extraordinary wealth comes out to play. In the mornings, from 7:30 until their office meetings begin, a special club gathers in the dark lobby, near the handy computer terminal.

According to a spokesman, 400 executive "Fortune 500 types" eat, meet, laugh—and pay—each morning to classical strains and salmon plates and muffins served with a smile. Of course, "21" is smiling, too. To be included in this exclusive city/country club, members pay a $2,000 lifetime membership fee, $250 annually, and about $15 per meal.

And yes, this is the same "21" talked about endlessly in the film *Quiz Show* of 1994.

AGGIE'S
146 West Houston Street, 673-8994

Down in the West Village is a hip diner that is best visited in the morning. It's owned not by a conglomerate but by people who believe that a wholesome breakfast is the day's best start-up.

This means the OJ is so fresh it has pits, the food is cooked well, there are a dozen different coffees, and the house kitten makes sure you feel at home. A must is Aggie's challah French toast, which is not served after 12:00 P.M., but what warms people most is the fabulous service by smiling faces.

Don't bother making reservations, and, as with most neighborhood places, don't bother proffering a credit card. Breakfast at Aggie's starts at 7:30 and the crowds zoom in by 9:15.

Breakfast on weekends? *Fuggedabadit.*

Note: The restaurant has grown to twice as big, no waiting, and they have added a rhythm and blues jukebox.

BELMONT RACETRACK'S BREAKFAST AT BELMONT WEEKENDS
Belmont Raceway, Queens, 718-641-4700

If you enjoy racing, action, or just something different, then Belmont Park's breakfast with the horses and their trainers is the winning ticket. Their continental breakfast of rolls, Danish, coffee, and tea starts at 6:00 A.M. and lasts until 11:00 A.M. Only May–July and September–October; call for exact dates. And kids are welcome, too.

Here you can talk to jockeys and other staff, who will gladly tell you the stories of their horses. This is a romantic experience for anyone who has ever been fond of horses, riding, or adventure. And PS: If you can't leave home, gambling with Off Track Betting (OTB) can be done at home via phone!

SIDEBAR SPECIAL Bagels, Bagels, Bagels

THE BAGEL

170 West 4th Street, 255-0106

A breath of fresh air and sunshine in the Village. This boutique—open twenty-five years—serves just about anything on a bagel to people who sit on a half-dozen stools or at an equal number of tables. Even if you're a stranger, they'll act like they know you here. Whether it's deli sandwiches, a plate of knockwurst and potato salad, or just a bagel-and-shmeer, these are your people. Try their delectable salad with the house dressing (mustard vinaigrette). Oh, and don't ask for anything fancy like, er, a raisin bagel. At this no-fuss joint, a bagel's a bagel!

Speaking of fancy, this is a real homey celeb hangout. Robert De Niro, John Kennedy, Jr., Julia Roberts, Lauren Hutton, Aidan Quinn, and Harvey Keitel go here. How do I know? Everyone talks.

Open 7:30 A.M.–midnight, $1 minimum at all tables.

BAGELS ON THE SQUARE

7 Carmine Street, 691-3041

How the Village has changed. It used to be you'd make your way through Father Demo Square on a weekend night and see only the donut shop and the bagel place. Now so many shishi nightspots are open till 5:00 A.M., that you have to make a choice. One thing is for certain: You'll need bagels for the morning. Stop by this 24-hour mainstay for a dozen different kinds, freshly baked and thick. At the Square you don't have to put *anything* on them, because each one's a meal by itself.

A friend from the Southwest swears by their egg bagels. They even ship vacuum-packed bagels anywhere in the United States. Look for the order form. A true bagel connoisseur must try their newfangled oat-apple-raisin-blueberry.

DAVID BAGEL
228 First Avenue, 533-8766

This bluntly named eatery is one of the few remaining cafeteria-type places for just hanging loose and gorging on bread with a hole. The raisin bagels are legendary here, and so are the boiled eggs that sit on the counter every morning like ritual objects.

The East Village once had dozens of Ma-Pa-And-Kid Shops like David where you could wander off the cold street and sit in the low-ceilinged warmth with a fresh poppyseed bagel. You'd buy a "smidgen of lox or whitefish," and whether you were Jewish or not, you'd feel kinship with a culture. Such establishments are now endangered in a big way! In the event a bagel isn't all you want, David offers great spicy Spanish knishes and few-dollar greasy omelettes. Open Monday–Saturday, 7:00 A.M.–10:00 P.M., Sunday, 7:00 A.M.–9:00 P.M.

H & H BAGELS
2239 Broadway at West 80th Street, 595-8003; fax 799-6765; they now ship overnight: call 1-800-NYBAGEL

The greatest nosh of all on the Upper West Side: Every type of bagel is baked on the premises, and you can enjoy several varieties of cream cheese. Take it home or eat it on the street corner. Stock includes a sesame seed bagel with a prodigious number of seeds. Residents can't understand how this 24-hour place has remained in business and yet they have also opened a 24-hour branch down on the highway (West 46th Street and

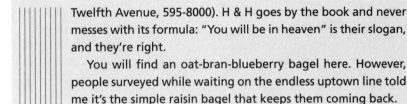

Twelfth Avenue, 595-8000). H & H goes by the book and never messes with its formula: "You will be in heaven" is their slogan, and they're right.

You will find an oat-bran-blueberry bagel here. However, people surveyed while waiting on the endless uptown line told me it's the simple raisin bagel that keeps them coming back.

CAFÉ CROISSANT
342 Madison Avenue between East 43rd and 44th Streets, 490-0055

This East Side king of the brioche offers its version of Sunday morning in central Paris. You can sit and be content with sixteen different kinds of croissants—plus brioches and other pastries not found in cheapo stopover places that call themselves croissant shops. Make yourself comfortable from 6:30 A.M. until about 12:00 P.M., when lunch crowds appear and laxness vanishes.

Best to come here early, get a good seat, grab a handy copy of *USA Today* or *Le Monde,* and share your table with the regulars.

EMPIRE DINER
210 Tenth Avenue at West 22nd Street, 243-2736; fax 924-0012

This goofy art deco spot has odd notions on its menu, including Feminade-lemonade served in unusually tall glasses sculpted as bare-breasted women. The bartenders and waiters make people laugh, especially in the morning, when this 24-hour diner becomes a notorious hot spot. Warning: The eggs are about as runny as a winter nose.

Read the fine print at the bottom of the menu and you'll chuckle: Right there with the odd omelettes, overstuffed sandwiches, and breakfast meats, you get such instructions as "Be nice, sit up straight, and stop fidgeting." The cooking may not be as good as Mom's, but the complaints about it are the real thing.

HEE SEUNG FUN (HSF) TEAHOUSE
46 Bowery right below Canal Street, 374-1319

Dim sum means "lunch" in Chinese; in English it just means good oriental food usually eaten for breakfast or brunch. HSF's dim sum is far from standard takeout—it's innumerable distinct offerings are served starting at 7:30 A.M. on small plates by attentive waiters.

One of the originals of New York-style dim sum, HSF offers stuffed bean curd dipped in clam sauce; clear, fried, or sticky rice; broiled wonton; tiny sukiyakis; and spicy pork tripe—served in steamer baskets and floating trays.

BREAKFAST NOTE

Michael's (24 West 55th Street between Fifth and Sixth Avenues) has a garden room available for private parties for breakfast. They have an early, sophisticated breakfast, the ultimate business breakfast— easy to digest and fun to attend in a suit or a skirt—Monday–Friday, 7:30–9:30 A.M. Call them at 767-0555. For your Los Angeles habit, they have that famous breakfast at their sister location in Santa Monica, featured snootily in the movie *L.A. Story.* For more on that legend see Chapter 11.

What Blocks Are Edible—
A Complete Look at Favorite
Neighborhoods

BEAVER STREET AND BROADWAY

A note for those who work near the Old Customs House (now the Bankruptcy Court Building) in Bowling Green. In the 1700s, that building was the site of the city's first vendor park. Now you can buy, right on the selfsame corner, Superb (their name) Coffee's rich $1 brews, oat muffins, croissants, and scones, each priced at $1.

But the real treat's a little further down Beaver, where a nice guy named Alex sells soup out of the Ratner's Delicatessen cart direct from the Lower East Side. Every day for $2.75, you can feast on matzo ball, potato, leek, or vegetable. And buy a juicy onion roll, too. Such a healthy bargain, *bubbelah*.

PAPAYA MADNESS!

These are not outdoor vendors but they ought to be.

You can stand at a Papaya place and have a hot dog and papaya juice. Or a glass of water and a papaya juice. Or a frozen yogurt . . . you get the picture. Why papaya? Gray's, the granddaddy of this gimmick, began with papaya, orange juice, and different kinds of hot dogs years ago at 2090 Broadway (West 72nd Street, 799-0243), and it took off big. Gray's Papaya

(402 Sixth Avenue at 8th Street, 260-3532) is a downtown replica; they sell these same products from the same type of open-air storefront.

Try East Side's very own Papaya King (179 East 86th Street, 369-0648). I'm sure I have missed some others, but these things multiply so often, it is impossible to track 'em.

HALLO BERLIN
Northwest Corner of West 54th Street And Fifth Avenue

The most scrumptious array of German delicacies this side of Heidelberg is offered by pushcart entrepreneur Rolf Babiel, who daily schleps what he has dubbed "the best of the wurst" to several hundred satisfied whitewurst and bratwurst eaters. A few years back, he and a partner opened a restaurant in the trendy West Village. Too many nitrite-conscious people there, so the restaurant failed. But it has reopened (new) in midtown at 402 West 51st Street, phone 541-6248.

As for the cart, Babiel has many fans from upper Madison, and as a matter of fact his partner became a crony only after years as Babiel's loyal fan!

REAL SIXTH AVENUE FOODMART

Walk from West 48th to West 51st Street any day from 11:00 A.M. to 2:30 P.M. (sometimes later) for the most motley assortment of midtown vendors. Sit and eat at any number of plazas—one by Exxon, one courtesy McGraw-Hill, another at Time's "America's Plaza." It's pure pandemonium from 12:00–1:00 P.M., but after the throngs go away, it's relaxed, especially in the summer.

Best mentions: babaghanoug is a splendid Afghan meal and only a buck-fifty, beef kofta kebabs are surprisingly lean, the falafel here are plentiful, and you get smiles free. The Mexican stand on West 50th Street is quite good, as are fresh fruit–fresh juice–fresh ice ("the triplets").

CHELSEA

The area on Eighth Avenue between 15th and 21st Streets is the new nirvana of eating, particularly since popular restaurants such as the newly opened **TAZZA**—formerly Twigs—(196 Eighth Avenue) have become what's expected. Once famed for "cuchifritos," the avenue cuisine is now a mixture of cosmopolitan **CAJUN** (129 Eighth Avenue), Italian flair at **COLA'S** (148 Eighth Avenue), and suave and trendy Mexican à la **MARY ANN'S** (118 Eighth Avenue). Also, a great pseudo-Mexican place called **BRIGHT FOOD SHOP** (218 Eighth Avenue), mimicking an old-fashioned candy store on the outside, sits along this strip. Just off Eighth is **EAST OF EIGHTH** (254 West 23rd Street), with a gorgeous bar, a series of mismatched entrées, and a nice garden to boot.

However, if you still crave Chinese-Cubano, do not despair. Find **SAM CHINITA** (176 Eighth Avenue), which has fab black beans yet looks like a diner-on-a-lot, and the unmatched-for-quality of **HABANA CHELSEA** (190 Eighth Avenue, once the cheaper, grungier, Asia de Cuba), run by a staff of the two hardest-working New Yorkers there ever were.

DOYERS, PELL, AND MOTT STREETS

Happily, all Chinese food is not shrimp and lobster sauce or "one from column A." There is a healthy, nonclichéd alternative to eating Chinese that has nothing in common with the corner takeout. Dim sum, which has no menu, is like eating on a race track. Trays zoom by you—be careful you don't get sideswiped—as you pick out delicacies: stuffed bean curd, barbecued spare ribs, spicy pork tripe, and all kinds of dumplings. Billing is $1.50–$3 per item.

NOM WAH TEA PARLOR (13 Doyers Street) is the perfect place for dim sum. Two can eat for $5–$9 on Mott Street.

On Thirty-first Street between Sixth and Madison Avenues, are several (perhaps ten at most) strange- and bright-looking Korean restaurants where, like on East Sixth Street, it seems they share the same kitchen. Hmm. The reality is the food is bland and the service—well, these places, with names that are quite ingenious ("Yet Jip"), seem more like little social clubs than real restaurants. Twice I walked in, looking kind of white when there were hardly any present, and twice I was told, "Mister, can you wait?"— let's just say, no.

My idea of a perfect Korean restaurant, as noted in the *Times*, is **DOK SUNI'S** at 119 First Avenue and 7th Street in the East Village, 477-9506.

Open 4:00–11:00 P.M., Monday–Thursday; 5:00 P.M. to midnight on Fridays and Saturdays. Cash only. "Dark and smoky, despite the anti-smoking rules, Dok Suni's offers Korean food with a soundtrack of Prince, Sade, and other one-name musicians, and waitresses who look as if they're auditioning for the Fashion Cafe." I really appreciate being warned . . .

EAST VILLAGE

East Sixth Street between First and Second Avenues

This block is so associated with Indian food that Indian restaurants from out of the neighborhood advertise here! **SHAH BAGH** from Bombay (328 East 6th Street), a basement-level spot, was the first of fifteen-plus Indian restaurants. The best (though everyone has a favorite) is **PASSAGE TO INDIA** (308 East 6th Street) with a varied and thoughtful menu.

Unique lunch dishes? Go to picturesque **BALAKA** (318 East 6th Street). Music? It pays to walk into any restaurant on the block (one rumor has it they share the same kitchen). Some feature a sitar and a bongo drum in the evening. Loathe the cellar notion? The ground-floor **GANDHI** (345 East 6th Street) will lift your spirits, with its spicy dishes and servers with keen senses of humor.

GRAMERCY PARK

On Irving Place, history makes the eating more interesting. O. Henry lived, observed, and wrote masterpieces ("The Gift of the Magi") in what is now **SAL ANTHONY'S,** located at 55 Irving Place. Sal's serves serious Italian dinners, not gimmicky selections, and theirs is a sensible wine list. See the store selling uncooked foodstuffs below it—bare essentials you cook "yourself." What a concept. Also, check out the beautiful buildings that border it. Also on Irving Place, check out **VERBENA,** 54 Irving Place. The food is healthy, although expensive, but the garden is gorgeous.

Cattycorner is **PETE'S TAVERN** (129 East 18th Street), circa 1864, touted as being "the place that O. Henry made famous." A sports bar/tavern with decent food and historic plaques, the window states, "Bel Bel Gramercy Pantry [original name], Ladies Invited."

LOWER EAST SIDE

First, nosh on a pickle from **GUS'S** (35 Essex Street, see "Smells of the City" sidebar on great smells, page 135) and then go for a real Jewish home-cooked meal. Your choices are plentiful, from **GRAND DAIRY** (341 Grand Street) to a few scattered restaurants that feature Jewish-Rumanian-Chinese! Maybe you're into the battle of the tongue sandwiches: refined **RATNER'S DAIRY** (138 Delancey) and the crazed **KATZ'S DELICATESSEN** (205 Essex). Ah, but Katz's has $1.75 knishes and Dr. Brown's to boot.

Want to work up an appetite? See several old paintings on the buildings above you. One is of the many delicacies offered by "Isaac Gellis—100 years of delicious memories." He's up in the Bronx, but you still can smell his gefilte fish.

UPPER WEST SIDE

Since this is home to many struggling actors and temp workers, there are several good, cheap restaurants to feast in. Decent quick stops are the **AMERICAN RESTAURANT** (2340 Broadway), **79TH STREET RESTAURANT** (2201 Broadway, meant to be the site where "Seinfeld" eats every single day), and six pizza parlors called Ray's or Famous or both. And there are two famous restaurants that grab all the hungry eaters here: **DOCKS** (2427 Broadway) and the gigantic plates filled with food at **CARMINE'S** (2450 Broadway); third-place goes to always-crowded and quite pleasing **ISABELLA'S** (359 Columbus Avenue). And remember to visit the good-food restaurant once called "Dish," which changes names frequently (100 West 82nd Street; noisy but scrumptious), also in this neck.

LA CARIDAD (2199 Broadway) is the heartiest and friendliest Comidas Chinas y Criollas [Chinese–Cuban] around. Near the Sony cinema, **SAKURA JAPANESE** (2298 Broadway) has a "movie dinner" for $11.

Many good eateries dot Washington Street, among them a mainstay, **TORTILLA FLATS** (767 Washington Street), a loud Mexican neighborhood hangout.

FLORENT (69 Gansevoort Street, off Washington) is the night crawler's much-loved French diner with reasonably priced food, noisy, crowded tables, good wine, and 24-hour service!* (Except for early Sunday mornings, when the wee hours send the staff elsewhere . . .) As for other restaurants, try the always fine **CARIBE** (117 Perry) for jerk chicken and other Jamaican specialties (they have stayed in business for nearly ten years, so give them credit and at least come in for a meal); and check out my local favorite for Mexican, **MI COCINA** (57 Jane Street).

Lastly, see the Italian menu at **MAPPAMONDO (MAP OF THE WORLD)** (11 Abingdon Square), which became so popular in its first location that it found itself needing to open two more locations: **MAPPAMONDO DUE** across the street (581 Hudson), and **MAPPAMONDO TRE** (114 Macdougal). Great focaccia bread—and such happy eaters, waiters, and owners!

EXTRA: THE VILLAGE—A BRIEF DISCUSSION

AVENUE A
Between East 7th and 11th Streets

Avenue A has changed from its no-man's-land image of the '70s to an artist, eater, and prayer avenue replete with galleries, restaurants, and ancient churches (such as St. Nicholas Russian/Greek Orthodox, East 11th Street). At St. Marks Place and Avenue A, near Alcatraz Bar, is a glass/mirror/china mosaic by Veronica Evanger. Look for the thought-provoking statement "We The People 1987" stenciled on the bottom.

On the northeast corner of East 10th Street, bordering on the 16-acre Tompkins Square park (see Chapter 6) are two sentiments: One is a colorful wall stating "Park for the People." Nearby, graffiti and pasted-up signs demand arrests of police officers for their behavior in riots (recently covered

---

* Florent got a big hit of fame as a "featured player" in the mega-bore flick *Men in Black*.

up by signs of political unrest like: "Arrest Gingrich"). Along the benches, see the signs that ask us to remember German-American citizens from the area who drowned by the hundreds in an accident back in the old country, circa the turn of century.

By the by, East 7th Street off A is a fantastic shopping block, with card-gift-book shops, cafés, and thrift boutiques.

EAST HOUSTON STREET

Between Broadway and Second Avenue

The scarecrow in the Liz Christy Community Garden is a reminder that the northeast corner of Houston and Second Avenue is the city's oldest community garden—dating from 1973. That corner is usually known for its car window–washer population! Go west on Houston Street for a typical cross-section that defines the new East Village.

The north side of Houston sports graffiti of various political persuasions, and early signs of two new lower-level shopping malls. On the south side find boutiques that sell clothes, "back bars" for New York's watering holes, and New York *chachkes*. Also on the south side are several locations great for wall reading, which can help you figure out what's happening in the arts. For more information, take a hand-out inside the vestibules of the many bars dotting this thoroughfare.

LOWER SECOND AVENUE

Between St. Marks Place and East Houston Street

Here is where the real East Village, or the Lower East Side, is most evident. Walk downtown from St. Marks Place, where you will see **GEM SPA,** the best-stocked newsstand in town, and note how the number of chic Japanese restaurants dwindles in favor of funeral parlors, secondhand clothing shops, and rundown theaters, or at least the vestiges of some that have closed due to disrepair beyond belief. A homeless shelter on East 3rd Street is a stark reminder of the city's poverty; renovations can only go so far. That shelter, you should know, is the Salvation Army that Sade sullenly sings about in her song, "Sally."

On the corner of East 5th Street is the hauntingly remembered **COOPER SQUARE RESTAURANT,** formerly Binibon, which closed after poet/ex-con Jack Henry Abbott knifed waiter Richard Adan there in 1981. Lower Second

Avenue remains a dark reminder of such events, except for the nightlife streaming off East 4th Street, a colorful artery crowded with tiny theaters that have become the new Off-Off Broadway home (visit the New York Theater Workshop, exemplary).

ST. MARKS STRIP
St. Marks Place between Third Avenue and Avenue A

The key word in describing St. Marks Place is "commercial." At Third Avenue is the Great Hall at Cooper Union, a prestigious scholarship-only college where Abe Lincoln gave his crucial preconvention freedom pitch. Right past Third Avenue is a strange conglomerate of expensive boutiques, cafés, and bookstores, and outdoor/indoor sellers of capes, socks, shirts, plants, costume jewelry, and junk. In the summer months, this is bigger than any shopping plaza in town. (See reference to "the Sock Man" on page 43.)

In the '60s and '70s, this was a wonderful mini-village of poets, dramatic artists, and "free thinkers." Today very few of these people are left, and veteran residents are angry.

Read the wall graffiti, notably between Second and Third Avenues, and allow me to commiserate with the people who have lived here for a while:

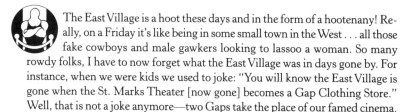

The East Village is a hoot these days and in the form of a hootenany! Really, on a Friday it's like being in some small town in the West . . . all those fake cowboys and male gawkers looking to lassoo a woman. So many rowdy folks, I have to now forget what the East Village was in days gone by. For instance, when we were kids we used to joke: "You will know the East Village is gone when the St. Marks Theater [now gone] becomes a Gap Clothing Store." Well, that is not a joke anymore—two Gaps take the place of our famed cinema.

Plus, St. Marks Place, the street we just mentioned, looks more like Paramus Park Mall every single day. (For more on St. Marks, see "Smells" sidebar on page 135.)

BLEECKER AND ENVIRONS
Bleecker Street from LaGuardia Place to Seventh Avenue South

Bleecker Street's fortunes have fluctuated. Some businesses in this old, predominantly Italian neighborhood flourish, coasting on unflagging local support. There are also a dozen timeless art and antique stores nestled comfortably between schmaltzy card stores and the few remaining cafés (Figaro, 186 Bleecker).

JOHN'S PIZZA has not only boomed in popularity, it's added a second restaurant nextdoor and one in midtown, and I think another in Paterson, N.J. (a joke). And Father Demo Square at Sixth Avenue is Bedlam Central: On Friday and Saturday nights people begin to cruise toward the East Village, far west to the "California" of the West Village, or up Sixth Avenue to Chelsea.

For years I've heard folks say the neighborhood has deteriorated, that AIDS has brought bad publicity. But look around—are there fewer *tourists?*

SHERIDAN SQUARE PEOPLE WATCHING
Corner of Christopher Street, West Fourth Street, and Seventh Avenue South

Really, this is about views. At the tip of Sheridan Square, where Grove, Christopher, and West Fourth intersect, you can sit outside at Riviera Cafe (or inside, depending on the seat), and watch people pouring out of six blocks. Everyone seems unrushed—unmatched in this part of this town—and there are hundreds of poseurs.

There were once better sidewalk cafes. Most went the way of the now-defunct Buffalo Roadhouse, a favorite hang-out that is now, gulp, a West Side version of Time Cafe—a carbon copy of an East Village "original."

TREE-LINED STREETS
Bank and Commerce Streets

Bank Street is a lane the Dutch once called "Farm in the Woods." It's the location of the famous acting school HB Studio, and where Toons has tennis-player tiles from sports clubs embedded in its doorframes.

A landmark plaque on the northwest corner of Commerce and Bedford Streets says that when yellow fever devastated the downtown financial district in the 1700s, banks came up here, terrified of being closed down.

At the Commerce–Morton–Bedford triangle, wonder at ancient yard gardens, the Cherry Lane Theater (named for long-gone trees), low-building design, one-story houses, and black metal sculptures on rooftops. This corner is so residential that there are no traffic lights. And you can walk around here and imagine you are somewhere else, like small-town France!

WESTBETH CENTER
Washington Between Bank and West 11th Streets

At the northeast corner of Bank and West Streets is Westbeth, built in 1900 as an industrial complex and now used to house artists. It has a community space, two theaters, an art gallery, and a synagogue. Inside are laboratory spaces—television was invented here. Three-dimensional film was perfected at Westbeth.

The first commercially successful talkie, *The Jazz Singer,* was filmed on a soundstage deep within the complex. *The Jazz Singer* was also the first film snubbed by the Academy during the first Oscar presentations.

Ancient signs say "You are here," but the rain has washed away all diagrams leading to where. You can't help chuckling over a sign in the airy courtyard reading: "No alcoholic beverages . . . no unnecessary noise. No pot smoking."

SIDEBAR SPECIAL Smells of the City

BAZZINI'S

339 Greenwich Street, 334-1280

You'll go nuts when you walk into this peanut emporium. The very second you enter, you're hit with the incomparable aroma of rich, deep coffee. What could make you happier, I wonder? Then you get a whiff of fresh chocolates and suddenly, it's heaven. Then you become aware of the marzipan. But the odor that drives people (at least the ones who work here) is the plethora of nuts . . . the freshly roasted ones.

Since Bazzini's has its own receiving warehouse, you can see the dozens of distinct nuts being transported into the store—right under your nose!

GUS'S PICKLE STAND
35 Essex Street, 254-4477

"Eat Gus's Pickles, Stay Young And Beautiful," goes the famous slogan. (Call them just to hear a guy answer the phone with, "Pickles!") The Gus experience was made famous a few years ago with the still-quaint movie *Crossing Delancey*, partially set on Delancey Street.

But, oh, those gherkins. People line up on Sundays, waiting to get "Three Generations of Quality." They're right to be impressed: The days of the family specialty store are gone. Gus's is an anomaly. Just get a whiff of the schmaltz herring!

(Next door is GRANDMA'S GEFILTE FISH, a substitute for your own Grandma, but not for mine, thank you.)

THIRD AVENUE BETWEEN ST. MARKS PLACE AND EAST 7TH STREET

Many strange and not unpleasant odors emanate from the most traveled block in the East Village: St. Marks Place is a pot smoker's paradise, in addition to being the home of three pizza parlors, a fried chicken stand, a few donut places, and several vociferous beer joints. Because crowds traipse through here at all hours, you can always count on the smell of pot, at least.

A funny nose-enhancer comes from the bagel-and-souvlaki place still on the corner. What IS that scent? It's frying grease, you realize, from donuts, burgers, hot dogs, french fries, zeppole . . .

CIGAR, BABY

Hey, I hate cigar smoke. There, I've said it. As one who's tried to smuggle 'em back from Havana for hifalutin' friends, I have to say what's the big deal? It's just an expensive form of pollution.

For you who love it, try your Cubans (the cigars, not the people) at CAFÉ AUBETTE at 119 East 27th Street (686-5500), a place that sometimes serves coffee during the day and has attitude for days, at night. Be careful how you dress at night when it becomes a *très* trendy bar: no sneakers. They will tell you it's a private party. Like, how 1980s!

Smell This: the tiny cigar bar in the back of steak-induced though somewhat stuffy (i.e., attitudinal) meat haven, **ANGELO & MAXIES**, at 233 Park Avenue South (220-9200, fax 220-9209). They sell them, smell them, wear them. And proudly.

VESUVIO BAKERY: DOWNTOWN BREAD, MAN
160 Prince Street, 925-8248

The loveliest smells of Soho can be found outside the ancient Vesuvio, a neighborhood always-be-there that mostly makes bread. Standing outside this small shop is recommended, particularly since many of the surrounding boutiques smell so darn fake.

RIVERRUN CAFE
176 Franklin Street, 966-3894

For one of the uncanniest downtown odors, stand near Riverrun Café, a not-unnoticed tavern with decent salads and more than a few beers on tap. What's in the air? Coffee. Several java manufacturing plants and delivery points are located in this area, and it's rumored that the same smell travels across the river.

PS: Riverrun's "bathrooms" were voted one of the city's best by *Time Out New York*.

EXTRA SMELLS . . .

. . . The Smell of Beer: **MCSORLEY'S OLD ALE HOUSE** at 15 East 7th Street. Since beer drinking is a serious art, this bar, put together here in 1854, is a beer-slave emporium, for whatever ales you (yuk yuk). It's a sawdusty beer shop; it smells like one. Women are allowed in. They weren't in 1854, nor in 1954.

WHAT BLOCKS ARE EDIBLE

EXTRA: MIDTOWN

The following are the ultimate in cheap eateries in midtown, which is something we all search for:

AFGHANISTAN KEBAB HOUSE
155 West 46th Street, 768-3875; fax 354-1912
A great find for people who aren't vegetarian. Most expensive meat dish is $12.

BARBETTA
321 West 46th Street, 246-9171
One of the oldest restaurants in New York. The amazing prix fixe is only $41, including wine.

 EDISON CAFE AT THE EDISON HOTEL
228 West 47th Street, 354-0368
Oh boy, this place serves the best matzoh ball soup in creation. Slurp away for $2.50. A famous "theaterati" hangout.

JOHN'S BRICK OVEN PIZZERIA
260 West 44th Street, 391-7565
As mentioned earlier in the chapter, this branch of the famed and crazy (busy) eatery from the West Village is now in the former chapel of a gospel church: To some people, not me, pizza is a religion. John's is pastor extraordinaire. Eight bucks.

LOFTI'S
358 West 46th Street, 582-5850
Mom-and-pop hangout for quick bites.

MANHATTAN CHILI COMPANY
1500 Broadway at 43rd Street, 730-8666

See Chapter 19 (on bars), and eat here after you've spent almost all your money on drinks. Oh, and on a whim, I left here and tried finding a decent cigar bar in midtown—nearly impossible. For more on cigars, see sidebar on "Smells" on page 135.

OLLIE'S NOODLE SHOP TIMES SQUARE
200 West 44th Street, 921-5988

With fast service and more than 215 dishes, this is the cheapie restaurant from the guys who manage Dock's and Carmine's. Three excellent restaurants from one chain—not a bad record.

CAFÉ NICOLE AT THE NOVOTEL HOTEL
226 West 52nd Street, 315-0100; fax 765-5363; e-mail: novony@aol.com;
http://www.novotel.com

This most amazing terrace bar (outside for people who like it out there) has a view of Times Square like none other. It also has relatively inexpensive drinks, like five bucks. I tell all my tourist friends.

VIRGIL'S REAL BBQ
152 West 44th Street, 921-9494

Hush puppies and ribs. Georgia chicken-fried steak for only $13. You can't beat it, but I will warn you, it gets darn noisy.

SOUP KITCHEN INTERNATIONAL
259-A West 55th Street, 757-7730

With the plethora of fabulous soup-only places dotting the borough of Manhattan, it is my duty to report on Soup Kitchen International ("home of the Soup Nazi" of "Seinfeld"-fame). The proprietor is Al Yegannah, who has been quoted as saying, fitfully, "I am not a Soup Nazi! NBC and Jerry

Seinfeld—they are nazis!" For that, you gotta love him. Closed in the summer.

(One of New York's top tourist hangouts—for no reason.)

You can also call the Business Improvement District (763-0233) for a small, not well-written, but helpful restaurant guide to midtown. You need it if you spend lots of time there.

Ethnic Specialties—
The Trendy to the Sublime

FLOWERS
21 West 17th Street, 691-8888; fax 647-9698

This place deserves mention because it is a beautiful replica of an Italian restaurant found in Venice. The food is nice, but the club itself is unique because of the events that follow your dinner.

The oft-changing schedule: Tango on Wednesday in the upstairs jazz lounge is pretty neat. There's jazz on Thursday, but light jazz, almost elevator music. On the roof you might check out a fashion show. Sometimes you'll pay a cover for events.

Keep in mind this was once Metro CC and Capito, two highly fashionable places, once very "in" and now very "out." Endangered location in the middle of a commercial street. Although Flowers is trendy, it is more often than not very empty.

PROVENCE
38 Macdougal Street, 475-7500; fax 674-7876

Not only is this a special French restaurant with somewhat overpriced and glamorous food, but on the 14th of July, it goes ape with Bastille Day celebrations. The crowd consists of unsmiling victims of fashion but the wait staff is entertaining and can assist with French words you don't understand. Dinner begins at 6:00 P.M., and ends at 11:00 P.M., except on Friday and Saturday, when they close at midnight.

CHRISTINE'S POLISH-AMERICAN RESTAURANT
208 First Avenue, 254-2474

Billed accurately as "homemade European cooking, reasonable prices, free delivery," Christine's is sadly adorned by oddly chosen celebrity portraits, but the service is wonderful in this Eastern European haven for people on the run.

The food is not kosher but it is a good facsimile: kasha varnishkas, stuffed derma, heavy Polish specials. Perfect for a daytime snack or a big meal, especially in the dead of winter when the heartiest prescription is chicken-in-a-pot: chicken thighs, veggies, matzoh balls, Mama's wholesome soup!* Open 7:00 A.M.–11:00 P.M., a good place for early solo dining.

BRISA DEL CARIBE
489 Broadway, 226-9768

Here's where Latins and Anglos converge to talk about current events and eat Hispanic-American food cooked, well, to *makeshift* edible. The café is fun, though, with a dozen stools for sitting, small tables for reading newspapers or meditating, and good service from people who will never rush you, although they may ask you to wait until they get off the phone.

Brisa serves a fine, cheap breakfast at any hour of the business day (ham and eggs or a Western omelette for less than $2.50). Also, coffee, soda, beer, and a fine selection of rich, though store-bought, cakes are available. Who said Cuban places were all about steak sandwiches? Open Monday–Saturday, 7:00 A.M.–9:00 P.M.; Sunday, 7:00 A.M.–6:00 P.M.

---

* If you are going to order home delivery of chicken soup, call the "Second Avenue Deli" at 677-0606. They'll deliver the cure-all ("chicken in a pot"—veggies, broiled chicken soup, stock, a prayer . . . bread, cole slaw, and pickles) for sixteen bucks.

LE MADELEINE
403 West 43rd Street, 246-2993; fax 586-7631

The scene circa 1984: This was the spot for great ratatouille at $1.75 a helping. I think a Coke was $.50. Then the café next door went kaput, and the fans waved a sad bye-bye to the cheap cuisine. The scene today: A "Bistro Francaise" with pretentious, though scrumptious, entrées. Now Madeleine can run you about $20 an entrée at dinner. No ratatouille, but their steak au poivre has a memorable cream-and-cognac sauce ($18). Take their garden, add an overhead roof, and voila!—comfy in all seasons. And Le Madeleine (née "Madeleine") has the friendliest staff in midtown. Open Monday for lunch, 12:00 P.M.–4:00 P.M.; Monday–Sunday for dinner, 5:00 P.M.–11:00 P.M.; and Saturday–Sunday for brunch, 12:00 P.M.–3:30 P.M.

VICTOR'S 52 RESTAURANT
236 West 52nd Street, 586-7714; fax 333-7872

In 1980, Victor Del Corral of Cuba opened the hottest Latin tourist attraction in midtown. Victor's Cafe has traveling musicians, a spacious overcrowded bar area, and impeccable service. The only problem is acoustic—too loud and boisterous. Fifty-two is just too popular.

Their restaurant is the one with sofrito—equipped with sauteed garlic, onions, and green peppers. We mourn the passing of the once-endangered Victor's on West 71st Street. It tried hard to be mellow and tasteful, and lost out to a trendy boutique. Just what the Upper West Side needs? Hmm. Open daily from noon to midnight. Currently undergoing renovations. So, who knows?

CACIQUE JAMAICAN RESTAURANT
106 Greenwich Street at Carlisle Street, 791-0510

One of the eating sensations in the financial district is a hangout where reggae music plays softly in the background. Here waitresses tell you to eat everything on your plate before you can have dessert! Cacique has no tables, just twenty-three counter stools, making it perfect for eating alone with a book or stock report. Order island specialty jerk chicken or any of the daily specials, such as vegetable gumbo soup or items called "Goodies": Sour Sop Juice and Coco Bread, both of which are usually hard to come by on Wall Street. Plenty of Jamaican food to go around these days, too. As you leave Cacique, get some asham, or sweet Jamaican candy ($1). Open Monday–Friday, 7:00 A.M.–9:00 P.M.; Saturday, 8:00 A.M.–6:00 P.M.

SIDEBAR SPECIAL Bakeries for Cultural Effect

FERRARA FOODS & CONFECTIONS

195 Grand Street, 226-6150; fax 226-0667

New locations: Times Square (Seventh Avenue and 42nd Street);

1700 Broadway (at 53rd Street); Greenwich Village (Sixth Avenue

at Greenwich Avenue)

If you spend too much time at the Little Italy location the management gets angry and suspicious, and you get a stomachache. It's not really a bakery, but more a sweets restaurant. They do have the best Italian ice cream, cakes, cookies, pastries, tarts, and (New York's favorite drink these days) bottled water, with or without gas. The latter costs $4 or more—but then again, so do cordials. Most things here are too expensive—you're paying for overhead.

A spacious place that's famous as a tourist attraction. Ferrara may not make your teeth happy, but your taste buds will thank you profusely. Try baba crema cassantina, a delicacy you can't make at home. The chocolate truffle cake is truly a materpiece. But first, have some tiny pizza pieces—this *is* Little Italy.

FUNG WONG BAKERY SHOP

30 Mott Street, 267-4037

Mott Street is Bakery Row. At the trip, by Canal Street, you will see **MAXIM'S BAKERY** selling turtle soup by the bowl, out of a gigantic arm sitting outside. Then there's **LUNG FUNG**, near Pell Street, with many Chinese delicacies (no one speaks English). Finally, **FUNG WONG** has authentic Chinese baked goods: lotus cakes, yellow bean cake, *baboy* (coconut), and not-sweet rice cakes made from brown sugar and white sugar. For the progressive, there are X-rated fortune cookies ("Man who lays girl on ground gets piece on earth . . .").

These folks are nice, and willing to explain what's inside the cakes. Most goodies go for between 40 and 65 cents a slice.

G. MORRONE BAKERY
324 East 116th Street, 722-2972

This bakery smells of one of the city's last remaining brick ovens that bake bread daily. Accordingly, Gabriel Morrone gets the dough rising at 6:00 every morning.

The Italian population who believe in ancient recipes come here daily seeking fazil, dried biscuits soaked in water. Morrone relates how they put "a little oil, oregano, and cheese—maybe even beans" on it. Delish. This is the kind of special bread found only here; you can also find fresh-baked whole wheat, onion, hero, and heavily seeded rolls. It was recently disclosed that exclusive boutiques, such as Balducci's and Grace's Marketplace, get their bread selections here.

ORWASHER'S BAKERY
308 East 78th Street, 288-6569; fax 570-2706

Nothing beats Orwasher's Hungarian specials, not since the No. 1 choice (Lichtman's of West 86th Street) was cut from the endangered species list. You can get many cakes and cookies at Orwasher's, open since 1916, and not everything is Hungarian. They boast oat bran cakes, too. Hey, in order to stay around, they had to change with the times.

But the sweet tooth will find that Orwasher's babka cannot be matchedy without a plane ticket to Budapest.

PALERMO BAKERY
213 First Avenue, no phone at press time

Palermo's is a few doors down from VENIERO PASTICCERIA (342 East 11th Street, 674-4415), which is the East Village's *famous* bakery. That one has the creamy Napoleons! But Palermo is the downtown place for bread, scones, raisin muffins, coffee cake, and even Tartuffo ice cream. Breads are freshly baked, with specials that you can smell along the avenues as early as 7:00 A.M. Palermo's constantly cuts its prices, too, so if something doesn't move in an hour it's offered at half-price.

Great onion rolls, seeded rolls, Italian rolls, tea biscuits. And a rare commodity on First Avenue outside a stuffy, trendy coffee bar: a decent cup of Joe. Palermo *is* open.

POSEIDON BAKERY
629 Ninth Avenue, 757-6173

Midtown's Greek food fans go crazy for this place, in business for seventy-two years (third generation and still in the family). Again, people love this place more since the demise of a favorite ethnic place in the area, Molfeta's. At Poseidon, foodstuffs are baked in flaky crusts and there are several vegetarian specials—potato, carrot, cabbage, onions, parsley—you can either munch standing up or savor at home.

Poseidon is smack between old-time RUDY'S BAR and the ultimately newfangled FILM CENTER CAFE. But Poseidon is strictly old country—less than $2 apiece for manakopita and spanakopita.* They also have a series of marzipan cakes, though really they specialize in full meals cooked with care and attention. According to the owners, "the only Greek pastry [shop] left in Manhattan."

* Meat and cheese pies.

YONAH SCHIMMEL'S KNISHERY
137 East Houston Street, 477-2858

For over a century, Yonah, Knish King, has been the best cabbage, spinach, and sweet potato knishery for the Lower East Side. One day, while making kasha-filled knishes, the manager thought "Do people out there know what a REAL knish is?" Sure they'd seen a frozen knish on vendors' carts, and even tasted variations of a knish at Nedick's, but . . . So he gave them a choice.

This dingy East Houston shop may rush you a *bissel*. (They won't cut a knish—don't even ask. It's sacrilege!)

EILEEN'S SPECIAL CHEESECAKE
17 Cleveland Place, 966-5585, outside NY, 1-800-521-CAKE,
fax 219-9558

It's not the least bit ethnic, and that's what makes it so darn special. As you may have noticed by reading carefully, the entries in this chapter all have ethnic flair; neither is cheesecake American in origin. Eileen's is quintessentially United States, the huge and small cakes are among the best I've ever had.* You may have to call for directions—Cleveland Place isn't easily found. South of Spring Street, parallel to Lafayette Street, east of Soho, and across from Lt. Petrosino Park! Open seven days a week, 9:00 A.M. to 6:00 P.M.

By the way, as of October 1997, Eileen's Cheesecake is now available in Tokyo and Yokosuka, Japan!

* Hey, don't believe me. The *Daily News* voted its stuff the best cheesecake, so did lots of other books, like the *Zagat's* guide.

SPRING STREET NATURAL RESTAURANT
62 Spring Street, 966-0290; fax 966-4254
http://www.citysearch.com/nyc/springstreetnatural

Serving multi-ethnic cooking with an "organic twist," featuring a line of "fresh-line caught and farm-raised fish" not to mention the expected free-range poultry. Twenty-two years on the outskirts of Soho, Spring Street Natural has a long, elegant bar and quite a few hangers-on, regulars who couldn't dream of going anywhere else. It is a beautiful, corner location, and the international wine list features organic wines.

On weekday afternoons you get a free cup of herbal tea just by coming in and plopping yourself down. (Ask nicely.) Open Sunday through Thursday from 11:00 A.M. to 12 midnight; open Friday and Saturday until 1:00 A.M.

RATNER'S RESTAURANT
138 Delancey Street, 677-5588; fax 473-4860

Eat at New York's oldest family-run restaurant, known in Jewish circles as "Ratner's Dairy Restaurant," so as not to confuse people who won't eat meat with milk. Established in 1905, this is the best fascimile of Grandma's food I've found, with some of the most notorious matzoh balls in town. A traditional restaurant with lots of nostalgia thrown in for free.

Once while I was guesting on a radio show, an older woman from Queens was telling the host about her plans to take her visiting sister for a big lunch at the Waldorf Astoria. I cut in and said, "Go to Ratner's with your sister; she doesn't need another fancy-shmancy brunch." The lady profusely thanked me with, "Oh, of course!" Open Sunday through Thursday from 6:00 A.M. to 11:00 P.M.; Friday, 6:00 A.M.–3:00 P.M. Closed Saturdays.

GUS'S PLACE
149 Waverly Place, 645-8511; fax 647-0619

The tiny restaurant with the great (Mediterranean) food and no atmosphere whatsoever; everybody has been there once if they have lived or worked in the Village. It's so tacky they use it for the reception for *Tony 'n Tina's Wedding,* a farce version of a typical Italian wedding that has been passing as a play for ten years! Gus's works for the part. Go for bread—strictly Italian loaves. Open for lunch daily at noon; closes at 4:00 P.M. Open for dinner daily at 5:00 P.M., closes at midnight.

It had to happen that New York would fall prey to a donut battle. It was only a matter of time.

The thing is, **KRISPY KREME**'s hype is managed well. To say the donut isn't a great one, you would probably get laughed out of serious cocktail parties. Krispy Kreme was the donut that Cub Scouts in the Deep South sold to raise funds. People all over the South swore by their flavor and their fresh-from-the-oven taste. And when Krispy Kreme donuts hit New York, the city folk went crazy. Krispy Kreme opened its first New York shop in Chelsea, on West 23rd Street, and people originally from the South told all their friends. Truth be told (I used to live next door to the place) the donuts are gooey, and startlingly sweet and rich; no match for Entenmann's Rich Chocolate, if you ask me. But the sign in the window says HOT when they are just out of the oven, and that's pretty cool.

In my former building, with its magnificent English-style garden, smelling the strong wafting scent of pastries is not anyone's idea of a good time, and shortly the garden-goers were suing Krispy Kreme in court. They demanded that Krispy Kreme get a better ventilation system, but the subtext on the matter was: Stop believing your press and remember that you are in New York, a city of cynics. (And donuts are supposed to be "happy food." Yeah.)

What happened shortly thereafter is one for the hype history books. The garden won its battle (Krispy was ordered to install ventilation, and publicly apologize for good measure), and Krispy Kreme rapidly started receiving bad press all around. Journalists starting writing articles comparing other donuts to Krispy Kremes, which hurt them even more. Krispy Kreme had been getting away with charging seventy cents per donut (you can get a bagel for half that at most bakeries or even at your local Korean deli), and the question rising in everyone's mind was why anyone would want to pay so much for something that takes but a second to consume.

It was at this point that a journalist at the *New York Times* discovered the ages-old GEORGIE'S PASTRY SHOP (50 West 125th Street) right near the new Krispy Kreme shop on 125th Street. The gorgeous Jelly Monsters sold at Georgie's (for 55 cents each, but only $4.50 a dozen) are so fantastic that the *Times* subsequently told all Krispy lovers to drop everything and get up there. But, it's in Harlem, and New Yorkers don't seem to travel north well.

Time for change. Along came FAIRWAY (2127 Broadway at 74th Street), a bastion of baked and other food goods for Upper West Siders, wholesaling Krispys for about fifty cents. (By the way, Fairway is the mainstay that exclusively sells the David Glass Chocolate Mousse Cake from Connecticut, with more phenylethylamine than any other chemical compound, for what is considered to be a reasonable twenty bucks.) Krispy Kreme executives were outraged, and told Fairway to raise the prices on their donuts immediately (it was hurting the elitism factor that allowed them to charge seventy cents in the first place). Fairway refused, and hung large signs in their windows proclaiming,* "WE NO LONGER SELL KRISPY KREME BECAUSE ITS SEVENTY-CENT PRICE POINT IS UNFAIR." Whoah. What's a "doooonnnuuut" (Homer Simpson reference) fan to do?

The price war gave donut munchers cause to think. Soon after, wouldn't you know it, Fairway started carrying Georgie's big jelly donuts, the very same ones the press had been eating up, literally.

To them I say, let the best filling win.

* I paraphrase.

ROCKING HORSE CAFÉ
182 Eighth Avenue, 463-9511; fax 243-3245

Roe's Rocking palace is a Chelsea favorite for its $10 burrito dishes and sauces you would never expect from "another Mexican joint." Prices for entrees start at $6 for typical tacos, and rise to $16 for the steak fajita.

The free-range chicken and *jicama* salads are the best for miles. Open 11:30 A.M. to 11:00 P.M., Sunday through Thursday; open until 12:00 A.M. on Friday and Saturday. Keep in mind that this is when the kitchen closes every night; there is a bar open until everyone leaves.

Rocking Horse Mexicana (their name when they're trying to be trendy) had a fund-raiser in celebration of the Day of the Dead last October 13th (1997). It is destined to become an annual exhibit and silent auction of commemorative altars. Proceeds benefited God's Love We Deliver and the William T. Harris School PS 11. It's something different when you're trying to digest.

MR. LEO'S
17 West 27th Street, 532-6673

Right in the heart of North Chelsea, on 27th Street between Broadway and Fifth Avenue, with decor right out of Memphis 1950, and great (though often greasy as hell) fried chicken, greens, and—believe it or not—real candied yams, and some down-home service! According to rumors, sometimes a gospel choir in long robes sashay in for a meal. Oh—$5.95 weekday lunch: It's heaven—and cheap! (Use Discover Card—get a free CD!!) PS: East 27th Street is home to the Gershwin Hotel and other quasi-trendy cheapie new lodgings . . . Come see.

INDOCHINE
430 Lafayette Street, 505-5111; fax 477-0397

A great French bistro that remains trendy even as the block around it falls apart (Indochine is across from the crumbling Joseph Papp Public Theater). It is still going strong after being open for fifteen years, and *New York* magazine calls it the "most fun place in New York." So fun, in fact, that one just opened in Los Angeles. (Those Californians, always copying New York trends!) The food is scrumptious, and Bianca Jagger still calls it her home. Entrées max out at $30. Open 5:30 P.M. to 12:30 A.M., Monday through Saturday. Closes at 11:30 P.M. on Sunday.

ROETELLE A.G.

126 East 7th Street, 674-4140; fax 358-7986

A German-Italian-Swiss-French restaurant, the best of its kind, the only of its kind. Food prices are not cheap, but the outlandish menu selections and wine list are exceptional. Go in good weather, bring your favorite person, sit in their makeshift garden, and listen to the yodelers or German crooners. And order the cold soup, the liver paté, and a bowl of fruit. Entrées? Sure, why not. How about the duck? Roetelle, in the heart of the East Village, is a find—good food, good service, and very nice to all types!

RIODIZIO

417 Lafayette Street between 4th Street and Astor Place, 529-1313; fax 677-1186

Brazilian barbecue is hot! First, many experts will tell you about the Queens-based Green Field Charrascaria (718-672-5202), the place where plates-of-food-you-order-from-floating waiters-as-you-give-them-the-"Go"-sign. (Now, also in Farmingdale, Long Island!)

If you haven't done this—and want to do it in Manhattan—I recommend Riodizio highly. The question is, what is Riodizio? It's a downtownish restaurant with nice place settings, art on the walls (the large painting near the front door looks like a cock fight), low lighting, a strangely-hip-looking crowd at the bar. There is a full menu, but don't order from it. The items on the menu are not what anyone goes to a Brazilian barbecue for. Order their avalanche all-you-can-eat prix fixe special.

At Riodizio, just like Green Field, for $25 a person you will get this superb, *heavy* all-you-can-eat barbecue. On your table will be a coaster, with one side green and one side red. As in all Charrascarias (in Portuguese, literally, barbecues), when you're full, just make sure the red side is facing up. Prepare to be stuffed, as waiters bombard your table with large fresh-off-the-grill skewers of barbecued sausage, pork, flank steak, chicken; you name it, they grill the heck out of it.

The waiters bring around corn, fried plantains, rice, and greens, but if you're anything like my friends, you'll only see eating vegetables as a stomach space-waster! In other words: why eat corn when there's a guy standing there with a skewer of sausage? It's messy as heck, you'll probably eat entirely too much and feel sick after, but you will never regret it.

ARIZONA 206

206 East 60th Street and Third Avenue, 838-0440; fax 751-1513

A while ago, the *New York Times* gave this restaurant three stars, and this was the first "non-tablecloth" restaurant to receive such acclaim. With outdoor seating in the summer, a fireplace in the winter, and arguably some of the best margaritas in the city, Arizona has become a popular dinner spot for the trendy/yuppy crowd. Excellent menu of Tex-Mex food, but I will warn you that it sometimes is pricey.

ZEN PALATE

Three locations: 34 Union Square East (614-9291; fax 614-9401); 663 Ninth Avenue and 46th Street (582-1669; fax 582-1708); 2170 Broadway between 77th and 78th Streets (501-7768; fax 501-7867)

Vegetarian to the core, the wait staff are not allowed to bring meat of any kind into the restaurant. The great thing about Zen Palate, besides the fact that the food is both healthy and tasty, is the prices. Zen Palate is cheaper than most veggie places in the city, and the restaurant in each venue is divided between a cheaper cafeteria-style and a slightly more expensive restaurant style place. And the outdoors environment only *looks* grungy.

REPUBLIC RESTAURANT

Two locations: 37 Union Square West between East 16th and 17th Streets, 627-7172, 627-7173 for deliveries; 2290 Broadway between 82nd and 83rd Streets, 579-5959, 579-5960 for deliveries

Republic is a very fun, very hip Pan-Asian restaurant. Although this restaurant has great music and service, it's the delicious, healthy food that keeps everyone coming back. Think noodles! The successful owners of Republic also opened a sandwich shop called, adorably enough, **SANDBOX** (East 40th Street and Madison, 973-9269).

ETHNIC SPECIALTIES

Romantic Eating

NOTE: Here are five special romantic places from all over town. See also other chapters in "Food"—and the "Gardens" sidebar in this chapter—and be creative.

OPALENE
85 Avenue A between 5th and 6th Streets, 475-5050; fax 475-5252
Very trendy and very low lit, the atmosphere at Opalene is quite romantic. The main dining area is only lit by a candle at each table and any light coming through the skylights. I highly recommend the seared tuna appetizer; Opalene beats all restaurants at this dish. It's not cheap, but the food and the atmosphere are worth the extra. Even good service here. Opalene only serves dinner, and is open from 6:00 P.M. to 11:00 P.M., Monday through Saturday, but the lounge and bar don't usually close until around 4:00 A.M.

ERNIE'S
2150 Broadway between 75th and 76th Streets, 496-1588; fax 595-1527
Great Italian food in a trendy uptown environment. This is a place to eat any time of year—for the view. The front glass walls open up and tables are moved onto the sidewalk. Fun to people watch here, although you may be too busy looking into the eyes of your date to notice. Though trendy as

heck, amazing dishes nonetheless: the spinach tortellini in a cream and wild mushroom sauce with prosciutto, and the risotto with tomatoes and shrimp. Open 11:30 A.M. to 12:00 A.M., Sunday through Thursday, and until 1:00 A.M. or until the place empties out on Friday and Saturday. They never rush you out at closing time here.

ERMINIA
250 East 83rd Street, 879-4284

The smell of a wood fire in a tiny candlelit room seeps through walls of exposed brick and thick-planked wood at Erminia, where pasta and grilled food are just one aspect of a truly interesting menu: e.g., a Jewish-style bread alongside a Parmesan-tinged artichoke.

This fast-paced place still manages to summon up a stylish repose, with an elegant wine list to match. Few couples looking for romance have been disappointed by Erminia. "We like to get a reservation because we only have eleven tables," said a spokeswoman. "Small, surely, but also romantic." Open daily at 5:00 P.M., closed Sunday; the kitchen shuts down at 11:00 P.M.

SIDEBAR SPECIAL Gardens of Eating

GASCOGNE
158 Eighth Avenue between 17th and 18th Streets, 675-6564

Nestled in the neighborhood that made restaurants in the 1990s "stars," this oldstay has a French flair, French owners, "franch" service (slow), and a makeshift garden in the back that is so cute and completely unexpected, it's worth the overly long wait. Try the fries, kids. A fireplace, too.

BAROLO
398 West Broadway at Broome Street, 226-1102; fax 226-1822

One hell of a tourist attraction, the wine list is appetizing, the prices are expensive, and its Italian style will never fail to impress a business acquaintance: The garden is beautiful, very New York (i.e., it's not really a garden but above someone's backyard), huge and noisy.

LE JARDIN BISTRO
25 Cleveland Place at Lafayette and Spring Streets, 343-9599; fax 343-9599

An arbored garden, a real one, in a space on the avenue known as East Soho. Another French bistro like Gascogne, this one's airier—and so is the garden. This place has changed hands many times in the last year, most likely because no one can find it.

MARCH
405 East 58th Street, 754-6272; fax 838-5108

March down to this dinner-only townhouse in a tony section and discover a $59 prix fixe with a garden AND an outdoor fireplace in hand. This gorgeous restaurant is quite unmatched, albeit pricey. The garden is the kind you would find at a Vermont inn: perfectly manicured and upbeat.

VERBENA
54 Irving Place, 260-5454; fax 260-3595

Just when you thought it could not get any trendier in this sidebar, discover the "New American cuisine" (read small portions): truly food of an exceptional nature, and again pricey. I dunno, the garden is REAL, and finding this unexpected treasure is worth it, if you're on an expense account. The menu is a treat, with unique combos. Otherwise, a place for grazing, i.e., appetizers only.

VITTORIA CUCINA
308–310 Bleecker Street at Grove and Seventh Avenue South, 463-0730; fax 463-0765

A relaxing atmosphere with ever-changing hands, the lovely garden here offers one of the Village's few respites; if you are nice, they will even let you sit there in the afternoon with a glass of wine. (Around the corner from 52 Christopher, an out-door/indoor coffee bar with affectionate owners, and a garden!)

PS: Vittorio is hardly visited by tourists because it doesn't appear classy, but it really is.

"44" AT THE ROYALTON (THE ROYALTON HOTEL LOBBY)
44 West 44th Street, 869-4400; fax 869-8965

A fine dining experience for anyone who happens to be cruising midtown. Pricey, this is a perfect way to start an evening, particularly since the small bar on the side of the entrance is a great place to get plastered without any of your acquaintances noticing you. This is part of the fancy Royalton Hotel, where the young hosts who greet you are taught to speak in southern accents (fake). Also, see **ASIA DE CUBA**—same owners—at Morgan's Hotel, 38th and Madison. A super, deservedly well-reputed Cuban joint with the city's first rum bar. (Reserve a week before, too.)

PEACOCK ALLEY RESTAURANT
At the Waldorf Astoria Hotel, 301 Park Avenue, 872-4895; fax 872-7272

French fine dining at its best, this restaurant has not only amazing food but the elegant atmosphere of the Waldorf and great service. Open for breakfast, lunch, and dinner. The head chef is French native Laurent Manrique from Gascogne (the town, not the restaurant).

11

Quintessential New York Spectacles

 CORNELIA STREET CAFÉ
29 Cornelia Street, 989-9318

In any weather, in any season, this café's tiny alleyway location makes a fantastic rendezvous point. Whether you go for food—the ever-changing menu is among the Village's most eclectic—or just espresso, you can either stay outside and watch infrequent passersby (in summer) or sit in front of the hearth and look at the subtle wall art (in winter). Wood floors contribute to a peaceful atmosphere. Also, a small, lower-level space hosts theater events such as staged readings, jazz groups, and tiny musicals. Few places in the Village are as pleasant to go to for cognac, as comfortable to hide in when it rains. Open every day. Call for new hours.

LUMA

200 Ninth Avenue, 633-8033; fax 691-7513

After six years as a total vegetarian restaurant of fancy cuisine, the place saw the market shrinking and decided to start serving meat, all organically grown and cooked (those chickens are out of their cages, they swear!). Great wine selection with veggie dishes; the steak's quite good too. Moderately priced. Prix fixe complete dinner for two available.

LUCKY CHENG'S

24 First Avenue between 1st and 2nd Streets, 473-0516

Lucky is the latest incarnation of what was once the First Avenue Baths and later Cave Canem restaurant and swimming hole cum discotheque. This time the drag waitresses and Chinese food *works*. And the noise is what you'd expect from a made-up name like Lucky Cheng: boisterous and bitchy. Entrées range in price from below $10 to $18. Call for drag show times and information. See below ("La Nouvelle Justine") for more on this place. PS: There are seemingly as many "Lucky's" as Burger Kings these days.

CUPPING ROOM CAFÉ

359 West Broadway, 925-2898; fax 966-5609

This place has been around, well, forever. Cupping Room started as a one-room muffin place ($1.25 for fresh pastry and coffee), then expanded into the best-around lunch emporium. Now the Cupping Room is a *tres* fancy restaurant with one of the best local wine lists, and it stays busy till 2:00 A.M. most nights, hosting jazz and gimmicks, such as a tarot card reader on Thursday nights.

Somehow the Cupping Room continues to retain an arty quality that is never ridiculous or overpriced. It still has two menus: a cheap café (burgers, sandwiches) and Foods of Australia and New Zealand: Posh. Espresso eggs and brunch meals are extraordinary, as are afternoon teas. Tuesday is customer appreciation night, when dinner is prix fixe at $13.95 per person. Evening reservations are a must. Service, however, is less than perfect. And stay away from pasta dishes, which are (pre-) over-cooked. The kitchen is open Monday, 7:30 A.M. to midnight; Tuesday–Thursday, from 7:30 A.M. to 1:00 A.M.; Friday, 7:30 A.M. to 2:00 A.M.; Saturday from 8:00 A.M. to 2:00 A.M.; and Sunday, from 8:00 A.M. to midnight.

Here are some of the answers I received when I posed this question to the members of the Native's Guide to New York Forum on CompuServe, the online service, and some pieces of the dialogue that ensued. If you have never been on an interactive "bulletin board"—or an on-line forum—here's a way for you to see what it's like:*

What's important to know, and perhaps that's the part that was discussed in the other forums but hasn't been discussed here, is why egg cream is called egg cream. After all, it has neither egg nor cream in it. Also, and perhaps this was discussed in the other forums but it bears repeating, who originally developed the drink? And why did egg cream come to be associated with New York? Does egg cream accompany particularly well any type of food or is it to be consumed as a refreshing drink only? And have any expressions come to be associated with the serving of egg cream, such as "Gimmie a double shot of Fox's with that," or "Straight up, seltzer back"? These are questions that a food critic would be qualified to answer, and we are lucky to have the participation of Jim, a food critic. Incidentally, I just reread Jim's recipe for egg cream and I would like to see it placed in the library section of this forum where it will be available for future generations of egg cream lovers. Can a violently shakened bottle of Perrier substitute for seltzer?

If you do the prep right, the foamy white top is almost meringue-thick (well . . . an exaggeration). But that's where the term evolves, I think.

Another possible source of the name "egg cream," from Jeff Kisseloff's *You Must Remember This: An Oral History of Manhattan:*

* And if you are an old hand at this, then a few guffaws are in store as people tell you (and me) evvverything they know on this classy subject.

A New York Yiddish-theater actor performing in Paris had a café drink, "chocolat et creme." He brought the recipe back to NY and somehow the word "et" got New Yawk-ized into egg.

Spalding evolved into Spaldeen, and where I grew up the Loew's Paradise was "Low-ee's Paradise." So the change in pronunciation doesn't sound so improbable to me. But it's just another theory for another of those insoluble New York mysteries.

Q: "DOES EGG CREAM ACCOMPANY PARTICULARLY WELL ANY TYPE OF FOOD OR IS IT TO BE CONSUMED AS A REFRESHING DRINK ONLY?"

A: "The latter! The life span of the head is short, so you gotta down the thing. It's not to swirl around at cocktail parties while you munch hors d'oeuvres . . ."

Q: "CAN A VIOLENTLY SHAKENED BOTTLE OF PERRIER SUBSTITUTE FOR SELTZER?"

A: "Lord no. Too salty. Bubbles too slow. And it's just . . . WRONG!"

SOME RECIPES:

The prime ingredient, malted milk powder, is not made in this country anymore (well, carnation does make a poor, poor version, but I won't count it). But Asians are crazy about Horlick's, the malted milk powder of our past (I like it straight out of the bottle). You can buy it at ANY Asian grocery store, and make yourself a very blissful malted.

If you ever get a hankering for an eggcream again . . . Buy Canfield's Chocolate soda, fill your glass to about 2 inches from the top and fill the rest of the glass with milk. It tastes as good as the original . . . I know, I was born and raised in Bklyn . . . was weaned on eggcreams.

Chill your milk almost to freezing in a . . . um . . . freezer. Put 3 or 4 fingers of milk in a glass, the best are those coke glasses that are narrow but flare out at the top. Fill it up with seltzer (siphon bottles work best, but DEFINITELY not club soda), violently at first, then more and more smoothly to make the head rise above the glass. Then drizzle in the Foxes U-Bet (none other will do)—it'll shplurk [sic] through the head down to the bottom of the glass, where it can be stirred into the milk/seltzer with a long spoon—best if it has a rather small, narrow top—leaving the creamy white head undisturbed. Add slightly too much syrup. Never ever add chocolate earlier in the process, because if it mixes with the milk before seltzer is added, you get a sticky brown head instead of a fluffy white one.

FORUM MEMBER ACCOUNTS OF THEIR "FIRST TIMES" (FIRST TIME HAVING EGG CREAM, THAT IS).

I can't remember when I last had an egg cream or whether I even liked the stuff. I may have tasted it when I passed through New York in '67. But then again, I was on a tight budget at the time and I may not have sprung for one. I think I first tasted one in the early seventies at the cafe of the San Francisco Jewish Community Center, but even there I'm not sure. How egg cream could have gotten that far west, I don't know, but I do remember at the time meeting a woman from New York who had fled to San Francisco to get away from the influence of her mother. I imagined that there were other women like her that were leaving the East Coast for various reasons—but mainly to flee overbearing mothers—bringing with them the yearning for the taste of egg cream and the skill to make it and perhaps one ended up working at the café of the San Francisco Jewish Community Center. I like to think that this is the way it happened.

When I finally got back to New York, after a 28-year absence, it was in June of '95. I was there on business and traveling with my wife. I said, "I have a hankering for some egg cream. Let's go out and find some." She said "OK." Now she's a smart woman and you might think that she would have figured out that there are better things to do in New York than to wander from deli to deli looking for a carbonated drink. Perhaps she accompanied me only with a sense of tolerance for a nutty husband who, with only a few hours to spare in one of the most dynamic cities in the world, would spend his time tracking down egg cream.

We went first to Hammacher Schlemmer, because I had seen bottled egg cream advertised in their Christmas catalog and I thought I could bring back a six-pack. However, they no longer carried it and the salesman recommended that we try a deli a few blocks down the street. We walked from shop to shop and the message was invariably, "We used to carry it but nobody drinks it any more. Try the deli a few blocks down. They might have it."

The day ended in utter frustration. I felt saddened by this experience. Not only because I couldn't get to taste egg cream or because I had squandered our few remaining hours in the city, but because I felt that an era had ended. Envisioning New York without egg cream is like envisioning San Francisco without Irish coffee, or the Cadillac Bar without tequila poppers. My wife tried to console me. She said, "I tasted egg cream once, but I can't remember that it was all that good." Crestfallen, I said, "I can't believe that New Yorkers have abandoned egg cream! It's been such an important part of their culture!"

. . . This, then, is what I was seeking when I set out in New York on my quest for an egg cream: a sense of exhilaration brought about by the action of performing a ritual that would signal to me that I had "been there and done that." Drinking an egg cream in a quaint little café in New York would have done it for me. Others, perhaps, would want something more.

My interest in egg cream came about quite a few years ago, when it was mentioned on some TV show I think (like "Jeopardy") or I read it in a magazine or something. Then they began selling it bottled, probably the stuff you saw, in the grocery stores (called "XXX the Original Egg Cream," with a guy in a little chef's hat or something). I was intrigued by this drink that had neither egg nor cream in it, but when well chilled, did sort of have the flavor of a Cadbury easter treat w/faux yolk. Hmmmmm . . .

Drinking an egg cream in a quaint little café in New York I had to laugh when I read this line because I too had visions of the spot that served this age-old drink. I at least pictured an old soda fountain type joint. Imagine my surprise when Susan Chen gets me down to the St. Marks area (wasn't it Susan?), makes a quick turn and leads me into a very small and narrow newspaper stand!! Behind the counter to the left, she quickly called out our orders for two egg creams, while I was faced with Pamela Lee's Christmas skin issue on the racks to the right. This was not what I pictured at all (uh, the soda joint, not Mrs. Lee)!! But our drinks were whipped up, and we scooted out single-file into the 40-degree weather, sipping happily.

As my days were short, she was required to take me back for several nights after so that I could sample the other flavors. Didn't get to them all, but that original is the best. And while I've slowly forgotten the actual nuances of the flavor, gotta tell ya, it only seemed to be a notch or two above the bottled, maybe because it had a freshness in the flavor. It was worth every bit of the effort to say I'd had THE original though, if just to have experienced it.

Information tidbit: Best *nouveau* egg cream can be found at Ellen's Stardust Restaurants (307-7575, for locations). See page 168 for the details.

RUSSIAN TEA ROOM
150 West 57th Street, 265-0947

Look, there's Carly Simon! No, *Paul* Simon. Oh, and Meryl . . . The list drones on. People don't seem to actually *eat* here, though the blinis are unbeatable. Everyone is too busy looking to see who's there and who's seeing them. Still, the best part of the Tea Room really isn't the looking, it's the shashlik, samovars, and Stolichnaya offered by attentive servers. Sure, it's pricey, but for a time on the town (warning: Saturdays are noisy!), few places are more entertaining.

See the board room and an art gallery that has hosted Tinsel Town's most glamorous imported stars for over sixty years. Open daily, and late too. Reopening in 1998.

SANDOMENICO
240 Central Park South, 265-5959; fax 897-0844

This New York variation of a café in Imola, Italy, offers the food everyone hopes they'll get whenever they order Italian: a wholesome meal of selections derived from classical Italian good taste. Reservations required. Mind the dress code. Study the menu carefully. Recipes are available. Say hello to the bartender as you enter.

Sandomenico is one of the hottest eateries in town. The owners proved themselves already at the poignant **PALIO** (151 West 51st Street, 245-4850; fax 397-7814), where the food is a magical experience. Palio has truly elegant Italian cuisine, an extensive wine list, and a beautiful bar with a wraparound mural of the ancient Palio horse race. Sandomenico is open Monday–Friday, 11:45 A.M.–2:30 P.M., 5:30–11:00 P.M.; Saturday, 5:00 P.M.–11:00 P.M.; and Sunday, 5:30 P.M.–10:00 P.M.

CHEZ 2020
149 Eighth Avenue at 17th Street, 243-2020; fax 691-0695

The better variation of a trendy, gay restaurant, now redone to a "T." The food is pretty good and the wine is served unpretentiously in orange juice glasses. Of course, the servers are cute—or very, very nice—but they don't run around acting snobby like those at some restaurants (I won't name names, and you probably don't need me to). However, service here is terrible, so if you're in a rush, go to Burger King (Sixth Avenue and 13th Street, 243-6626) for a chicken sandwich with special sauce. One other problem: Wouldn't it be nice if the owners removed all those silly tables so people could please dance! Open for lunch from 12:00 to 4:30 P.M., for dinner from 5:00 P.M. to midnight.

BROADWAY 104
2725 Broadway at West 104th Street, 316-0372; fax 866-7129

Fine place for lunch: decent, simple food at a simple price and in an entertaining neighborhood—the Morningside Heights that George Carlin once condescendingly called, "white Harlem." The area is filled with old record stores, and since this place is a throwback to an old Dylan song, you can reminisce about the '60s here and enjoy a chicken sandwich. Dinner? Same menu as lunch, only not as enticingly cheap! Closes at 11:30 P.M., so don't consider a late meal here.

SAZERAC HOUSE BAR & GRILL
533 Hudson Street at Barrow Street, 989-0313; fax 645-3528

A salad and fish place for the local weary-eyed patron, Sazerac is one of those places that amazes people because it's still in business. Everyone goes there but no one would ever recommend it. Cheap food, drinks expensive. But the waiter's been the waiter since it opened in the '70s. Lunch is served from 11:30 A.M. to 4:00 P.M.; dinner from 4:30 P.M. to midnight.

TIME CAFE
380 Lafayette Street, 533-7000; fax 995-0591
Also at 87 Seventh Avenue South, 220-9100

Great magazine rack, fantastic jukebox, good service, decent wine list: The food is just so-so. But prices at the Lafayette location start at $5 and go to $16 for lunch, which is when most people in the Noho (north of Soho) go to Time Cafe for eats. Dinners are $9–$19 and are filled with entrées including pizza-pasta and other faddish dishes. But really, why bother eating too much when you can read, look at the people, and listen to the music? Speaking of which, behind a bead curtain in the back is the Moroccan-style **FEZ BAR,** and downstairs is the very small but very cool Fez jazz club, where you can usually catch live acts most nights. Call for schedules. The West Village, untested as yet, is more cafeteria style than a cool spot. Former home of the Buffalo Roadhouse, a favorite for decades, when a $4 plate of mussels was the norm!

MARION'S/THE KAHIKI LOUNGE
354 Bowery, 475-7621, fax 979-2492

A fun, loud East Village version of Universal Grill (see below) and it makes for a raucous good time for those who don't mind dining above the din. Prices for entrees are $9–$22 and a great deal of most involve German/Hungarian/Polish cooking. That means it's heavy, so bring a huge appetite. Kahiki Lounge is usually open mid-week and on Friday nights, when the drinks are cheaper.

PARIS COMMUNE

411 Bleecker Street, 929-0509 (phone and fax)

One of our editor's faves, this is the oldest in-Village restaurant except for One Potato and for a reason: seasonally changed foodstuffs for the adventurous; excellent, satisfying nouvelle pastas; and a few good chicken dishes. Prices run from $7 to $18; a few specials are priced higher on weekends.

Mixed neighborhood crowd, fireplace, candlelight, casual, friendly bistro. Very, very well-known for brunch; most popular item is the whole wheat French toast with fresh fruit. Most brunch items are also on the weekday lunch menu. Lunch hours are 11:30 A.M. to 4:00 P.M.; dinner hours are 6:00 P.M. to 11:00 P.M. from Sunday through Thursday; until 12:00 P.M. on Friday and Saturday.

CAFÉ LUXEMBOURG

200 West 70th Street, 873-7411; fax 721-6854

This very pricey joint—on a strange, poorly lit block—merits talking up because you can sit at the bar and for $35 a person eat a few appetizers and be seen among the beautiful people. Very, very beautiful-looking place with the best lighting in town. Oh, and there are tables if you're stubborn and want to sit!

ODEON

145 West Broadway at Thomas Street, 233-0507, fax 406-1962

One of *the* hip places of 1988! The food at this cafeteria is still good, though, and recommended by all eaters I know: Food starts, for entrées, at $9 and ends at $20. Open Monday through Friday, at 12:00 P.M. Saturday and Sunday the brunch begins at 11:30 A.M. Kitchen closes at 2:00 A.M. Sunday through Thursday; 3:00 A.M. on Friday and Saturday.

 EIGHTEENTH & EIGHTH

159 Eighth Avenue, 242-5000; fax 675-3083

The number one gay hangout downtown, this completely expanded restaurant provides a friendly neighborhood atmosphere. Good American cuisine at reasonable prices. Saturday and Sunday brunches are not to be missed! The decor certainly isn't shabby, either. The French doors open for sidewalk access, and the floral arrangements are beautiful. Open Sunday through Thursday, 9:00 A.M.–midnight; Friday and Saturday, 9:00 A.M.–12:30 A.M.

LA NOUVELLE JUSTINE
206 West 23rd Street, Between Seventh and Eighth Avenues, 645-2999; fax 727-3975

Dorothy, you're not in Kansas anymore. But you're definitely in New York when you find a much-hyped restaurant with waiters and waitresses dressed in full S&M gear, and you get to choose whether to eat your food off a plate or out of a dog bowl. According to General Manager Bela Bolski, La Nouvelle Justine, another creation by the owners of Lucky Cheng's (also in this chapter) offers "classical French cuisine in a fetish environment." The food is both very good and reasonably priced (prices range from $12.95 to $23.95). The restaurant itself is very dark—black chairs, black tables, black curtains, not to mention the black and silver latex, leather and chain-link outfits of the random dominatrix waitress or slave busboy. Prepare for an interesting evening, albeit seemingly tourist-driven.

ELLEN'S STARDUST DINER
1650 Broadway at 51st Street, 956-5151; fax 956-5834

Ellen Hart was "Miss Subways 1959." In the midst of huge neon lights in the surrounding Times Square area, this diner has decent food, but the atmosphere is far more interesting. Staff auditions are required, for all waiters, waitresses, even the bartenders, sing. Luther Vandross has no real competition here, but it's entertaining nonetheless. The decor is the real highlight—1940s–1950s, with lots of shiny leather and silver chairs, airbrushed plates of Elvis hanging on the walls, and 1950s televisions playing clips from various old movies in every corner. Between the singing, the contests, and the magic tricks, you may very well forget to eat. Make sure to try one of their "triple ball" milkshakes (I live for chocolate), their evening showstoppers (of late, "Forbidden Broadway"), or their huge platters of onion rings. Classic diner food in big portions. Not gourmet, but you'll be stuffed and leave quite content.

EXTRA: HANDS SOLO, OR EATING
BY THE LIGHT OF SELF

ELITE CAFÉ-RESTAURANT
185 Columbus Avenue at West 68th Street, 724-8850
In the midst of a jungle of cafés and boutiques, it's a joy to walk in here, nod to a server, sit at the tiny counter, and order one of the largest breakfasts to be found on the Upper West Side. A simple juice, fruit, and egg combination of your choice will rev you up for the day to come. And the soups—well they are "fresh made daily" and worth stopping by for. You cannot sit alone at a table during peak hours, though.

Places with counter service are crucial to single eaters. So bring a newspaper, spread out as much as you can, and gorge! Open daily, 6:00 A.M.–midnight.

One just like it on the East Side is **EAT HERE NOW** (Lexington Avenue and 64th Street, 751-0724; fax 826-3023). Among the nicest staff I know.

VESELKA
144 Second Avenue at the corner of 9th Street, 228-9682;
fax 505-6950
In the East Village there's a quiet place with the best borscht in New York (according to the *New York Times* and *New York* magazine) and even better wall murals that are pictorials of the life at Veselka. *Jambo* features rockers, and *Bisontennial* is a day in the life of an unlikely East Village animal. The murals are newer editions to this circa 1954 family-owned and -operated Ukranian restaurant.

Try the boiled-beef-and-horseradish entrée; it's a memorable experience. After you nosh on some of their home-cooked dishes (which cost $6–$10), go outside and check out the street scene painted on the northeast corner of East Ninth and Second: a perfect sideshow of recent experiences at Veselka. One of the many reasons they say New York never sleeps, Veselka is open 24 hours a day, seven days a week.

SHOPSIN'S GENERAL STORE
63 Bedford Street, 924-5160

Very hard to find, and you may wonder why you'd want to when you peer into the window. Way deep in the Village, this old-fashioned luncheonette is set up like the ones they have on the Wyoming-Idaho border (I've been there, and believe me, they are all this grim-looking). The Shopsins own it, eat there, even hang their laundry there. The menu's endless—like Mom's *would* be—and while the awningless appearance might not suggest good eating, you can be sure the food will be quite fine, although damn expensive. Sit, relax, and read the writing on the walls. And wait.

The seven pages of menu selections offer the silent eater anything from hot-hot tacos to simple egg sandwiches. Open Monday–Friday, 11:00 A.M.–10:00 P.M. No credit. You're not in Idaho anymore.

For the fiftieth time, they have asked to be removed from our book. Go figure.

LAST OF THE TRENDY RESTAURANTS

REMI (145 West 53rd Street, 581-4242; fax 581-7182) boasts one of the fine Italian menus in a dining room that isn't as pretentious as some. . . . **MICHAEL'S** (24 West 55th Street, 767-0555; fax 481-6778) IS pretentious, but may as yet have the best food around. Expensive as all get-out, but you might as well go for it, once. This import from Los Angeles will offer a meal of fancy unbeatables, and the wine list is a miracle from heaven. (This is the restaurant mocked in the film *L.A. Story* where people needed to give their credit histories to get a reservation.) . . . **LOLA** (30 West 22nd Street, 675-6700; fax 645-6738) is best known for its gospel-inundated Sunday brunches, and a bunch of scrumptious Cajun goodies. Lola—no longer run by the vibrant "Lola"—also has rhythm and blues on Wednesdays and Saturdays, and a changing photo exhibit in the lounge by young neighborhood photographers. Remember that next door at 32 West 22nd Street is **LOLA BOWLA** for small dinners and lunches with a Thai flair. You gotta like these bowls. . . . **TRIBECA GRILL** (375 Greenwich Street, 941-3900; fax 941-3915) specializes in funky ideas for food, and yet the Southern (sometimes) and Northern (often) dishes from Thailand (maybe) and Provence (that, too) make up what New Yorkers are now calling THE place to go, sit in a booth, and gawk at the blue hairs. . . . I, for one, think **MESA GRILL** (102 Fifth Avenue, 807-7400; fax 989-0034) is THE place to run to for Arizona cooking (ever so trendy now) and everything from zesty pisoli to hearty pork dishes. Nicest hosts and bartenders for miles, which you can't say often. A very busy bar, too, even though it is almost nine years old now. Too much—it lasted! (Also, **MESA CITY**—uptown.)

The previously mentioned **FLORENT** (69 Gansevoort Street, 989-5779; fax 645-2498) is a find for cafeteria-style French-gourmet cooking (a lot of adjectives, yes), offering bistro cuisine in a 1940s all-American diner. As featured in *Men In Black,* you can see how this place is especially interesting late at night, when the crowd is rambunctious and the service is, well, exciting. Try the new prix fixe menu (FYI—it's cheaper to eat before 7:30 P.M.). . . . Extras, for pleasure: **RAOUL'S** (once-trendy and still wonderful French food at 180 Prince Street, 966-3518); **GRILL 53** at the New York Hilton (what a steak! at 53rd Street and Sixth Avenue, 265-1600); and **MARYLOU'S** (seafood better than expected in a city no longer considered a port city, 21 West Ninth Street, 533-0012; fax 353-8967) are the food lover's no-gamble stops for eating. . . . The last stop for stomach pleasing is **UNION SQUARE CAFÉ** (21 East 16th Street, 243-4020; fax 627-2673), which offers wine for the connoisseur, meals that include steak, a tuna that is thicker than any steak I've ever seen, and such exotic dishes as spiced venison and Thai lamb, all sincerely out of place in such a staid-looking nightspot. Sit in the room immediately to your left and be seen by the walkers-by, who will all be heading to the **COFFEE SHOP** (trendy, maybe, but a Cuban sandwich without lotsa ham?) on Union Square (29 Union Square West, 243-7969; fax 243-4187). Sit, eat, and leave Union Square with a smiling, satisfied expression. A nice gawking experience!

Last note for food: My mom has told me all my life that the best burgers are found in the boroughs at White Castle. So now I know—there is one in midtown! I won't go, but Ellen, my erstwhile assistant, tried it out— sorry, but the place is way too ugly for my tastes. More bright lights than an average 7-Eleven. **WHITE CASTLE,** 325 Fifth Ave between 33rd and 34th Streets. Best information about White Castle is their 800 number: 1-800-thecrave . . . ! Open 24 hours. Only a few located in Manhattan. Burgers ("sliders") are $.47 each, and yes they are tiny and square, just like legend has it. She tells me they're the best, but only if you want to risk it.

CHAPTER

12

Block Parties

Break out the castanets and head for Little Spain for one of the city's most rambunctious festivals, the **FIESTA DE SANTIAGO** (the last weekend of July) on West 14th Street. You'll find food, crafts, and best of all, mariachi music on an outdoor stage. The festival ends with a big public mass on Sunday. (By the way, some years ago they held a bullfight with a mechanical bull, and are threatening to do it again. Olé!)

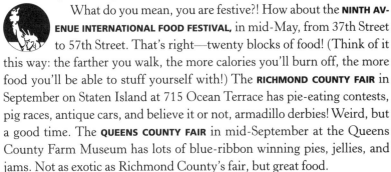 What do you mean, you are festive?! How about the **NINTH AVENUE INTERNATIONAL FOOD FESTIVAL,** in mid-May, from 37th Street to 57th Street. That's right—twenty blocks of food! (Think of it this way: the farther you walk, the more calories you'll burn off, the more food you'll be able to stuff yourself with!) The **RICHMOND COUNTY FAIR** in September on Staten Island at 715 Ocean Terrace has pie-eating contests, pig races, antique cars, and believe it or not, armadillo derbies! Weird, but a good time. The **QUEENS COUNTY FAIR** in mid-September at the Queens County Farm Museum has lots of blue-ribbon winning pies, jellies, and jams. Not as exotic as Richmond County's fair, but great food.

During the last two and a half weeks of August, a major uptown celebration known as **HARLEM WEEK** takes place. On the final weekend, West 125th Street becomes "Uptown Saturday Night," and people hoot, holler, and feast along 125th Street between Lenox and Seventh Avenues. Towards

BLOCK PARTIES

173

the end of the two-plus week celebration, the days have themes and include pop musicians and standard jazz players.

SIDEBAR SPECIAL Upper East Side, Delivery Free!

I must say, and I've thought about this a lot, that people who live on the Upper East Side hate crowds . . . and won't ever travel below 14th Street or above 95th Street (wrong side of the tracks, dear). So, since they are missing all the action and would rather stay home and watch "Caroline in the City"—a great example of the Fake City portrayed by Hollywood every night on ABC, Fox, NBC, CBS, and the Fox News Channel—I opened up the floor to the Native's Guide Forum.

Thanks to their help, I have now discovered that nearly every restaurant delivers in town, in some way or another. In Chelsea (where Native Central exists) even the four-star restaurants deliver. Anybody can use Dial-A-Dinner, but this is an incredibly expensive service. (They are also unbelievably inconsistent; once, I called them, and they said it was "raining too hard" to deliver. Huh? Yep, the city that tends to sleep.)

Try www.nycdelivery.com for better rates than Dial-A-Dinner (see Chapter 22, "Cyber Situation").

Here are some suggestions for delivery:

• Szechuan Kitchen (First Avenue and 76th Street, 249-4615)— amazing Chinese food, quick delivery. Closed Tuesdays.
• K & D Liquors (96th Street and Madison Avenue, 289-1818) will deliver for free if the order is over $80. Schumer's on East 54th Street (355-0940) will deliver one bottle for free, if you wish.
• There is a magazine called "We Deliver," which will give you the menu, delivery policy, and fees for dozens of restaurants on the Upper East Side. You can find it in building lobbies or some markets.
• I just found out about a very cool delivery service called the Milkman (987-3276). This company delivers milk, juice, Snap-

ple, water, and soda products at supermarket prices to anyone in a building with a doorman.

• Andrade Shoe Repair (1521 York Avenue, 249-8603; other locations throughout the United States) not only offers decent prices, but delivers!

 The **MIDTOWN CHINESE SPRING FESTIVAL** occurs in mid-May on 31st Street between Lexington and Park Avenues, where you can sample food from China's different regions, and see all sorts of kung fu costumes. The **GREEK ORTHODOX CHURCH OF SAINT DEMETRIOS FESTIVAL** at the end of May (the last weekend) has Greek souvlaki, pastries, and more. The festival is in Jamaica at 152nd Street from 84th Road to 84th Drive. **OUR LADY OF LEBANON CATHEDRAL FESTIVAL** (last weekend in May), in Brooklyn Heights at Remsen Street from Clinton–Henry Streets, is a great place to find homemade Lebanese delights. **A LOVE FELLOWSHIP** is an amazing church festival in late June on 125th Street from Lenox Avenue to Adam Clayton Powell Boulevard in Harlem, where you can find African soup and the famous (and fattening) Krispy Kreme donuts.

Have a craving for Caribbean food? Want to hear a steel band play? Try the **EBENEZER WESLEYAN METHODIST CHURCH FAIR** in Bedford-Stuyvesant (Bergen Street from Nostrand–Rogers Avenues) in late June. The **INTERNATIONAL AFRICAN ARTS FESTIVAL** on the first weekend of July in Bedford-Stuyvesant (Fulton Street from Utica to Schenectady Avenues) also features Caribbean as well as African and Southern soul food.

On **BASTILLE DAY** (July 13) visit 60th Street between Park and Fifth Avenues for French food and wines at the local cafés, as well as New Orleans jazz. Around the same time, try a **TASTE OF TIMES SQUARE,** on 46th Street between Broadway and Ninth Avenues, when Restaurant Row chefs will give you samples of their cuisine starting at around $2.

Central Park's big folklore festival happens the first Sunday in June at the Rumsey Playfield (call 529-1995 for more information). **BROOKLYN ARTS AND CULTURE'S PARKS JAMBOREE** is a hot show in June (718-783-4469). **ATLANTIC ANTIC** on Atlantic Avenue in Cobble Hill gets a big Brooklyn turnout in September (718-624-4555).

Other faves include the **AMSTERDAM AVENUE FESTIVAL,** every third Sunday of the month from 77th to 92nd Street along what used to be a crummy avenue, now beautiful and yet nowhere near as pretentious as nearby Columbus Avenue. Big stars are included in the proceedings, too (595-3625 for info). A favorite of the Upper West Side is the **EDGAR ALLAN POE BLOCK PARTY** along West 82nd Street at West End Avenue (799-4285), which is a puzzle because Poe didn't live that long on this block. What the hey, people want to celebrate their most famous neighbor, I say why not? The party includes local vendors and crafts.

In Brooklyn on the last day of May (the last Sunday, probably, unless it's Memorial Day) you can find **MAHRAJAN,** the Lebanese festival that is mostly in Brooklyn Heights but also takes place in surrounding Lebanese areas. To quote Ellen Degeneres: "That's *Lebanese.*" (Ah-hem.) Anyway, there are foods, folks songs, dancing, more. Call 718-634-7228.

You want more? Well, since more is the most overused word in this chapter, how about it? The **ASIAN-AMERICAN FESTIVAL DAY** is for Japanese, Korean, Thai, and Vietnamese groups to dance and eat, and to invite others too. This occurs the last weekend of June, around Bayard and Mulberry Streets in Chinatown. This park's named after Columbus.

Why is this so much fun? Those four cuisines are among the most popular now (J, K, T, and V).

Now to trendy ol Chelsea. **EIGHTH AVENUE** (one of the hottest avenues in town, as discussed in earlier chapters) puts out a typical block party along Eighth Avenue with loads of food—tons of grease—but the difference is it's a pretty good-looking bunch. West 200 Block Association at 243-7215. Early Novemberish.

This has been just a sampling of the great block parties throughout New York—there are many, many more. If you're a big fan of the food, music, and good times to be had at festivals, check out the Street Festivals listing weekly in *Time Out New York.* Lea Lerman's Street Festival Party List is worth it—a few bucks a year and you get all the "non flash in the pan" listings you can handle: Write L.L. at 201 West 70th Street, NYC 10023.

And look at the Community Board listings now found on various phone booths (in place of those well-lit ads).

Nighttime

13

Book Readings to Wander Literarily into All Night Long

BARNES & NOBLE

Manhattan Events Line, 727-4810

B&N is one of a few places to HYPE their events with authors with fervor and panache. Each week (see *Time Out New York* or the *New York Times* for ads) you can see a most recently published author (or theater/film director, cartoonist, screenwriter/playwright, poet, etc.) get on a pedestal and discuss, read, or analyze his or her work with the beloved readership. My fave is Union Square because this 100-year-old building housed a literary magazine as the century turned. Ah, history.

BOOKS OF WONDER

16 West 18th Street between Fifth and Sixth Avenues, 989-3270; fax 645-3038

Greeted by the Cat in the Hat and Lilly with her plastic purse, children have a place of their own at Books of Wonder. Described as vibrant and fun, this bookstore carries contemporary and classic novels for children from newborn to age fourteen. They also have old books and rare collector first editions like *Winnie the Pooh* and *The Wizard of Oz*. If your child has a favorite author, Books of Wonder holds author signings generally on Saturdays. Some famous authors who have read in the past are Madeleine

L'Engle, Lloyd Alexander, and Chris Van Allsburg. There's also story time, where children from ages two and up are invited to sit and listen to their favorite book being read; readings are held every Sunday, usually around 11:45 A.M. (well, it's not nighttime, but kids can't stay out late). Hours are Monday–Saturday, 11:00 A.M.–7:00 P.M., and Sunday, 12:00 P.M.–6:00 P.M. (but doors open at 11:30 A.M. for those attending readings).

THE CORNER BOOKSTORE
1313 Madison Avenue, 831-3554; fax 831-2930

In the Yorkville and Carnegie Hill area, this bookstore features mostly contemporary literature readings. Their schedule is a bit sporadic, but hop on down for a list of once-a-week items; call ahead to make sure.

A DIFFERENT LIGHT
151 West 19th Street, 989-4850; fax 989-2158

Since there are so many gay writers in New York, A Different Light prides itself on its comprehensive selection of speakers and other informative lectures by, for, and about gay and lesbian people. According to the management, "Everything that covers gays and lesbians and is in print, we carry." The store has 18,000 titles in stock, including over 500 AIDS/HIV–related titles. The periodical collection is an excellent resource for people traveling to other parts of the United States who want to read a local gay rag about other cities they may be visiting. A Different Light holds weekly readings throughout the year (except in July and August).

Author reading/singings are held most evenings, but A Different Light also shows movies Sunday nights at 7:00, and holds a music event to showcase the talent of "out" lesbian and gay songwriters or musicians one Sunday afternoon a month. For more information on events for gays and lesbians, see Chapter 20.

 **DIXON PLACE**
258 Bowery, 219-3088; fax 274-9114; http://www.el.net/dixonplace

Dixon Place is a nonprofit organization founded in 1986 to provide a space for literary and performing artists to create and develop new works in front of a live audience. This intimate and homey place holds many poetry, fiction, and science fiction readings. Their Web site is an extension of their warmth, detailing more about this creative house and their activities. Eleven months out of the year (Tuesday through Saturday), they have an alternating schedule of themed readings, such as "First Wednesday Words," "African American Poetry and Fiction," and "HomoText" (poetry and fiction by gay and lesbian writers, occurring every third Wednesday of the month). They hold performance art, theater, and dance and even a few cool gatherings—hey, get on their mailing list.

THE DRAWING CENTER
35 Wooster Street, 219-2166; fax 966-2976; e-mail: drawcent@interport.net
The Drawing Center is a nonprofit museum for the exhibition of works on paper. Though it focuses on emerging artists, the Center also features a special—an historical exhibition each year. They run a writers-in-performance series from September to June dedicated to new prose. The readings are $5 and feature a group of writers they dub "totally eclectic."

On Sunday afternoons, monthly from September to May, the Center also has a storytelling series for young children: "NightLight for Kids"—no less! These programs feature both children's book authors and writers or performers well-known in their fields who read from classic books. Recommended age group: that is, "4 to 8 or 9." (Not 25 or 6 to 4.) These readings are accompanied by slide shows of the books' illustrations. Admission and refreshments are, thankfully, free.

NEW YORK BOUND BOOKSHOP
50 Rockefeller Plaza [n/a]
I have included this entry for posterity: Out of business since the large book chains took over, this bookstore specialized in books about New York, covering New York's history, planning, architecture, neighborhoods, the immigrant experience, journalism, crime, nightlife, and any other topic related to New York. They had tons of guidebooks, photographic books, both new and out of print, as well as a collection of New York photographs, turn of the century images, and old maps. They were very good to this series. Amen.

Ha, ha.

Here is the place for those of us who refuse to go to any literary happenings when attacks of "Must See TV" occur.

I insist you leave house or hotel room; here's a fantastic way to be a couch potato among strangers who share the affinity.

"COSBY"

Kaufman-Astoria Studios, 34–12 36th Street (between 34th and 35th Avenues), Queens, 718-706-5389; for groups: 718-706-5707. Taping time: Thursdays, 4:00 P.M.

Send a postcard for tickets; call for a large group; get in line for last minute requests. At press time, "Cosby" was adding tons of little kids to the cast—sounds pretty old hat to me. Jello pudding commercials, here he comes.

"THE DAILY SHOW"

356 West 58th Street between Eighth and Ninth Avenues, 560-3135; http://www.comedycentral.com

Send a postcard, call, or order tickets for up to four people on the Web site. Usually a two month wait; tickets do not guarantee a seat at the shindig. Taping schedule varies; schedule is available through the Web site.

PS: Host Craig Kilborn, the star for the late '90s, insists the show's deft motto, "when news breaks, we fix it," is meant to make HIM look good. I wish Dan Rather spoke as honestly. . . .

"LATE NIGHT WITH CONAN O'BRIEN"

NBC, 30 Rockefeller Plaza between Fifth and Sixth Avenues, 664-3056. Taping times: Tuesday–Friday, 5:30 P.M.

Send a postcard for tickets. Fifty same-day tickets are distributed at 9:00 A.M. Conan is king, so his fans (Andy Richter?) say.

"LATE SHOW WITH DAVID LETTERMAN"

Ed Sullivan Theater, 1697 Broadway at 53rd Street, 975-1003; http://www.cbs.com Taping times: Monday–Thursday, 5:30 P.M.; Friday, 8:00 P.M.

Send a postcard six months to a year in advance, or order through the Web site. Only two tickets per person. Standby tickets are available at noon, but it is very difficult to get seats. Letterman is number three (of all the latenight shows) now, as his sign in midtown proudly proclaims.

"THE RICKI LAKE SHOW"

2 East 37th Street, between Fifth and Madison Avenues, 889-6767. Taping times: Wednesday–Friday, 5:30 P.M.

Send postcard for tickets one month in advance. Standby tickets are available one hour before taping. Rick—ki!

"SALLY JESSE RAPHAEL"

515 West 57th Street between Tenth and Eleventh Avenues, 582-1722

Taping times vary. Request tickets by phone or send a postcard one month in advance. Standby tickets are available one hour before taping. The lady with the glasses is still on, God love her. (And explain her?)

"SATURDAY NIGHT LIVE"

NBC, 30 Rockefeller Plaza between Fifth and Sixth Avenues, 664-4000.

Dress rehearsals at 7:30 P.M., live at 10:00 P.M. A ticket lottery for the season is held in August; only postcards received in August are accepted. Lottery winners are notified one to two weeks in advance of taping. Same-day standby tickets are distributed at 9:15 A.M.

This could be the fortieth-to-last season for this oldstay, so, uh, rush.

"SPIN CITY"

Chelsea Piers Studios, Pier 61, West 23rd Street at the Hudson River, 336-6993

Send request for tickets in the month of July to London Terrace Post Office, P.O. Box 20241, New York, NY 10011-0003. This is Michael J. Fox's return to TV. Expect another return soon.

"APT. 2F"

MTV; Chelsea Piers Studios, Stage F, 23rd St. and the Hudson River, New York, NY 10011, 654-6000

This zany TV show, which swears it's going to change the image of MTV away from silly shows like "The Real World" (which I imagine has an audience, too, since it's so darn fake) . . . This one, from the makers of MTV's non-music programming, promises live antics and stuff like whoopee cushions blowing fart sounds . . . if this is your thing, get over to this address. Don't say I didn't warn: Beavis and Butt-head sound more mature. (Note: "Apt. 2F" has been cancelled. But who knows? They might bring it back to TORTURE us.)

Just to say they exist:

- "Live With Regis and Kathie Lee" is at 456-3537.
- "Geraldo" is syndicated but filmed here; call 265-1283.
- Celebrity for the sake of it: Be on "The People's Court" with former mayor Ed Koch, each day—no judgment! Call 643-7418. Located downtown, but away from the court system.
- Fox's morning show (changes daily). Call 802-4200 for info.

And now a note from a non-sponsor:

Warning about boredom.* You have to sit through several takes on many of these shows, and they will not even let you

---

* And being boring is such an easy sin for TV people to bestow upon you that I have purposely left out the vain and dull "Maury Povich Show," which tapes daily (he is probably quitting in '98) and is, I discovered firsthand, a waste of time to sit through because it's all about Maury!

stand up until the taping is completed. In most cases ("Cosby" is the exception I have witnessed), they do not care about you—they care about the home audience getting "the experience." *Quelle* drag!

PARTNERS & CRIME

44 Greenwich Avenue, 243-0440; fax 243-4624; http://www.crimepays.com

With a crime novel section like no other, Partners & Crime sends out mailings for readings and invites you to see their Web site for all the details. They are open seven days a week, noon–10:00 P.M.

Special sections devoted to award winners, mysteries for young readers, for gay people, and for Sherlockians; also, reference books for crime writers, books on tape, out of print titles, and a special section devoted to "100 of the Best We've Ever Read." Partners & Crime also has a rental library which includes all the latest hits, select older gems, and books on tape. They also hold art shows featuring original paintings of mystery book covers.

POETRY PROJECT

Second Avenue and East 10th Street, 674-0910

The Poetry Project at St. Mark's Church sponsors poetry readings throughout the week (Monday nights, "New, Up and Coming Writers"; Wednesday nights, "Established Poets"; Friday Late Nights are group readings around a theme). The Poetry Project hosts a marathon benefit on New Year's Day, which over 100 performers and poets attend—all day and into the evening. The Project sponsors ongoing workshops for poets. Programming is October through May; $5 contribution for all readings.

You can pick up a newsletter at the church or find listings in the *Voice*. And yes, there's plenty of small talk here.

POETS HOUSE

72 Spring Street, second floor, 431-7920; fax 431-7920

Nestled in a sunny, quiet Soho loft, Poets House was founded by poet Stanley Kunitz and poetry administrator Elizabeth Kray to provide a place for poetry open to all. The house is an independent literary center and has a 35,000 volume open-stack collection of books and journals augmented each year through the *Poetry Publication Showcase,* an all inclusive exhibition of the year's poetry releases from commercial, university, independent, and micropresses. The collection—free to use and open to the public—also includes audio tapes, poetry, videos, and reference materials.

Each year, Poets House presents over thirty programs, seminars, and workshops documenting the wealth and diversity of contemporary poetry and stimulating public dialogue on issues of poetry in culture. Phone for information plus the calendar of events. Hours for events and free use of collection: Tuesday–Friday, 11:00 A.M.–7:00 P.M.; Saturday, 11:00 A.M.–4:00 P.M.

REVOLUTION BOOKS
9 West 19th Street, 691-3345; fax 645-1952

Revolution Books is the kind of bookstore where you would want to start a revolution. This isn't any ordinary bookstore, since these booksellers are proactive and passionate about social and political causes. Revolution Books often participates wherever there is a demonstration, such as with police brutality cases. They carry books in many different languages, like Spanish and French, knowing English isn't the only language, especially in New York. Their readings are mostly cutting-edge and politically themed, representing a forward-moving realm of literature. C. Clark Kissenger, radical activist, writer, and speaker, was one of the many readers at Revolution. His latest book is *The O.J. Simpson Case and the Shame of White People.* Hours are Monday–Saturday, 10:00 A.M.–7:00 P.M., and Sunday, 12:00 P.M.–5:00 P.M.

RIZZOLI BOOKS
454 West Broadway, 674-1616; fax 979-9504

A fancy bookshop at the epicenter of the Soho shopping experience, Rizzoli specializes in art and architecture books, many of which they publish. Also, Rizzoli is one of the few shops to feature nothing but classy writers in a fine regular reading series.

Rizzoli Books is something of a mixture. They combine the aesthetics of a gallery and a bookstore, because here you can find many things on art and architecture. This two-level gem has wall-to-wall books, and up top sits an espresso bar mixed in with the magazines, mostly foreign fashion and art magazines. They hold readings at least once every couple of weeks, free and open to the public; however, seating is limited. Hours are Monday–Saturday, 10:30 A.M.–9:00 P.M., and Sunday, 12:00 P.M.–7:00 P.M.

SHAKESPEARE & CO.
939 Lexington, 570-5148; fax 570-0369
Nestled in the prestigious Upper East Side, this cozy two-floor bookstore has a great general collection of books, not just literature. It's warm and inviting enough that you could read books all day. It doesn't have the supermarket flavor as do some of the bigger superstores, and definitely not the annoying crowds. Shakespeare & Co. holds readings at least twice a month. On Tuesdays, they have children's readings at 4:00 P.M. They say that their readings are endangered, due to the lack of interest in that area. Hunter and Upper East Side residents are not particularly fond of readings, but not to worry, they keep reinventing ways to bring in more people. Hours are 8:00 A.M.–9:00 P.M. on weekdays; 10:00 A.M.–6:00 P.M. on weekends.

TOWER BOOKS
383 East 4th Street at Lafayette, 228-5100; fax 228-5338
To expect anything less from the giant Tower is a fallacy, because at Tower Books, this hip joint carries a huge selection of everything, even videos. And strategically, Tower Warehouse and Tower Records are across the street! Some of the eclectic finds at Tower Books are "fringe/cult" and transgressive books. They hold readings quite frequently or almost everyday, featuring mostly contemporary writers. Their lineup of writers includes Tim Cahill *(Pass the Butterworm)*, Eric Bogosian *(Suburbia)*, and Joe Carducii *(Rock & Pump Narcotics)*. Hours are 9:00 A.M.–12:00 A.M., every day.

WORLD FINANCIAL CENTER WORD SERIES
Information: 945-0505; fax 945-3392 (Battery Park City)
The Financial Center (see Chapter 14, too), first presented mostly concert attractions to draw a crowd. Copeland's *Appalachian Spring*, performed by St. Luke's Chamber Ensemble, was very popular. Lately they've moved on to riskier fields: In conjunction with Squash Week, held in early May, they

present a week of "action-packed tournaments," player clinics, workshops, and associated dance performances.

To make spending time at World Financial more diverse, they also present a series of East Village performance artists. Every few months, uptown's avant-gardists journey to the financial district, to give the big business world a thrill. Always a "reader" in the bunch.

URBAN CENTER BOOKS

457 Madison Avenue, 935-3595; fax 223-2887;

http://colophon.com/urbancenterbooks/

Urban Center Books is a fab haunt for the aspiring architect and city planner. They are truly a specialized book store, dealing with mostly architecture and its related arts. Urban holds many lectures all the time by famous and obscure scribes. Find an updated schedule of their lectures/presentations on their Web site.

In Brooklyn: The **BROOKLYN MOON CAFE** (745 Fulton Street, 718-243-0424), a simple coffee spot with "Afro-themed readings," couches, art, and COOKIES.

CHAPTER

14

Watered-Down New York

During 1998 the first of the plans for Hudson River Park are being revealed. That's the state park being planned to span from Robert F. Wagner Park and the low end of the Battery, straight up to the Intrepid Sea/Air/Space Museum and above, where the Henry Hudson Parkway/West Side Highway artery begins. Starting in 2002, you will be able legally to SWIM in the Hudson, which for a native like me seems unthinkable and very Saturday Night Live. But, hey, who am I to argue with (hoo hoo!) Progress.

Here's how it will look:

The state- and federally funded plan is to allow people to swim at 31st Street (swim!) and also at Pier 51 way downtown in the West Village. Now the mere notion of swimming in polluted waters of yore is disgusting. But it should be noted without sardonicism that Harold Kilinsky, a scientist with the City Department Of Environmental Protection, told the *New York Post* that, "The water quality has improved drastically." Imagine the traffic jams. Already, you can actually run down to Pier 26 just below Canal Street and rent kayaks—free at press time, a few dollars when the demand runs feverish—and on a clear day go and test the water for yourself. This so-called boathouse is obvious from the West Street roadway and you will, pretty soon, see kayaks, windsurfers, and rowboats. I hear talk of sailboats, and a "public fountain for kids to play in" around Gansevoort Street in the Village, but these I gotta see.

I hold my breath.

SIDEBAR SPECIAL The Transportation Dat Floats

In 1997 the *New York Post,* the bastion of civilized journalism, asked writers to do a study on a possible future great city. (They tied it to a launch of a new Bruce Willis vehicle set in a futuristic New York.) The study seemed a little silly, but those who participated hit on an idea that I have imagined for years: converting the waterfront from industrial use to public use, implementing more ferries and possibly banning private cars. "The city will become more pedestrian-oriented," said the *New York Post.*

The way the majority of commuters from the other four boroughs get to Manhattan is by subway or bus. The subway system in the past has not proven to be especially clean or safe, but significant improvements have been made, and since the MTA started offering free transfers between the bus and subway, these forms of transportation have become more popular. Cabs in New York are really no competition—they are far more expensive, not much faster with the amounts of traffic in the area, and really prove to pollute the air in New York City more.

Ferries are a great way to travel to and from the city, whether you're coming from New Jersey, Staten Island, or Long Island City. Many New Yorkers envision a future with expanded waterway transportation systems, hoping for more ferries and less cars. Imagine Woody Allen's precious Sutton Place Park as a waystation for commuters from Queens and Long Island, or the Pier at 42nd Street (Hudson Pier) as a waystation for travelers from Jersey!

Who would miss this scenario: You're in your car, going over a bridge, when suddenly one of your tires blows out with a

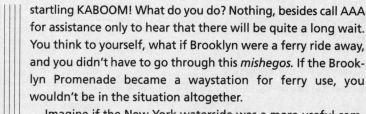

startling KABOOM! What do you do? Nothing, besides call AAA for assistance only to hear that there will be quite a long wait. You think to yourself, what if Brooklyn were a ferry ride away, and you didn't have to go through this *mishegos*. If the Brooklyn Promenade became a waystation for ferry use, you wouldn't be in the situation altogether.

Imagine if the New York waterside was a more useful component of life.

BARGEMUSIC: FULTON FERRY LANDING

Foot of Old Fulton Street at Furman Street, 718-624-2083 or 718-624-4061

Since 1977, the only full-time "chamber house" for chamber music has floated on the landing off Fulton Street, along the East River (which never freezes). Year-round concerts are supported by "as many [funding] places as possible," says a spokesperson, including the ticket buyers—who sit in the enclosed floating loft and listen to the beautiful sounds, 7:30 P.M. on Thursdays, 4:00 P.M. on Sundays. The music is further enhanced by the drama of passing ships. Tickets are $23; $20 for seniors; and $15 for students, but money-saving subscriptions are available.

Bargemusic, one of the best spots to hear chamber music in the country, proudly hosts many great musicians. Get a schedule.

LINCOLN CENTER FOUNTAIN

64th–66th Streets and Broadway

Philip Johnson's structure is one of the best-looking fountains in the city, near several TV screens that vividly tell the details of what's happening in four concert halls and the Performing Arts Library. The fountain is made of brass tubing, knobs, and a board that modulates the water. So it's entertaining to look at even when it's turned off. Fun fact: The surrounding pavement's concentric circles are trampled on by 6 million people each year.

Those 6 million are either strollers using this plaza as a thoroughfare from Amsterdam to Broadway, or concert-goers en route to a free event in Damrosch Park, or theater buffs on their way to a big happening at the New

York State Theater. Talk about luxury—the awning above the sidewalk at the State Theater announces to limos what time tonight's performance will end!

MINETTA BROOK FOUNTAIN
2 Fifth Avenue in Washington Mews (lobby of building)

In the inner lobby at 2 Fifth, near Washington Square, you can find a marble fountain that symbolizes Minetta Brook. The brook, which no longer exists, was a natural spring that ran through the Village way back in the 1700s. The Dutch called it Little Stream and it ran on several major avenues (remember this the next time you're crossing Eighth in heavy traffic), until the brook dried up in the mid-1800s.

Tour buses stop by the site—a big apartment complex—so it must be authentic. On the shooting water basin is inscribed, "A brook winds its erratic way beneath this site." The plaque also alludes to "Devil's Water," the brook's old nickname, and says that Minetta Brook "has settled underground." Take a peek at historic Washington Mews, a private alleyway that holds housing for New York University staff. The buildings were once hayloft stables; now they're luxury townhouses. Is this progress or what?

 PETREL
Far east corner of Battery Park, 825-1976

Take a trip during spring or summer, on your lunch hour or after work, on a sailboat around New York harbor! It costs only $8–$20, depending on the size of the carrier. These boats are pretty fast and are manned by Coast Guard–trained skippers. On weekdays, they go out at noon and 1:00 P.M. and their ride lasts forty-five minutes ($8); another boat leaves at 1:00 P.M. for ninety minutes ($12); or regularly after 5:30 P.M. for ninety minutes ($20), which they call the "Sunset Sail." And on Friday nights, they leave the dock at 9:30 for a "Moonlight Sail" ($20).

It's recommended you go on windy, overcast days, because they tend to be breezier and less crowded. A spokesperson commented, "You don't need heat and sun to sail." Since the last book they have unveiled a 105-foot single-mast sloop for longer journeys. Petrel, by the way, is the name of a sea bird—not oil.

RIVERVIEW TERRACE
Sutton Place Park, East 58th Street off Sutton Place

Head to a quiet area like Riverview Terrace, which is the best use this city has for the East River: an enclave of buildings that share a common, picturesque garden. In front of the Terrace is an addendum to Sutton Place Park, also standing at East 57th Street. Here are only a few benches—and it's much quieter. The water is steps away and looks more inviting than it actually is.

Along Sutton Place, from East 58th–53rd Street, a welcome breeze is bestowed on each and every parkgoer, at several tiny pocket parks along the avenue.

SOUTH STREET SEAPORT CRUISES
207 Front Street, 425-3737

See New York Harbor in all its splendor on a ninety-minute cruise aboard the recently refurbished DeWitt Clinton, an historic recreation of a classic nineteenth-century steamboat. A tour guide gives you a new perspective on the obvious landmarks, such as the Statue of Liberty, Ellis Island, the Battery, and Fulton Ferry Terminal. And there's a bar on board! Excursions during the Mayor's Cup race allow you to watch from the starting line.

From late May through December, a two-masted schooner, named the *Pioneer,* glides past tugs, ferries, and pleasure craft into the harbor. The cost is negligible, about $15 for two hours, or $22 for three hours. For true boating enthusiasts, call the museum about its additional boating events.

 WATERFALLS AT THE BRONX ZOO
Fordham Road and Northern Boulevard, 718-220-5100

At New York Zoological Park, colloquially known as the Bronx Zoo,* you can find two amazing waterways. First, walk along 180th Street to see the waterfall that drops forty feet and falls into the Bronx River. It's easy to get to this lovely site. Take the #2 train to the 180th Street stop. Walk west one block, then north one block.

---

* This is one of those bureaucratic wonders of the world: The Bronx Zoo gets this great household name and decides it's not "Classy Enough" so they change it and spend oodles of money, letting us know in advertising and public relations efforts. You go figure.

Then, in the World of Birds exhibit—deep in what the park calls the Conservation Area—a forty-foot thundershower pours down on the "rain forest," an artistic exhibit that helps the zoo's birds feel at home. This shower occurs daily at 2:00 P.M., and floats off a fifty-foot fiberglass cliff. There's also a thunderstorm in the reptile house (it too runs by the clock!). Let's get off water for a sec.

The most incredible exhibit at the constantly changing Bronx Zoo is the new Butterfly Zone. Inside a 170-foot structure designed to look like a giant caterpillar are more than 1,000 different types of butterflies and moths. Walk through this hall as mother nature's most beautiful insects fly around you. *And bug out!*

For more zoo-inspired fun, see the **QUEENS WILDLIFE CENTER** at Flushing Meadows, Corona (718/271-1500). And visit the **STATEN ISLAND CHILDREN'S ZOO** (718-442-4308), which features a Kid Olympics each July. The latter has games, races, and the price, well, it's right: $3!

WATER MONUMENT
666 Fifth Avenue

The late and great Isamu Noguchi built a gorgeous "planar water sculpture" against the wall outside this giant structure. Find it in the passageway between 52nd and 53rd Streets west of Fifth Avenue. For more on Noguchi, see Chapter 5 on serious *aht*.

There is an unsubstantiated legend that during a 1970s water shortage, or drought, in New York City, the *Times* polled New Yorkers, who were unable to take many showers or wash their cars, on what they missed most. Midtown residents all spoke about the 666 Water Monument, which had been turned off because of water regulations! I would say that's unequivocally a reason to see it.

ROOSEVELT ISLAND TRAM
For $1.50 you can take a four-minute ride on the tram at Second Avenue between 59th and 60th Streets and come back fifteen minutes later. You might ask *Why?* Question well-received. You get a dynamite view of the East River and the Queensboro Bridge and the gentle swaying of the car is,

well, therapeutic. And then go back. Because unlike the Ferry to Staten Island (where this book lists several reasons why you should stay), the tram takes you to an island that is nothing but a series of track houses and apartment buildings.

Keep in mind the traffic swelling up on Second Avenue, and never wonder why the area has fought tooth and nail against a proposed trolley going from here to the town's two airports. Imagine a tramway and trolley stop, projected to stop right here, at the entrance to the Queenboro Bridge *and* the tram stop.

If you're taking your kids . . . try nearby **SERENDIPITY** (225 East 60th Street, 838-3531) and **PEPPERMINT PARK** (66th Street and First Avenue, 288-5054) for any child's favorite: ice cream.

WORLD FINANCIAL CENTER

Located north of Battery Park City, just opposite the World Trade Center by Chambers Street, this has one of the best uses of water New York planners and architects have ever thought of: First, there is a matchbox-looking presence called the American Express towers at 200 Liberty Street. Then there is the promenade that overlooks the water in a way that only Chicagoans have previously enjoyed. There is a walkway or a bicycle-way (with words by famous New York poets wrought into an iron railing), and there is even a further passageway for long walks down to Battery Park (a friend and I found a huge sandbox to play in along the promenade).

Inside the Financial Center is the Winter Garden, a 120-foot crystal palace replete with palm trees (not indigenous to these parts) where music events occur almost daily (945-0505). In addition, special happenings are held on holidays for the whole family. (The Financial Center also has a shopping mall that unfortunately resembles too much of suburban New Jersey.)

On a nice day, be sure to bring a book and sit at one of the few restaurants that dot the plaza of the Center. You will have to ask yourself, "Where am I now?" as you gaze out on the water.

BROOKLYN HEIGHTS HISTORIC DISTRICT

You're missing out on a lot if you don't take at least one ramble through North Brooklyn Heights, the oldest historic district in New York City: This was a prime residential community in the 1820s. Starting at Court Street and Remsen Street (most train lines will let you off at the Borough Hall stop). See St. Francis College at 180 Remsen Street, opened in 1859. Or Spencer Mews, a Gothic Revival church erected in 1850, at 154 Remsen. There's the Church of St. Ann at the northwest corner of Clinton and Montague Streets, dated 1844, where pop, folk, and classical concerts are held nearly every weekend and where stained glass stares at you from every angle. Also Manufacturer's Hanover Trust at 177 Montague, just around the corner, is a gorgeous turn-of-the-century structure closely modeled on the Palazza della Gran Guardia of Verona, Italy. Franklin Trust Company—lots of banks here—at 164–66 Montague dates to 1890. This Romanesque revival building is terra cotta style; its Spanish tile roof is a wonder. At 128 Pierrepont Street is the Brooklyn Historical Society, built in 1878 and filled with books, paintings, prints, and documents about the area and Brooklyn.

If you continue along Montague Street you will eventually reach the Brooklyn Heights Promenade, a parkway and walkway with a panorama unlike any other: See the Statue of Liberty, the newly refurbished but hardly finished Ellis Island, all of Lower Manhattan, and even the skyscrapers dotting midtown. Believe it or not, city planners wanted to erase any signs of this peaceful landmark when the Brooklyn–Queens Expressway was built in the 1940s. See what a little activism can do: The Promenade was the compromise that sits atop the noisy Expressway!

Hey—isn't that the East River over there. Uh-huh.

CHAPTER
15

Places Other than Cinemas
to See Movies

NEW FESTIVAL/A.K.A. NEW YORK LESBIAN AND GAY FILM FESTIVAL
Information: 254-7228
The New Festival is held every year in the first two weeks in June, and has been ongoing since 1989. In 1993, there were 172 films and videos shown! The Festival shows feature films, short films, and videos by and about gay men and lesbians. Visitors should call the info line, any time during the year, for schedules, prices, and special event listings that have nothing to do with the actual festival. This is surely one of the most important festivals in the city. In 1997 the festival was held at the Cinema Village (12th Street near University Place) and other locales.

 **ANTHOLOGY FILM ARCHIVE**
32 Second Avenue, 505-5181
Anthology Film Archive has a huge collection of independent, avant-garde films from the past, as well as other material related to the history of avant-garde and independent film. In addition, they have weekly screenings of independently produced films and videos, which are shown mostly on the weekends (400 screenings a year). A great showcase for independent films and videos.

PLACES OTHER THAN CINEMAS TO SEE MOVIES

197

They also have a book service—publishing and hawking books generally about independent film and video, as well as about the stuff which they show. These are available by mail-order through their catalogue. The schedule of events comes out every two months. Screenings cost $6 or $7.

WALTER READE THEATER AT LINCOLN CENTER
165 West 65th Street / Plaza Level at Lincoln Center, 875-5600.

New York's newest moviehouse not owned by Sony, they offer diversified programs — something for everyone — premieres and classics from around the world: thrillers and comedies, sleepers and hits, American, Italian, French, African, Jewish, Arab, others.

Annual events include The New York Film Festival in September, New Directors/New Films in April. One particularly popular monthly event is Independents Night, a showcase of the best of new independent films; another is Movies for Kids on Saturdays and Sundays.

Membership in the Film Society of Lincoln Center provides admission discounts, calendar mailings, a subscription to *Film Comment* magazine, advance mailings of Film Festival tickets (membership is $50, $35 for students). $7.50 admission, $5 for members, $2 for weekend Sunday matinees. Great snacks and even-better coffee. (Often, depending on the series, snacks are thematically related to the movies.) Huge and luscious screen, perfect for movie lovers.

MILLENNIUM
66 East 4th Street, 673-0090

Millennium makes 16-mm and Super-8 film and video equipment available for anyone to use at very low costs. They also sponsor the Personal Cinema Series, in the fall, winter, and spring, where people come in and coordinate screenings. "Experimental, avant-garde, mostly new works" are shown. Screenings are $6. They also publish a journal, called *Millennium,* about independent film, and they offer film and video workshops for people working in these mediums. Established in 1966.

P. J. CLARKE'S
912 Third Avenue

At this bar/restaurant, at the corner of East 55th Street, director Billy Wilder shot the infamous Nat's Bar scenes in *The Lost Weekend* (1945). P. J.'s, now just called Clarke's Bar, is an after-work drinking person's friend that has not changed an iota since it was last seen on film. Wilder had to reshoot much of the footage on a Hollywood soundstage, though, because in the background of every shot, the director heard rumbling: the El trains passing by like clockwork!

But according to the history books, that was Ray Milland running up Third Avenue, trying desperately to hock a typewriter.

You must, if you can, take a good look at P.J.'s, which sits on a strange corner, all by itself, looking awfully wistful.

It is cornered by a lot: There is a humongous building on every side of it. This is the holdout of the century, if you ask me. Wonder of wonder that some big corporation didn't make the owners sell. Perhaps we shouldn't even mention it; by the time this edition comes out, the petite building could be bulldozed!

36 SUTTON PLACE SOUTH

This is the building featured in *How to Marry a Millionaire* (1953), where Lauren Bacall, Betty Grable, and Marilyn Monroe lived for $1,000 a month, including the grand terraces.

As long as you're on the Upper East Side, take a poignant trip to Mecca in the form of the **FRANK CAMPBELL FUNERAL HOME** (1076 Madison Avenue at East 81st Street), where you'll find commemorated the deaths of stars such as Joan Crawford, Judy Garland, James Cagney, Monty Clift, and Tommy Dorsey.

This is quite a trip for movie lovers. You can just imagine all the death that was honored here. Remember, it's one thing to be famous while alive . . .

55 CENTRAL PARK WEST

For slime fans: Here's where much of *Ghostbusters* was filmed. The gooey scenes, however, were done in Times Square. Not far away is the outdoor piazza of Tavern on the Green, where Joseph Cotten ate with Ethel Barrymore in *Portrait of Jennie* (1948).

In the funniest film on the power of hype, *It Should Happen to You*, (1954), Gladys Glover (Judy Holliday) lusts after sudden celebrity, which she purchases by renting a billboard at Columbus Circle. The billboard bears only her name—but that's enough to make her the hottest talk-show guest in town. Inside the stairwell at **115 WEST 69TH STREET**, Gladys watches as her pal, Pete Sheppard (Jack Lemmon in his first starring role), shakes his head in disgust and disbelief.

239 WEST 49TH STREET

While you're in Judy and Jack's neck of the woods, take a look at **ST. MALACHY'S CHURCH**, the scene of at least one mobbed media event, the 1926 funeral of Rudolph Valentino. This is known as the celebrity mortuary, for good reason.

Then, ponder the windows at Tiffany's, which have the same glimmer witnessed by Holly Golightly (the late Audrey Hepburn) in *Breakfast at Tiffany's* (1961), as she waltzed in sighing, "Dont'cha just love it?"

LEXINGTON AVENUE BETWEEN EAST 51ST AND 52ND STREETS

The subway grating here, on the northeast corner, is where Marilyn Monroe's skirt billowed up in *The Seven Year Itch* (1955). A blowup poster of this film's sexiest segment stood for years near the Loew's State. Copies of the poster (originals are worth a fortune) can be found in a photoplay store near you.

Then take Lexington all the way down to 14th Street, walk east, and go to Third Avenue, to see where Martin Scorsese set the harshest scene in *Taxi Driver* (1976): a coffee shop where strung-out Jodie Foster got cozy with Robert De Niro. It's now the all-night Disco Donut, allegedly serving "The Best Hamburgers in Town." And *Taxi Driver* has become reimmortalized by David Letterman, who can't help but ask taxi drivers if they know the harshest lines from the film. (And many of them actually do!)

BELOW EAST HOUSTON STREET

These are the streets that the young Don Corleone (Robert De Niro) walked in the 1918 segments of *The Godfather, Part II* (1974).

The gripping, but strangely edited, *Once Upon a Time in America* (1984), was shot on Delancey and Rivington Streets. *Hester Street* (1974) and *Pretty Baby* (1978) were filmed on Hester Street. Underneath the Brooklyn Bridge you can still find, almost scene for scene, the exterior dramatic moments from *Ragtime* (1981).

129 EAST 18TH STREET

Speaking of *Ragtime:* Did you know that many of its turn-of-the-century bar scenes were filmed in PETE'S TAVERN (the city's oldest "original" bar, founded in 1864)? Pete's is still the same friendly neighborhood hangout that it was last century. Also shot here were famous beer commercials, among them the Miller Lite "Goalies" spot. Other beers promoted on TV via Pete's Tavern are Piel's LA Beer, and Stroh's, making this the unofficial beer Hall of Fame.

A forgettable film with scenes at the landmark bar: *Endless Love* with Brooke Shields (1981). This bar has hung photos of every celeb that ever graced its threshold, including a beshaded Cher.

502 HENRY STREET

There's this great bakery with fresh bread in Cobble Hill. It's called Cammareri Brothers (718-852-3606). If you go in there, talk to the Italian saleswoman about wheat bread and rolls, have some coffee, take a free crumbcake slice, then look at the walls. Yes, you've seen them before—it's where *Moonstruck* was filmed.

Let's just say that the owner—who had a small part in the film—wasn't too crazy about the former Mrs. Bono. (Read the interview on the wall.) Okay, now go around back and take a look at the basement entrance. It's where many precious Cherless scenes were filmed, in which Nicolas Cage and actual workers from the bake shop hollered in touching camaraderie.

FILM AT THE JOSEPH PAPP PUBLIC THEATER
425 Lafayette Street, 260-2400

Though this theater no longer offers a well-plotted selection of good first-run films, political cinema, and their once-famous free shows on weekends about topical events (*Panama Deception* won the Oscar in '93), often they will take a failed first-run feature that is considered by some to be "art" and run it in one of the Public's theatrical spaces. They do festivals, such as "Garbo Talks" and show old-fashioned revival house fare for buffs who can't stand the small screen.

In years past, they have held an on-again, off-again series called "Public Service," in which political documentaries and dramas on topical subjects are the bill of the day.

REVOLUTION BOOKS
9 West 19th Street between Fifth and Sixth Avenues

Believe it or not, they are still in business: Revolution, as mentioned in Chapter 13, is a bookstore that caters to "revolutionaries," a code word for political activism (read: Socialism) that still exists in several nations!

A revolutionary assortment of nighttime films, videos, and lectures can be found in this crowded bookstore that sells political texts in both English and Spanish (hmm, Spanish, why, I wonder . . . ?).

Some of the films here include, for example, *The White-Haired Girl,* a Chinese ballet film, or *The Murder Of Fred Hampton,* about the political high point of the Black Panther movement. The $2 investment is worthwhile.

DCTV, OR DOWNTOWN COMMUNITY TELEVISION
87 Lafayette Street, 966-4510

DCTV holds wild fundraisers on a pretty regular basis for TV and film organizations that need community support in order to make established non-establishment videos. These shindigs are held in the screening room of their downtown facility, worth visiting just for the beer! There's dancing and food and often an experience or two called "body-rocking" (and also a lot of mouth-smashing) screenings, for about ten bucks. You can pay $8 if you're broke and $5 if you're totally broke.

If you want to stay abreast of what's happening at DCTV, keep a lookout on Channel 69, the public access "Manhattan Neighborhoods" channel on which DCTV occupies many time slots, or ask them for their listings to be sent free (757-2670).

AMERICAN MUSEUM OF THE MOVING IMAGE
3601 35th Avenue at 36th Street, Astoria, Queens, 718-784-4520

This is a museum that thinks of movies as ART, not an entertainment medium. So among its earlier exhibits was a costumed cardboard head of Eddie Murphy for you to place your head in (like those photo-with-the-president stands in Times Square). But the museum also has three theaters for screening film series like the cycle called "The Media and The Vietnam War" and special comedy flicks from the golden era of the '50s.

Since 1981, Moving Image has screened experimental videos, silent films, animation, and retrospectives of great actors and directors, in addition to mediocre films from rented collections derived from national archives, studios, and collectors. Movies free with your paid admish ($5 Adults; $4 over 65; $2.50 students; under 4 gets in free).

PLACES OTHER THAN CINEMAS TO SEE MOVIES

During the winter they displayed memorabilia on Hopalong Cassidy, the licensed cowboy king; recently, video game software was added to the mix. Give the people what they want.

See film and television costumes, cameras, and memorabilia. Enjoy full-length feature films. Add sound-effects to a TV commercial. Learn how film is edited. Play the latest in home video games in what is the only museum in the country devoted to film, television, and video.

American Moving Image exists in London, but that has more of a bemused quality to it; in England, the fascination with Hollywood movies is more about bewilderment with Americans.

ASIAN CINE-VISION
32 East Broadway, 925-8685

Free movies about the Asian experience as shown at Cine-Vision's Chinatown headquarters, or at the American Museum of Natural History, a refractory of children's fun in upper Manhattan. Screenings are held seasonally.

Cine-Vision's Asian-American Film Festival takes place at the Rosemary Theater (133 Canal Street, great home of films from the East, some of which are action-adventure like none seen in this country). The best Asian-American Video Festival is held at Millennium. The "Cinema and Society" film series is an unusual effort combining films and lectures. Admission ranges from free to $7.

BROOKLYN MUSEUM CINEMA PROGRAM
200 Eastern Parkway, Flatbush, 718-638-5000

Film series of the utmost importance now appear at this large, ostentatious museum, which ties screenings to exhibitions (such as "German Cinema, Birth and Rebirth" coinciding with a German show).

Thematic shows here usually emphasize both American and other ways of making movies. Also available are documentaries, art films, and an abundance of kids' programs that fit under the umbrella title "Family Flicks." Guest speakers include scholars, filmmakers, and renowned critics. Free with museum admission, $3.

ETHNIC FOLK ARTS CENTER
Screenings held at various locations; located at 131 Varick Street, 691-9510

Ethnic Folk Arts is a group that promotes music, dance, and films from Eastern Europe, home of the ever-changing nations. The Center presents a series of popular films, free. For example, Polish, Czech, Hungarian, and formerly Soviet experimental forays. EFA offers concert series from western Italy, called "Musica Popolare."

FILM FORUM
209 West Houston Street, 727-8110

This is one of New York's only remaining art forums for cinema. Endangered as ever, so remember it when you are thinking of what to do on a dry or rainy evening. No, they don't put butter on their popcorn, but they are the only cinema in town (three screens) that allows you to see the latest films from around the world in addition to releases from the 1940s through the 1970s that nobody has the guts to show. Examples are Russ Myer's avant-garde *Faster, Pussycat, Kill! Kill!* and a newly mastered series featuring French clown Jacques Tati. You could see their 3-D version of *Kiss Me Kate,* while sitting on *comfortable* seats, as well as the latest '60s retro-art documentary.

Also, special events, including appearances by filmmakers, cinematographers, and aging celebs from bygone studio days.

Charges are $7.50 for a ticket; for $40 a year you get a $3 savings off the cost of admish and a booklet listing what's up sent to you seven times a year. You can get the list if you ask.

NYU—NEW YORK UNIVERSITY STUDENT FILMS
566 LaGuardia Place, Loeb Student Center, 998-1795

An annual and exciting film event that occurs each May when the future Martin Scorseses, Spike Lees, and Jim Jarmusches of the world have their work viewed by the public. Usually it's a nerve-wracking first time, so be respectful.

After the first night's Animation Festival, they're off: five straight nights of films from 1:00 P.M. to 1:00 A.M. For a five-spot you can hardly go wrong—well, maybe you *will* see a night of turkeys.

PLACES OTHER THAN CINEMAS TO SEE MOVIES

Once each season it's dream night for film students. The Mobil Awards are given to the best films, as judged by industry directors and department faculty.

Also, some of the most intriguing student films are held at the Columbia University film program, but it's catch-as-catch-can (campus number, 854-1754; held at Symphony Space, 2537 Broadway, in May; phone 964-5400).

BIG MIDTOWN MOVIEGOING TIPS

The **SONY IMAX THEATER** is a must, but only because it's so gargantuan and 3-D futuristic that it is worth a spin. But the others are **LOEW'S ASTOR PLAZA** (doesn't the name sound regal?), which has just recently become yet another Sony, or Sony Astor Plaza. Loew's—always Loew's to me—screens the big action adventure films, from Indiana Jones to Eddie Murphy bests. This is a large screen in a larger-than-life neighborhood, and the one thing to watch out for is the rowdiness of the crowds. They sometimes drown out the sound of the picture! Sometimes, on Thursday nights, official openings are held here, often with invited public (ticket winners on the radio, lucky people on mailing lists).* If you act fast, you can get into these—just be charming and say, "Oh darn, I left my ticket home." Sometimes they just shrug and say, "Go in . . ."

The **ZIEGFELD THEATER,** last of the remaining big one-screeners (Sixth Avenue and 54th Street, 765-7600), is the largest of the first-run screens in town. All the big films that truly need large screens *(Lawrence of Arabia, King Kong)* come here to play.

PS: Expect around forty first-run "screens" (read TV-sized) on the now empty 42nd Street any day now.

CHARAS TEATRO LA TERRAZZA
605 East 9th Street, 982-0627

This is the local Lower East Side collective that concentrates on the artwork of ethnic groups in Manhattan and the outer boroughs. Films Charas

* The call of the adventurous: get on mailing lists!

is a regular tribute to the works of independent films and videos of the Lower East Side (known as Loisada around here), and other American regions, not to mention far-off continents. Charas's latest program is exciting: video poetry by men and women from dozens of different backgrounds who read and discuss their work in self-critical thirty-minute segments. More on Charas can be found in Chapter 22.

They also screen movies of interest to the local denizens. A series of Cuban films never seen before in this city was shown a few years ago, some predating the 1959 revolution, sparking some controversy, which every grassroots organization thrives on.

ALLIANCE FRANÇAISE/FRENCH INSTITUTE
Florence Gould Hall, 55 East 59th Street and at Alliance Française, 22 East 60th Street, 355-6100

The Institute opens many of its evenings to French cinema. Mostly subtitled, their ongoing modern film series, "Cine Club," has screened films most Wednesdays since 1964 for only $6.

Institute members enjoy recent Parisian TV shows, no Jerry Lewis, and a spokesperson calls this mix: "the old, the new, the medium." Alliance has a rich series of events and a rude receptionist.

It's worthwhile pointing out they have several chamber music series and an ongoing lecture series on topics relating to French culture. They also have a library and a French bookstore. And they also offer French lessons.

Lastly, for Francofiles, see Columbia University's **MAISON FRANÇAISE** (117th Street and Amsterdam, 854-1754), as a place to see recent French films for school credit! There are informative videos on such topics as the history of the French government and the history of Frenchy products (a recent video, I kid you not, was on the subject of Hermès scarves!).

MAISON FRANÇAISE OF NEW YORK UNIVERSITY
16 Washington Mews, 998-8750

Because I wanted to make sure you had enough of French film, I add one more: Off the beaten track, NYU's French house screens obscure and literary movies. These, essentially, are the nonhits of Paris! Maison gets films from the Cultural Service of the Embassy. Only ninety seats in this house and the Friday screenings are only a few dollars. Go.

NEW SCHOOL FOR SOCIAL RESEARCH FILM "CLASS"

66 West 12th Street, 229-5600

Offering unusual programs, many of them popular-culture related, the most popular of them are the famous film programs in which new (and often forthcoming) films are screened alongside live commentary from a director or a star. Giant course catalog available upon request.

CHAPTER

16

Music—Concerts
That Cost Nothing

WHAT'S FREE?

Welcome to the world of the free.

Participation is the key to enjoying New York. And this section is about the best things in life.

First, some ideas to keep in mind: Sometimes events are falsely assessed as "free" and often require a small donation. This could be something to keep the charity or group going, or where liquor is served—a small drink to keep it friendly. But still, New York can be a world of absolutely free living—except when the first of the month comes around—and only if you know where to find the freebies.

Suspicion abounds: Why are some of these things free? Many societies and cultural organizations are given money via grants and donations, and then they have to use the funding to create shows, functions, group events, even art. And you, the lucky and informed, can cash in just by knowing about it.

Best thing to remember: If something on this list strikes your fancy, call and demand to be put on their mailing and phone list. This way they will get in touch when something is about to happen.

ARTS AT ST. ANN'S
157 Montague Street, Brooklyn Heights, 718-858-2424

Hours are Monday–Friday, 10:00 A.M.–6:00 P.M.; box office hours, Tuesday–Saturday, noon–6:00 P.M. Performances take place in the sanctuary of the National Historic Landmark Church of St. Ann and the Holy Trinity, a Gothic revival masterpiece by Minard. Arts is also home to Lafever's first cycle of figural stained glass windows made in America. Their fall concert series is, "unimpeachable," says *New York* magazine. It's a great theater to be on the mailing list for. Arts at St. Ann's continues to be one of the most eclectic and highly regarded music programs in New York City. Divine acoustics and dramatic architecture. (Note: Sometimes a fee. And sometimes art.)

JAZZ INTERACTIONS' QUEENS CONCERTS
Jazz Foundation of America

Write 1200 Broadway, Suite 7D, call the "Jazz Line" at 479-7888 or the Foundation at 213-3866

Jazz Interactions is a nonprofit center that wants you to be more attuned to the jazz world. They say, "We strive to create a social and cultural climate in which the art form can prosper." We say, enough credos—just give us the music! In Queens, Interactions presents free Wednesday concerts at 1:00 P.M. in McDonald Park, groovin' to the sounds of swing bands.

JUILLIARD SCHOOL CONCERTS
155 West 66th Street, 769-7406

Juilliard often exudes an air of snobbery, but pay no mind: concerts at Juilliard are worth the visit. Every so often students play whatever's dear to them—or whatever their teachers place on their music stands. These special evening shows are held at Alice Tully Hall; free tickets can be picked up one week prior to the announced event. If you're a true music buff, you'll want to stay informed of their regularly scheduled offerings, where you can see tomorrow's talents breaking through to professional caliber. Standby is always available for last-minute deciders.

NEW YORK YOUTH SYMPHONY
Merkin Concert Hall, 850 Seventh Avenue, 581-5933

The Youth Symphony finds new talent from a pool of youngsters in the metropolitan area and presents them before their careers take off. Rehearsals are at Carnegie Hall, where they are instructed by members of the New York Philharmonic and then perform in competitions and regular concerts at Carnegie and Merkin Halls and also at local colleges, such as Colden Center for Performing Arts at Queens College.

The Youth Symphony also discovers new composers; after auditions, the three best compose works for a full orchestra (another complimentary series).

 ## SUMMER GARDEN CONCERTS AT COOPER-HEWITT MUSEUM
Carnegie Mansion, 2 East 91st Street, 849-8300

When magnate Andrew Carnegie built the mansion that encompasses Fifth Avenue between East 90th and 91st Streets, he wanted much of it to be a garden. Not only did he get his architectural wish, but today we can relish his notion during a special series of free concerts all summer long, Tuesdays at 6:00 P.M. A little jazz, some classical, and some chamber music are played amid the ivy, rhododendron, and Vermont granite that officials say was "selected by Carnegie to last forever."

The garden is a quarter of the block's length and can hold up to 1,000 people. Don't worry about crowds, though, because no matter how many show up, the peaceful atmosphere is always in bloom.

SUMMERPIER
South Street Seaport Museum, Pier 16, South and Fulton Streets, 748-8600

The South Street Seaport is famous for its Christmas show, which lights up the block with dancing puppets, music, and the renowned Christmas Tree of Carolers (a dozen red-nosed singers on triangle-forming benches).

But you can find treats in the summertime, too. Jazz, big band, and classical concerts are given at eight o'clock every Saturday night, after July 4 on the main pier. Officials suggest that you plan to come early, bring a blanket, and stay a while. There are usually terrific, energetic crowds—and, of course, the stores stay open late.

SUMMERSTAGE
Midpark, call for calendar, 360-2777

The Parks Department offers a special collection of musical wonders during the summer. Presented by the Central Park Conservancy, a trust that believes in keeping arts in the park alive, this series has in the past featured Brazilian ensembles, "Texas polka revivalists," Southern singers, Bayou boogie, grand opera—the list goes on to include famous and obscure authors of poetry and fiction. (Yet no guidebook writers!)

This series is never hyped, so only park aficionados or hard-core music fans attend these beautiful summer events (at 3:00, 9:00, and 11:00 P.M.). At season's end, "New Music" evenings entertain with art-funk and electronic experiments. This series is endangered—if it sounds interesting, please attend it.

New York Philharmonic (875-5709) also presents free concerts in the park, with one night given to fireworks; "Shakespeare in the Park" (861-7277) produces some great nights with the Bard, free; and "Metropolitan Opera in the Park" delivers evenings of uninterpreted art (362-6000). Picnics not included.

SYMPHONY SPACE WALL-TO-WALL CONCERTS
2537 Broadway, 864-1414

The great Symphony Space is one of the few remaining places to have a good time free (or cheap). This is an endangered species extraordinaire! One reason it has fended off the wrecking ball is that unique events keep the community eagerly involved in its upkeep. Once a year it presents, free, twelve hours of "Wall-to-Wall Cole Porter," with New York's brightest talent reading or singing Porter's work.

Or maybe you're a classicist. "Wall-to-Wall Mozart" presents the master in twelve hours that are a bit more sedate. Hint: Bring your instruments and opera voices, and play/sing along. And get on their mailing list if you are a music buff.

THIRD STREET MUSIC SCHOOL SETTLEMENT
233 East 11th Street, 777-3240

Why is Third Street on 11th Street? Well, why does Waverly Place intersect Waverly Place? Strange city, this. The settlement has offered classes in music appreciation and music theory to kids and adults since 1890. Now it also presents concerts to the general public, no tickets required, Wednesdays at 8:30 P.M. In the past, the weekly bill has mixed many of the local players with superstars of international renown.

The settlement often presents special summer concerts in tiny St. Marks Park, where St. Marks-in-the-Bowery stands. Sometimes, if the students are very, very good, they invite a large audience to share in a birthday celebration of a famous composer, usually dead, who is heralded with a musical feast.

BRYANT PARK RESTORATION CONCERTS
Behind the New York Public Library at 42nd Street and 6th Avenues, 983-4142

The Bryant Park Restoration Corporation keeps this nearly restored park an oasis and it has, as advertised, become one of "the best-kept secrets in midtown." It's clean, safe, and has accessible public bathrooms, which in itself makes it an eyebrow-raiser. Park hours: winter, 8:00 A.M.–6:00 P.M.; summer 7:00 A.M.–9:00 P.M.

For our purposes, find free movies at sunset (large screen, often silent films, sometimes raucous and loud ones), comedy at lunchtime, many concerts, and even readings by famous authors. Also, the park runs botanical garden tours weekly. (Also take advantage of the same-day half-price tickets booth for music and dance, located on the corner of 42nd Street and Sixth Avenue. Tuesday–Sunday, 12:00–2:00 P.M. and 3:00–7:00 P.M.)

TIMES SQUARE MUSIC FEST
Underneath West 42nd Street at Seventh Avenue, at the intersection of the S and 1-2-3 trains.

So much music goes on underneath Times Square that many commuters add a few minutes to their travel time to check out the action. It's not quite free—you need a token; plus your enjoyment meter may force you to drop change in various hats and boxes. These aren't everyday buskers or opera crooners. Down in the plaza, where a variety of subway lines converge, you'll find both *salsa* record stores blasting their wares and professional musicians who spend their days entertaining the crowds.

Serious musicians from Mexico, Haiti, Brazil, and Puerto Rico bring guitars, amps, and recorded accompaniments. It's a true fiesta, where you can usually choose from up to four bands.

Note that when this book was first issued in 1989, the problem for riders who wanted to revel in music was that A-train riders had to purchase a separate token to come into the 1-2-3 area. No longer, because the MTA opened it to all undergrounders already in the system!

Oh, okay, here's a little known fact: many New Yorkers wonder why there is no such thing as an "8" train, and yet there is. The "S" or Shuttle train was once the 8—current lingo only for MTA employees in the know. So next time you go to hear music beneath Times Square, be sure to ask a trainman, "Where's the 8 train leave from?" Shock him or her, rightly.

MUSIC UNDER NEW YORK (METROPOLITAN TRANSIT AUTHORITY)
362-3830

It is not what captive audiences fear most: This program of freelance musicians encouraged by the MTA to make music at the train stations includes street musicians, ethnic bands, groups with an Afro-Caribbean or calypso beat, and specialists in jazz and Peruvian music, at fifteen different underground places. Funny thing is, there's no real schedule, so you either happen upon these passageway tunesmiths—or keep calling the above number.

MUNY operates at three places in Grand Central Terminal: Graybar Passage (Graybar Building), the token booth by the S train, and the ever-popular main concourse. And although these are paid gigs for the artist, drop some money in their buckets. They can use it.

Buskers, as they're called, can make good money when people like their music. Ask Paul McCartney, who once went down in the London Underground and made hundreds of pounds each day.

TRINITY CHURCH CONCERTS
Trinity Church, Wall Street and Broadway, 602-0873

Depending on which venue you attend and on what day, this can be a Gothic Bore or a modern adrenaline-raiser. Held year-round at Trinity Church, Tuesdays at 12:45 P.M., and at St. Paul's, Mondays and Thursdays at 12:10 P.M., these free concerts are an unusual grab bag of up-and-comers who will thrill you in St. Paul's aesthetically exciting chapel, or lull you into oblivion in Trinity's somber, dark-oak atmosphere. Regardless, they do have special events worth noting. (If you promise to attend, they'll mail you regular listings. Call 602-0747 for regular postcard drop.)

In particular, the Wednesday concerts at Trinity present winners of the Metropolitan Opera auditions and a variety of stars (Abbey Simon, Faith Esham) to rev up the downtown crowds. Concerts last about forty minutes. Schedule varies, so call first; it's quite a *schlep* if they're not playing that day.

WQXR
Information: 633-7600

New York's classical station, WQXR-FM, fights for ratings and loyalty; it's owned by the New York Times Company so the media-ites host shows aimed at getting you to really like the music.

At 7:00 P.M. on Tuesdays in July and August, Damrosch Park in Lincoln Center lights up with different WQXR personalities and pianists, brass and chamber orchestras. Sit in the chairs, heckle the DJs, and have a great time on the air.

WORLD TRADE CENTER SUMMER CONCERTS
Information for series: 435-4700/466-4170

One of the more adventurous summer series is found at the five-acre centerpiece called Austin J. Taubin Plaza, located at the crossroads of all the World Trade Center buildings (except #7). Here you will find a summer music feast of Monday Mixed Bag, Tuesday Classical, Wednesday New Jazz, Thursday Broadway Greats, and Friday Comedy Performers.

These take place from 12:00 to 2:00 P.M. and involve the entire financial community. Bring your lunch and good cheer. Thursday's offering is particularly groundbreaking, because the organizers of the series actually get new and veteran stars from current musicals to "bring part of the show" to the Trade Center.

There is a rumor that this may not be around long. So bag your lunch and come.

LOUIS ARMSTRONG ARCHIVE

Rosenthal Library, Queens College Campus, 718-528-8490

An interesting, and unusual, new note for music lovers: all of Armstrong's personal effects and the home he lived in in Corona were left to Queens College, where they are now on display, including 5,000 personal photographs, 85 scrapbooks, and 600 reel-to-reels that he personally recorded, not to mention diaries, letters, and some trumpets to boot. Armstrong's house is nearby. Call 718-997-3670 for directions to Corona and the trumpeter's residence, recently redone as a tribute/monument.

SIDEBAR SPECIAL Jukebox Music

ASTOR PLACE HAIRCUTTERS (Astor Place and Broadway, 529-5761) is a tri-level $10 haircut emporium—a regular assembly line—with a jukebox that seems to say, "I don't care if you don't like Frank Sinatra." Sure there's plenty of Madonna, Prince, and Quiet Riot, but what Italian-run shop could possibly lease a box without a Tony Bennett tune? At Astor, even if you are not getting a cut, the energy is so high-level that if you want to dance, you can dance; if you want to sing, you can sing; if you want to party . . . they ask you to take it outside. Open Monday–Saturday, 8:00 A.M.–8:00 P.M.; Sunday, 9:00 A.M.–6:00 P.M. And please say "hi" to Jay.

V. RAO (455 East 114th Street, 722-6709) is a quiet, cozy Italian restaurant in East Harlem, with an eclectic jukebox programmed by on-air radio personality, Bob Jones. With Italian food to rival many Italian grandmothers', and a bizarre location, V. Rao's is extremely popular—it is very, very difficult to get a table.

TENTH AVENUE JUKEBOX CAFÉ, housed at 637 Tenth Avenue (315-4690) has nothing fancy to offer you OR the Royals. This café could fit into many of the "Food" chapters: It's trendy, has healthy food, is a great place to eat alone, has bagels during lunch, and is reasonable. Its jukebox is interesting because all it contains are middle-of-the-road tunes—surprises except for two French singles. What makes it special is that they don't drop names of hot rock bands from, say, Zimbabwe; rather they divvy up Streisand, Diamond, Sade, the formerly famous George Michael, and songs by Elvis (the living one).

After looking into their "average American" menu, you can explore obscure "B" sides from some staid 45s, often the artists' riskier ventures that never got airplay. Open Monday–Friday, 11:30 A.M.–midnight. "B" sides, mind you, can be awfully fun and frisky.

And lastly, 'cause it's probably been there the longest, is the **GRASSROOTS TAVERN** at 20 St. Marks Place (475-9443, fax-hah!). Wow, man, like shades of the '60s: low tin ceilings and an incredible jukebox filled with misspellings. For example: Credence Clearwater, Bix Bliderbecker, Eurmics, along with some even odder choices. This place is as laid-back as it was in the hippie days. Everything is designed in natural wood. Beer choices are still five draught, five bottles, that's it.

The best irony is that it sits right across from the All-Craft Community Center, a crony from the Grassroots' earlier days and now the home of AA, NA, and the East Village spiritual center. But in the '60s the Center was the discotheque Electric Circus, where Hendrix and Joplin used to play. Grassroots is open daily, 4:00 P.M.–3:00 A.M. I don't know for sure, but I *think* the reason the Grassers are still on the lot is they were smart and bought the building.

A SMATTERING OF TUNES: THE LAND OF THE FEE

TATOU
151 East 50th Street, 753-1144

Dinner is served accompanied by a jazz ensemble every night of the week, with dancing after dinner (American cuisine with a French touch). From time-to-time a cabaret performance is scheduled on Tuesday nights. Music begins at 6:00 P.M. and continues through 10:00 P.M. Auditions are held on Mondays and something called, "From Hollywood To Broadway," occurs on weekends. They ask for $15 cover with dinner ($20 on Friday and Saturday), and say, "Even if you eat, you pay the cover." Warning: An enjoyable evening, yet Tatou is not as chic as when it first opened. (But neither is anything.)

PAULA COOPER GALLERY
534 West 21st Street, 255-1105

Music under the oils! A fringe benefit to living in New York is that you can watch performing artists "try out" difficult programs before they get their official premiere. For the past few seasons, the SEM Ensemble, an experimental music group, has played here twice a year ($10). Get on Cooper's mailing list; the gallery often holds what the manager refers to as "special things for our friends," meaning musical events.

JUPITER SYMPHONY
Good Shepherd Presbyterian Church, 152 West 66th Street, information: 799-1259

This independent concert series is committed to making concert music accessible, with concerts four times a year in October, December, February, and April. Each offered twice, on either a Monday afternoon and evening or a Tuesday evening. Ticket prices range from $6 to $18, or pay what you can. The symphony also performs at Battery Park each summer, also for free.

JAZZ FOR THE HOMELESS

St. Peter's Church, 54th Street and Lexington Avenue, 935-2200

While indeed esoteric, this is an unsanctimonious hour at the church that features musicians Terry Clark, Roger Kellaway, and Robin Eubanks, on Saturdays at 10:30 P.M.; special shows for the homeless are held at 12:30 P.M. on Wednesdays. Also, St. Peter's (also known as the "Jazz Church") occasionally sponsors memorial concerts for jazz greats. Call to find out more.

THE FEZ AT TIME CAFE

380 Lafayette Street, 533-2680

For some reason, the Fez did not want you to have its number, but since they are listed each week in the *Village Voice,* I figured, this is something you should know about: A wonderful promoter puts on small shows (less than 100 seats at tables) downstairs under the Time Cafe, a trendy yet solid eatery. Recently, such Brit pop favorites as Julia Fordham and Everything But The Girl graced us with their presence in the Fez's comfortable living-room-like space. Most tickets are $15. The popular Charles Mingus Band plays on Thursday nights at 9:00 and 11:00 P.M., but make sure to get there early. Call to find out schedule. Often surprise, unadvertised event nights, too (e.g., Joni Mitchell).

55 BAR

55 Christopher Street, 929-9883

Live music—a band and singers, seven nights a week. Sunday–Thursday from 10:15 P.M. to 2:00 A.M., and on Friday and Saturday nights from 10:15 P.M. to 3:00 A.M. There's no cover, but there is a two-drink minimum per set.

NADINE'S

151 Bank Street, 691-2272

Nadine's long-running restaurant has presented wonderful theater pieces such as Robert Chesley's *Jerker.* They offer a wide range of performances and events in this room, including cabaret, performance art, jazz, poetry, plays. Some food available, and a full bar. Get calendar.

BLUE NOTE

131 West Third Street, 475-8592

Most proprietors would love to promote their venues as "the jazz capital of the world." Blue Note swears it is, probably because so many jazz greats have performed there. Cleo Laine and Lou Rawls are the top of the line at Blue Note, a well-decorated and intimate space that can be awfully pricey. They often charge $35 plus a drink minimum to see someone of the caliber of Grover ("Just the Two of Us") Washington, Jr. But some of their "all-star lineups" (everyone is billed this way) cost only a $7.50 cover charge and $5 minimum.

Monday nights are scheduled by record companies for the "New Artist's Showcase," with various show times. On Tuesday and Saturday nights a jam session is held after the last show; at 1:00 A.M.; musicians in the audience play with the band. You can buy dinner here, though the menu is not fascinating in the least.

LINCOLN CENTER SPECIALTIES

Lincoln Center's Avery Fisher Hall hosts a summer festival that beats many other performances throughout the year there. Not high-class opera, not fancy chamber, but six weeks of pure beauty in the form of uncluttered evenings when Mozart and friends ("Mostly Mozart") are performed in those near-perfect acoustics. Even if classical doesn't really grab you, imagine: For $10 to $20, you can relax and recoup for two hours, with no commercial or other interruptions.

Summer also brings the two-week "Serious Fun!" series to Alice Tully Hall. Here, downtown's best performance artists, dancers, and singers entertain a whole new crowd . . .

"MICHAEL'S PUB" AT BILL'S GAY NINETIES

57 East 54th Street, 758-2272

This dark and unseedy jazz club is still definitely one of the city's top tourist attractions, and for those who find jazz a stimulant, the Pub is definitely an

upper. While the space has changed, we all know that Mondays are great because of the traditional Louisiana band that plays each week.

Most shows start at 9:00 and 11:00 P.M. These jerks always charge a
cover—$15 to $20, depending on their mood—except for promotional parties; and the two-drink minimum is for real.

ARIAS IN THE AREA

The Metropolitan Museum holds early-evening recitals on Fridays with
accomplished opera singers. . . . The French Institute/Alliance Française
(355-6100) presents opera, specifically French language pieces, including
those that need a premiere, several times a year. Performances cost $12 and
are held at Florence Gould Hall. Once yearly they hold a "Concert Evening
of French Opera," presentations of one-act productions, for $15. . . . The
Village Light Opera Group offers $10 evenings of classics and obscure
pieces at a variety of theaters downtown (call 243-6281, for their mailers).

For kids, some news. Five dollar tickets to the opera are available for
teenagers with valid ID. This "thing" is called High 5 Tickets and arranged
via Ticketmaster; call 445-8587 or look up http://www.high5tix.com and
get thee to the City Opera, Bro Opera . . . all sorts of cool opera. Do it before the fat kid sings!

OTHER CLASSICAL CONCERTS

Note the happenings at Symphony Space (2537 Broadway, 864-1414), another endangered species that offers orchestras, revels, Mozart and Gilbert
& Sullivan festivals, and an assortment of uncanny experiences for the
musical-at-heart . . . Great Performers at Lincoln Center (875-5050) is a collection of winter and spring appearances by some of the all-time greats, including composers' showcases by pop (read "hip, nouveau") performers
such as David Van Tieghem, the guy who makes money making music from
garbage cans and whatever's handy. Tickets are $15–$25, dates and times are
all over the map . . . Merkin Concert Hall (129 West 67th Street, 362-8719)
has Tuesday matinees at 2:00 P.M. during the winter, of all things; they include piano quartets, soloists, even a harpsichord concert. Tickets are $7; $6
by mail. Tuesday nights, it's "Music Today" with some of the sweetest
soloists known to mankind. The strings are beatific, and single tickets are
only $12 and up.

THE TOWN HALL

123 West 43rd Street, 840-2824

This place no longer holds town meetings—though Breslin challenged Murdoch to a "word duel" here a few years back—but the acoustics are perfect for new plays, traditional and classical music, even a series with new composers titled "New Riffs" and featuring marimba, music with animals, and a jazz chamber group (call for mailers).

Multicultural events by outstanding artists reflect the cultural diversity of the city. Jazz, prose, poetry, film, dance, and even live radio broadcasts from Minnesota Public Radio (Garrison Keillor's "Prairie Home Companion" was produced here).

A 76-year-old home for most anything (even Elvis Costello and Lindsey Buckingham did concerts here a few years back), Town Hall was first built as a public forum for political debate by suffragettes! We've come a long way, baby.

BROOKLYN ACADEMY OF MUSIC

30 Lafayette Avenue, downtown Brooklyn, information: 718-636-4100;

fax 718-857-2021

In the past, such innovative works as Philip Glass's *Einstein on the Beach* and *Hydrogen Jukebox* (libretto by Allen Ginsberg) had their New York (read "their official . . .") premieres here. BAM's famous "Next Wave Festival" takes place in the fall and features avant-garde opera, music, dance, theater, and multimedia. Good to get seats early in the season. There is an international children's festival each year too.

Also at BAM is the "What's Going On?" music series including tributes to soul greats of the past, a festival of gospel music, and even the best look at the musical world of Charlie Parker. Seats start at $10. You can call them with your order or fax it to them anytime.

THE MANHATTAN SCHOOL OF MUSIC

122nd Street and Broadway, 749-2802

This school, one of the top music schools in the country, features opera performed by students; most of the productions are $10.

NEW YORK PHILHARMONIC
Hotline: 875-5709

The Philharmonic is one of the pillars of the New York cultural scene. In addition to a full schedule of concerts throughout the year at Lincoln Center, the Philharmonic gives occasional performances at their original home, Carnegie Hall. And by the way, they have a free summer concert series in the parks throughout the five boroughs, with fireworks displays after all events. The programs always begin at 8:00 P.M., and picnics are a part of the tradition. Call their information number above for a full schedule.

SAINT ANDREW MUSIC SOCIETY
Church located at 921 Madison Avenue, 288-8920

For twenty-five years, the Madison Avenue Presbyterian Church has foregone church-oriented conclusions about having a good time in order to produce recitals that are amazing and amazingly expensive: From $30 to $499 (for Society sponsors), you can see major performances throughout the regular school year (September–June). The concerts are all on Sundays, of course, and start at 4:00 P.M. When you call, ask for the Director of Music. Suggested donations for each single ticket are $8.

CHAPTER 17

Theater

It is here we need to talk about some serious subjects: the world of theater and how it affects New Yorkers and visitors. As a lover of the theater (theater aficionado), I often find myself dismayed at how people spend their hard-earned cash on outings that are definitely not worth it: That would be Broadway.

Theater is New York's number one arts industry; after all, where is Broadway if not in New York? However, the problem these days with Broadway is not merely that it stinks. It's that producers get very greedy with the money they get when there's a hit. That's not to say this is only the case with Broadway; Off-Broadway has its share of greedy producers.

In this chapter you will find ways to get around that, via entries of special Off- and Off-Off Broadway companies that are doing fantastic theater without lifting the contents of your wallets. When looking into small companies you think might be worth a ten- or twenty-spot, hedge your bets: Tell 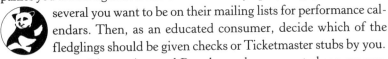 several you want to be on their mailing lists for performance calendars. Then, as an educated consumer, decide which of the fledglings should be given checks or Ticketmaster stubs by you.

In past years I have witnessed Broadway phenomena to keep my perplexed head shaking. I am still amazed: First, the old thinkers at the American Theater Wing, makers of the Tony Awards™, refused to give a Best Play Award to the only art in years on the Great White Way, namely John

Guare's *Six Degrees Of Separation*. They instead went with *Lost In Yonkers*, a repeat of so much Neil Simon muck that even he was shocked (ask the cast members of the show, who all say they don't understand its success). Then a brilliant Broadway-oriented play can't make it to the Way—Edward Albee's *Three Tall Women*—and he opens, to a Pulitzer Prize-winning burst of applause, Off-Broadway at The Promenade. Still the Tony Awards doesn't want to give anything to the "little shows" that play in smaller theaters. So in a paltry-pickings year (1995), Neil Simon takes his play *London Suite* Off-Broadway* . . . so little to choose from; only *Sunset Boulevard* was eligible for the Best Book and Best Score awards—a very, very bad sign.

My answer to the dilemma of what to see is: Try HBO or something way off Broadway. Here lies a list of theaters whose mailing lists you should be on in order to find out what *else* is out there besides Lloyd Webber's latest creation:

TRIBECA PERFORMING ARTS CENTER
199 Chambers Street, BMCC campus, 346-8510; fax 732-2482

One of downtown's busiest performing arts centers presents the finest in theater, music, and dance, from U.S. premieres of works from other nations to cutting-edge new American works. Tickets are $20 for adults, but if you like to go often, your best bet is to buy the T-PAC, a ten pack of tickets, which brings the prices down to an unbeatable $7 a ticket.

Ethnic heritage month festivals staged at BMCC include Southern Exposure (Hispanic performing arts), Revelations (Black arts), Far Eastern Exposure, and eastern European Exposure. The main season is from September to May and includes family fare such as Family Folk & Fairy Tales and magic shows, where magicians make their heads disappear.

CLASSIC STAGE COMPANY (CSC REPERTORY)
136 East 13th Street, 677-4210; fax 477-7504

Going to the Classic Stage Company is an exciting way to see staid classics revived in fresh productions. Famous for devoting itself to the oldies, CSC

---

* Simon's newest play, *Proposals,* was just on Broadway (1997) while there was no "straight play" competition.

is usually adept at offering a new view of the ancient Greek tragedies or obscure Restoration comedies.

The '97–'98 season marks the thirtieth anniversary of the successful CSC. A year ago, CSC was nominated for a Drama League Award for its critically acclaimed production of *The Entertainer* with Brian Murray and Jean Stapleton. Years back they snared Sigourney Weaver to play Portia in their revival of *The Merchant of Venice*. Normally, they rely on a regular group of actors, looking to artistic director Carey Perloff, whose strange and often surreal notions lead to wondrous and adventurous evenings. Performances run from September to May, Tuesday through Saturday at 8:00 P.M.; Sunday at 3:00 P.M. Tickets range from $15–$35.

DANCE THEATER WORKSHOP

219 West 19th Street between Seventh and Eighth Avenues, 924-0077; fax 633-1974; e-mail: dtw@dtw.org

Famous as a showcase for burgeoning dance companies, DTW is also home to several experimental theater projects that concentrate on dance and performance art. In the Bessie Schönberg Theater, which DTW recently purchased and plans to renovate soon, they have provided a workspace for more than 1,000 artists in its 25-year history—all on the same ever-changing block.

The DTW's Family Matters program, supported by a grant from The New York Community Trust, is great for parents and children to attend. These matinees are designed specifically to broaden the education of children through the arts. Call for information about prices and times.

INTAR

420 West 42nd Street, 695-6134; fax 268-0102

A nonprofit company housed on 42nd Street's Theater Row, Intar is dedicated to celebrating the art of Latin playwrights and directors. Founded in 1966, this ground-breaker of the Spanish arts has presented such luminous pieces in recent years as *Tango Apasionado*, based on the works of Jorge Luis Borges, in addition to tackling work by new playwrights and directors. They also house a playwright-in-residence program, a reading series, and an art gallery.

Theater Row (a line of brownstones between Ninth and Eleventh Avenues) is one of the few lasting impressions of the Koch administration—then-Mayor Ed Koch saw dilapidated buildings rotting away and said, "Let's put on some shows." Now along this section of 42nd Street is a series of theaters showing new and almost-ready-for-prime-time attractions. Tickets can be purchased for between $15–$25 and are available at Ticket Central (406 West 42nd Street), a place you can visit on a weekend, pick something interesting, and just go.

 JEAN COCTEAU REPERTORY
330 Bowery at Bond Street, 677-0060; fax 777-6151;
http://www.gis.net/~cocteau

The never-mellow Cocteau Rep always amazes theatergoers by producing masterworks of both old and new dramatic literature from around the world. The Cocteau with its over twenty-five years of experience stands out as one of the longest-running classical theaters in the nation.

What has made the Cocteau special is the odd choices of its plays: a never-performed Tennessee Williams, a revival of a failed Broadway ensemble piece, a rare Shakespeare, or a blood-and-guts Jacobean tragedy, not to mention many post–Soviet Union Russian plays. With the Cocteau, never bother to second-guess, but do go.

Craig Smith, who has been with the company since he began acting, who never pretends to be a Leading Man, is the reason for going to this old warhorse. With all due respect to the rest of the company, it is Smith who runs this engine. His is one of those New York stories that you shake your head at and wonder: Why not go Hollywood? Once I asked him, and he responded with, "No reason to go."

JEWISH REPERTORY THEATER/PLAYHOUSE 91
316 East 91st Street, 831-2000; fax 831-0082

Ethnic productions of every kind challenge audiences throughout this city. This theater company has been lucky enough to induce such renowned writers as Arthur Miller and Ira Levin *(Deathtrap)* into its stable. All of its shows have an undeniably Jewish flavor, and although most are done in very low profile, a few have gone on to bigger venues: Levin's *Cantorial* enjoyed a run at a midtown Off-Broadway house, while *Chu Chem* brought a taste of Chinese-Jewish music uptown. In 1988 a JRT world premiere titled *Crossing Delancey* made the transfer to a successful movie.

When going to JRT for the first time, try a Jewish Vaudeville, which is a genre unto itself.

In *Native's Guide* third edition, we called this "endangered." Mea culpa—they're still going strong.

LA MAMA ETC (ENTERTAINMENT THEATER COMPLEX)
74A East 4th Street, 254-6468

La Mama, for more than thirty years, has been the mother of all Off-Off- (and Off-) Broadway. It was in Mama's smoky East Village cellar that the cliché "smoky Village basement theater" was born. La Mama gave birth to the writers Lanford Wilson, Sam Shepard, and Harvey Fierstein *(Torch Song Trilogy)*, as well as several other renowned artists. Unfortunately, many of La Mama's recent offerings have been dull and uninspiring.

Several theaters and a nearby La Mama gallery offer an abundance of newfangled art. Still, the most fun you can get is on Mondays, when "The Club" premieres comic performance artists and even puppet shows.

Also, a recent musical called *Positive Me* by Lisa Edelstein that was meant as education about HIV, played to raves. A positive depiction sorely needed.

MEDICINE SHOW THEATRE ENSEMBLE
552 West 53rd Street, 262-4216

If oldtime Broadway musicals from the 1920s through the 1960s is your thing, then the doctor orders zany comedies with cherished tunes from yesteryear at the Medicine Show. Past offerings have included *Helen of Troy, New York 1923,* forgotten classics by Cole Porter, and the political sounds of Leonard Cohen.

Medicine Show uses talented musicians, avoids fancy sets, presents hosts of unknown talent, and charges half of what other companies do! Like many artists, they are constantly losing their space, always having to move somewhere cheaper.

RIDICULOUS THEATRICAL COMPANY

Intermittently at Actors Playhouse, Seventh Avenue
South above Bleecker Street, information: 594-7704

Some of the funniest productions in New York are performed by this group, where farce is king. This was once the one-man outfit of Charles Ludlam, who died in 1987 after almost twenty years as the theater's founder, resident writer, producer, director, and star. Now, under the watchful eye of Ludlam's longtime second-in-command, his lover, Everett Quinton, new parodies and strange pieces (such as a modern version of *A Tale of Two Cities*) show up in high style—and high camp.

The eccentrically chosen ensemble has also produced several revivals of earlier works, including Ludlam's previously lauded *Turds in Hell,* and other drag-inspired lunacy ventures. Long live "Ridiculous," wherever it may land.

13TH STREET REPERTORY COMPANY

50 West 13th Street, 675-6677

Excitement is rare at this little company run by Edith O'Hara. Yet an amazingly high proportion of actors who become "somebodies" once performed here in either *Line* (which celebrated its twentieth anniversary in 1997) or *The Indian Wants the Bronx.*

There is always a flurry of activity at 13th Street, for Edith O'Hara allows anyone with a concept to try it out onstage. Their purpose is to develop writers—for which she deserves credit and patronage. After three editions of *Native's Guide to New York,* I still walk by and mutter, as Sondheim said in *Company,* no matter what happens, she's still here. Ticket prices as of late are $12.50 for adults, children's shows are $7, and they have a dinner theater for $35 a person, including tax and tip, which is the kind of deal rarely found in theater in New York.

THEATER FOR THE NEW CITY

155 First Avenue, 254-1109; fax 979-6570

Over twenty years ago, the West Village was the place for basement theater; much of it has since moved east. Theater for the New City, the last remaining full-time bastion of experimental theater art, started at Westbeth but ultimately plunked down in the East Village.

Shows include avant-garde productions of new writers and revamped looks at standards. Ethnic and community-oriented shows abound, at about $5 per ticket.

SIDEBAR SPECIAL One-Acts

NEW DRAMATISTS
424 West 44th Street, 757-6960; fax 265-4738

ENSEMBLE STUDIO THEATER
549 West 52nd Street, second floor, 247-4982; fax 664-0041

PLAYWRIGHTS HORIZON
416 West 42nd Street, 564-1235

The city is filled with one-act plays that give both new writers and veterans a chance to vent creative spleen. Many one-acts are experiments that later evolve into fully developed two-acters; usually, though, the writer turns out to have already said what he or she wanted to, in brief.

Be sure to look into the series held at New Dramatists that introduces new works, some of which are by out-of-town playwrights staying overnight in their spacious complex.

Ensemble Studio Theater, an experimental collective, holds a yearly marathon featuring one-acts mostly by renowned writers. These twelve plays are performed in the late spring and feature big-name film and theater actors. Unlike other one-act fests, Ensemble is interested in getting a playwright exposure, not in getting a play on Broadway. Also, New Voices presents staged readings each winter for free.

The most unusual one-acts, however, are the ones by kids, for adults. The Young Playwrights Series is held yearly at the Playwrights Horizons Theater, where many Broadway-bound shows get their start. Stephen Sondheim began this series in 1980, modeling it after London's Royal Court Young Writers' Festival. Young Playwrights has since given professional productions or staged readings to works by 49 playwrights under the age of 19.

JOYCE THEATER

175 Eighth Avenue at West 19th Street, 242-0800

Joyce stages a terrific range of performances every year, from avant-garde contemporary companies to international companies focusing on traditional dance forms. Expensive pricetag.

P.S. 122

150 First Avenue at East 9th Street, 477-5288

Founded in 1977, P.S. 122 is one of the venerable performance art institutions on the downtown circuit. If you're not so up on the performance art world, P.S. 122 is a good place to experiment blindly. The theater is a small stage on the second floor of this old schoolhouse with a set of bleacher seats in front of it. It is far from attractive, but the performances will make you forget all about your surroundings. Some plays written and performed here are beautiful, some are oddball, but all are memorable. The last one I went to started around 10:30 at night and ended around 3:30 in the morning, and both the audience and the actors were excited.

ROUNDABOUT THEATER COMPANY

1530 Broadway, 869-8400; fax 869-8817

Though Broadway by name, this well-endowed company with its large and recently renovated theater spaces (several in the area) has a subscription series specifically geared to single people (including one for a gay and lesbian audience). There's a reception after each "special evening's show" and the informal gathering includes wine, soda, Dewar's—the politically correct sponsor—and even some foodstuffs. (Dewar's, I should mention, also sponsors bar nights, and you can call 1-800-8DEWARS for more of that.) Some receptions have live music. Ticket prices vary, and can be purchased in five- or three-play packages.

231

WESTBETH THEATRE CENTER

151 Bank Street, 691-2272; fax 924-7185

A wide variety of entertainment events in both table/chair/bar environments and legitimate theater settings. Tickets cost $5–$15.

AUDIENCE PARTICIPATION THEATRICAL EVENTS

ARTIFICIAL INTELLIGENCE

Artificial Intelligence is a smart bunch who decided years ago that rather than just make people laugh, they would make them join in. They got points for *A Very Vicky Christmas*, a perfect spoof of an Eydie Gorme '60s Christmas special. You were her TV audience and were told when to applaud, laugh, etc.

Now they are currently into year zillion of *Tony n' Tina's Wedding*, a laugh-riot affair for audiences, who first attend tumultuous nuptials and then get a sumptuous and eventful supper at Gus's Place, located at 149 Waverly Place, 645-8511. All for a lot of money, upwards of $50–$60 (in lieu of a gift). Go ahead and try to "break" the actors from their roles! Figure out who the Vitales and the Nunzios are—and who is married to whom in "real life." Still, my personal opinion is, skip this. Why pay big for a gimmick when you can see *two* Off-Broadway shows for the price of "half-a-one"? (See "Peanut Butter" sidebar.)

THE COMIC STRIP

1568 Second Avenue, 861-9386; fax 861-8358

They call it "showcase comedy"—an open-mike policy lets anyone get up and try to make people laugh. Sounds easy, huh? As the movie *Punch Line* demonstrated, it can be the most frightening assignment in the world. The mike is open seven nights a week, with up to fifteen comedians every night, many of them brand-spanking new.

Though the place looks like a dive—it's a drinking-man or -woman's favorite hangout—it was once home to successful comedians Eddie Murphy and Robin Williams (who still "does a few minutes" now and then).

Showcase comedy mainstays in the West Village include: **BOSTON COMEDY CLUB**, and in the same location (82 West 3rd Street, 477-1000), **SUN MOUNTAIN**

CAFE, which usually features comics seen on Letterman, Leno, Conan O'Brien, Showtime, and Comedy Central; and CHASE MANHATTAN (no phone, but found weekend nights at the corner of the bank on Houston and Broadway). Also, in Chelsea, try comedy night at REBAR (127 Eighth Avenue, 627-1680). If you're an experimenter and want further proof of the proliferation of open-miking, you can go hog wild at PIP'S in Sheepshead Bay, Brooklyn; JIMMY'S COMEDY ALLEY in Bayside, Queens; MAIN STREET out in Hackensack, New Jersey—and for the truly addicted, GRANDPA'S on Staten Island. These are hardcore open-mike hangouts—look out for ads in local papers.

FRANKLIN FURNACE ARCHIVES
http://www.franklinfurnace.org

Now twenty-one years old, Franklin Furnace began as a group that collected artist books, which are fanzine-like books of art. Once the collection was complete, it was sold to the Museum of Modern Art, where it is still displayed. After the collection was sold, Director Martha Wilson decided to move on to performance art, a medium she says is still "not tamed."

Franklin Furnace underwent a major change in 1997—they left their original workspace at 112 Franklin Street. They have no permanent home now, renting other people's workspaces, but can always be found at their new and still-under-construction Web site. The plan, according to Wilson, is to perform in different places every time and cybercast all the performances live via the Web. The ultimate goal of Franklin Furnace is to be used as an archive and research facility of the avant-garde. The schedules and show locations can always be found on their site, so go watch in person or on your computer terminal.

HASSELFREE MURDER MYSTERIES
Information: 563-5572

All over town—at cabarets, rib restaurants, bars—a funny—ha, ha—way to die is entertaining crowds and forcing them to dress up! You take your seat at the club, and before you can decide on tequila or rum, someone named Jolie starts a scene. Soon she's dead. That's the show, folks, except that in the tradition of really corny Broadway, you have to vote on who iced Jolie.

Hasselfree even provides hats so you can play the butler. The stories are

THEATER

preposterous, with catchy titles—*Dead, White and Blue*—and a game show special, *Death or Consequences.*

It's an example of something you've got to see once, if only to see what waiters do when they're not saying "Enjoy."

STAND-UP NEW YORK
236 West 78th Street, 595-0850
There are many comedy rooms in New York, as evidenced by the list on the preceding page. This one looks like a theater, with one exception: The audience decides who remains onstage—and who is thrown out.

Instead of open mike, it has an amateur "Occupational Contest" starting at midnight. Dozens of hopefuls make the audience laugh—the top prize is money! These people have included taxi drivers, teachers, lawyers, and even a pimp.

WEST BANK CAFE THEATER BAR
West Bank Downstairs Theater, 407 West 42nd Street, 695-6909
In the basement, where you'd least expect it, is a most adventurous theater home. Many well-known and aspiring show folk have developed pieces—plays, one-acts, songfests, and improvisational theater—in this laid-back setting. A free comedy show Saturday nights at midnight lets the audience members "do a few" with the comics.

Fifteen thousand people a year stumble into this downstairs mecca—and it remains a well-kept secret. That's either bad public relations work on their part—or perhaps merely careful planning.

SIDEBAR SPECIAL **Mentions of Unusual Theater Events**

Some worthwhile mentions for theater aficionados include these bits and pieces:

In addition to a regular season of well-chosen works, a great many new and known performers participate in the *O Solo Mio* festival at **NEW YORK THEATER WORKSHOP** (505-1892), held each spring at their home at 79 East 4th Street, which is becoming a little Off-Broadway center of sorts. . . . **PERRY STREET THEATER** (31

Perry Street, 691-2509) is quite an extraordinary little theater, particularly since it is the premiere home of lesbian- and gay-themed Village plays (the home of the long-running *The Night Larry Kramer Kissed Me*). . . . East Village's quite political **RAPP** (220 East 4th Street) often injects political ideas into its controversial, all-too-hip productions (e.g., *Uncle Vanya* as a man of color and slowed down to a crawl). . . . A Brooklyn-based group, **BACA DOWNTOWN** (37–39 Coenton Street, downtown Brooklyn, 718-522-4322), often produces highly unique work. . . . **DIXON PLACE** (258 Bowery between Houston and Prince, 219-3088; fax 274-9114) and a local organization called the **W O W CAFE** (59 East 4th Street, 777-4280) are, respectively, a performance artist showcase and a wild Lower East Side institution offering a full schedule of readings and performance art throughout the year. People like Eric Bogosian and Ann Magnuson often show up to hone their craft at Dixon; a few years ago Joan Rivers came back for a stint to ensure she could make loyal audiences laugh. W O W presents plays and performance pieces every weekend from September to June. The longest-running all-women (mainly lesbian) theater collective, it has been home to Split Britches, 5 Lesbian Brothers, Holly Hughes, Reno, and a host of celebrated women. Performances are usually at 8:00 P.M. on Thursday, Friday, and Saturday nights, and there is a late night cabaret beginning at 10:30 every Friday where there is an open mike and usually short acts by women. Get a schedule; find surprises galore.

 ## WHERE TO FIND THE EVER-SHRINKING BAND OF TRAVELING SHOWS

THE GLINES
Information: 354-8899

For information about some local gay theater, see the producer who keeps producing when all else fails due to lack of funding. John Glines presents an array of gay theater, and was responsible for Harvey Fierstein's *Torch Song Trilogy* both Off- and on Broadway. (The Glines also co-produced a popular Broadway gig, *As Is.*) The Glines have been presenting too many shows written by Glines himself. One show not the case was *Get Used to It: A Gay Musical Revue*, by Tom Wilson, performed at Courtyard Playhouse (426 West 46th Street, 765-9540; good to be on that theater's mailing list). Write The Glines at 240 West 44th Street, New York, NY, 10036, for more information.

BREAD AND ROSES PROJECT
Information: 631-4565
This company performs rap, R & B, and ballads about the plights of hospital workers to very appreciative crowds of hospital workers and union members. Their shows are constantly changing, so catch as catch can. Call for details.

HOSPITAL AUDIENCES, INC.
221 West 41st Street, 575-7660; fax 575-7669
With an eye to the less fortunate, this mostly volunteer organization brings theater, music, and joy to the hospitalized and homebound in a program called "Art for Healing." They also offer a selection of special events tailored to the needs of the disabled and the homeless.

HAI gets the most visibility when 25,000 disabled and elderly patrons receive free culture in the city's parks. To see HAI in action is to see professionals with a purpose.

MABOU MINES
150 First Avenue between 9th and 10th Streets, 473-0559; fax 473-2410
This mostly avant-garde theater troupe recently converted its small rehearsal studio into a small, 60-seat theater for the occasional play. Mostly, Mabou Mines rents spaces throughout the city to show its award-winning performances. In 1996 the group won five Obie awards for its play *Peter and Wendy,* based on *Peter Pan.* Mabou Mines performs puppet plays, original works, and even pieces by Beckett. Call the above number for locations and shows.

Taking Peanuts out of Peanut Butter—
Why Theater Could Die A Slow Death

For months people have been wondering in the newspapers about the theater situation in New York. Ah, who cares? According to thousands of people I've spoken to recently, New Yorkers don't care about theater. And for good reason. Broadway is that reason.

Saying that BROADWAY is all the theater that "makes" New York is like taking peanuts out of peanut butter. So the real question is:

Would you pay $65 to see a wedding if you didn't know the family?

Doubtful. We talked about it in a series of messages on the Native's Guide to New York Forum on CompuServe. I asked people why they spend so much time with Tom Cruise and not enough with the playwrights of our time.

The angst-filled answer? Money, the filthy greed of not just Broadway but Off-Broadway producers.

The wedding is a perfect metaphor for what's wrong with theater today: *Tony 'n Tina's Wedding* is a funny little idea that invites people to witness a "real Italian festivity, buffoons and all" (said the silly ad) but is way, way expensive, even by wedding standards.

Tony and Tina's blissful time started out as a $30 fun night in the Village nine years ago when the interactive site-specific theater got popular and, voilà!, the price doubled!

One forum member started the discussion: What goes through producers' heads when they up the price of a show like that? Don't they realize that while people might go (once), these theater people are killing their favorite industry?

Other forum members remarked: "I think the city's number one arts commodity, the not-known theater world, is close to

THEATER

dead. Spend that kind of money for a night in a not-proven play? Nah. The film's the thing nowadays."

"Who are these people to think they can charge so much and expect us to come back again and again?"

"It's bad enough that we have to sit through old washed-out revivals uptown, but to be told any play that gets a great review is worthy of 60 bucks of hard-earned cash . . . doesn't cut it."

"We feel taken advantage of by anything Off-Broadway that achieves success."

Light at the tunnel's end: After years of overpricing customers with a $65 wedding, the ninth year of Tony and Tina's marital status brought on reduced Discount Coupons/Twofers: $39 for an evening at a church. Harumph!, the forum members remarked.

"Come on, it's a fake wedding and a little pasta!"

PUERTO RICAN TRAVELING THEATER
304 West 47th Street, 354-1293; fax 307-6769

Every summer, this Hispanic collective's brightest and most unusual concepts are happily played for New York City passersby. Bilingual presentations of shows relating to the Hispanic experience are done in parks, in cul-de-sacs, and on street corners.

Their theater base churns out a yearly body of fine new or classic Latin plays, often importing Latin American and European writers and directors. The company is a collaborative effort, and members execute all the aspects of production.

And several fabulous, though not famous, actors have starred in these shows, just to pursue their art.

Tickets are $20 for adults, and $17 for seniors and students.

RIVERSIDE SHAKESPEARE COMPANY

Riverside claims to take its cue from the Master: Everyone who appears in its shows is trained to be a Shakespearean actor, so he or she can handle both the Bard's words and the language of modern writers. In winter you can find them at the Riverside Shakespeare Theater, 165 West 86th Street. In the summertime it's all Bard, as Riverside takes to city parks and presents free and highly inventive Shakespearean works.

"Sunday in the Park with Shakespeare" is held in Riverside Park on the Upper West Side. They also go to the boroughs, even making a stop at Staten Island's picturesque Snug Harbor.

Funded in part by either Ben or Jerry, or perhaps both. Ads for summer shows appear in local weeklies and the Sunday *New York Times*.

WOMEN'S PROJECT
55 West End Avenue, 765-1706; fax 765-2024

Here is a company that presents only new and reconceived works by women, usually directed by women, and with topics that concern women.

Its founders believe that women are greatly underrepresented in these fields. Women's theater has come a long way of late, particularly with the independence of this company that began as a well-funded appendage to the American Place Theatre.

Now the Women's Project is a traveling theater company, renting spaces throughout the city.

The company also has an educational program, "Ten Centuries of Women Playwrights." This gives high school students a history of female playwrights, and provides them with the opportunity to write and direct plays themselves. The Women's Project takes pride in the fact that the number of women playwrights and directors in the theater industry is ever increasing, and their ultimate goal is to have an equal amount of men and women in these positions.

The company has performed plays devoted to women's issues all around town. Nothing here is ever tedious in spirit or subject matter.

EXTRA: MAINSTREAM THEATER HINTS

Here are more mainstream events and notably the best of New York's popular theater scene:

AMERICAN PLACE THEATER (111 West 46th Street, 840-3074) is a regular theater space rental house that presents women-oriented theater, too. Also, contemporary shows by new and tried/true writers, not to mention comedy nights. . . . **ART AT ST. ANN'S** (157 Montague Street, Brooklyn Heights, 718-858-2424; fax 718-522-2470) is housed at St. Ann's Church and is a great theater to be on a mailing list for: They are known to compose ideas relating to culture. Fall season is October through December, spring season is March through May. . . . **WPA THEATER** (519 West 23rd Street, 206-0523; fax 627-7154) offers great plays and some losers from little- or well-known writers. Buy a cheap ticket subscription for a season (four plays per season) to see the shows before they become hits. WPA got famous as originator of *Little Shop Of Horrors* in the '70s. It also was the first to show *Steel Magnolias* and the AIDS-era comedy *Jeffrey* by Paul Rudnick; its worst production was *Watbanaland* by Douglas Wright.

LATE-BREAKING BROADWAY: HOW TO GO CHEAP

THEATER DEVELOPMENT FUND

Mailing address: 1501 Broadway, 21st floor, New York, NY 10036, 221-0885; information on tickets and events, 768-1818

Subscribers to TDF take advantage of cheap seats to new Off-Broadway and Broadway shows, offered when TDF subsidizes shows and buys large blocks of discounted seats that are then turned over to the subscribers.

TDF sells half-price tickets (with a $2.50 service charge), but often for better seats than those available from "TKTS" booths at Duffy Square on West 47th Street, 2 World Trade Center, and in Brooklyn Heights. Call them at their newly furnished information line above.

But now the rules have changed to accommodate a Broadway so darn expensive even half-price means that for many, it's only a third off the price you expected. Or even only a quarter off. Here are the rules:

How do I go about getting Broadway and Off-Broadway tickets on the cheap? Here are two ways. Write to the Theater Development Fund. Send them $14 and they'll send you vouchers for really cheap Broadway shows. TDF also runs the famed "TKTS" booths (note locations above), which were recently redesigned for quicker service. The ticket booths sell day-of-show tickets for half price, often for less than half (at the World Trade

Center you can buy weekend tickets on Friday), plus a $2.50 service charge.

The second thing to do is send a self-addressed stamped envelope to the Hit Show Club, the people who manufacture and distribute "twofer" coupons that are redeemable at the box office for a third off nearly any Broadway show. Call 581-4211 for more info; ask about special non-member prices on Broadway.

STANDING ROOM AND STUDENT TICKETS

Cameron Mackintosh, the esteemed and embattled producer of *Miss Saigon, Les Misérables,* and among others, *Phantom of the Opera,* introduced a policy giving those with student ID's balcony or rear orchestra seats during the week for just $16. He probably figured that young or adult students need an incentive to go to the theater, or the future generation will put him out of business!

Many large theaters sell standing-room tickets, at $10–$15, but only if a show is nearly sold out. Once you get in, keep a lookout for empty seats. Check with box offices.

Of course, if you are willing to wait until the last second, stand outside the box office and look for men and women, hands aflutter, desperate to get rid of extra tickets. If you wait until five minutes before curtain, it's a buyer's market.

There's always getting a ticket from a friend who knows someone in the band. Or sneak in during the intermission, everyone knows it's doable!

SPECIAL ADVICE FOR THURSDAY NIGHTS

On Thursdays around 8:00 P.M., unknown to most ticket buyers, that weekend's "house tickets," or good seats held by the press office and producer's office, are released to the public. So get in line and wait until eight. Who says there's no way to get a great seat at the last minute, at regular price, for Saturday night?

Broadway prices are going up up up. It was amazing when *Miss Saigon* posted a top ticket price of $100 for an event that would be over in a matter of hours (though granted, it's a wonderful, heartbreaking show). However, a new alliance of Broadway productions—the Broadway Alliance—is offering a top price of around $24 (except for recent big hits like *Love! Valour! Compassion!*)* because everyone involved is taking a cut in pay. The participating theaters (Nederlander, Belasco, others) are listed in the "ABCs" of the *New York Times*, which are the theatrical classified ads in the arts pages. Take a look—and peek at some new Broadway drama. It's worth it.

Obviously, theater lovers should follow the news in the theater column in the *New York Times*'s Weekend section on Fridays. In that section are the biggest reviews of the week of plays and musicals, and news about special offers. In fact, all the newspapers devote entire snippets on future dates and possible shows in the works (most of which should be considered hyperbole until the ink dries on the contracts—and even then . . .). The *Times*'s Sunday Arts and Leisure section and all of Friday's papers truly help, as do lots of the freebies that you can pick up on corners in green, blue, and red boxes—and in your local diner or coffee haven. The theater critics report freely on upcoming events, unusual and mainstream offerings, and famous and obscure people.

The magazine *In-Theater Weekly* is, unbelievably, the only New York weekly catering exclusively to theater. Its 70-odd pages are devoted to future Broadway and Off-Broadway shows, with detailed stories about theatrical persons in the news.

Playbill, Encore, and *Official Broadway Theater Guide* list lots of theater and also give out helpful phone numbers. *City Guide,* a free magazine available on stands throughout Times Square, offers an articles-and-listings guide to the best of current and future Broadway, and often prints offbeat articles about unhyped events.

City Guide is usually overlooked as "for tourists only," but it has been in business for over a decade and there's a reason why: The information, although corny, is relevant and accurate—even the gossip is dependable.

Also, see Ward Moorehouse in the *New York Post* or Patrick Pacheco, a freelancer, in *Newsday* ("Play By Play") for gossip galore. Both are good

---

* Anytime something becomes a hit, the rules change. For instance, everyone was nervous when *Jerome Robbins' Broadway* opened, because it seemed like the "Carol Burnett Show" for New Yorkers (a revue of lots of shows). As soon as the reviews called it fantastic, the price skyrocketed. What, me, nervous? said the producers boldly . . .

sources—a little too much glitz for me, but you can't beg for types of coverage during a dearth!

Hints: Free kids tickets to Broadway offered to adults who pay full price. Call 563-BWAY for details. . . . Call 302-4111 (888-411-BWAY if you're out of town) to get instant info/tickets for Broadway. . . . And lastly, read *Hot Seats* (989-5257), a rag given freely by the aforementioned Alliance to Off-Broadway fans. It's available throughout midtown and downtown at select theaters (and theaterati-hangouts).

TICKETS-BY-PHONE DILEMMA

Tickets are a sore issue with most people who have ever tried to get them by phone. Surcharges are deadly—you pay a charge for the ticket and an additional one for the handling (this by Ticketmaster, Telecharge, call it by any other name). Truth be told, we're the ones getting the handling: it's a total ripoff and my advice is go to the theater. Box office lines are never very long—okay, maybe the day after the Tony awards.

There's something else to keep in mind if you hit the phones and buy a ducat or two, know that there's a law now: Theaters, concert halls, places-of-interest, even sporting events, have to tell you the seat numbers. If they say no, report them to the Consumer Affairs Office. I did. I tried to buy a pair over the phone for *Stomp*, the ages-old cute tourist attraction that makes music out of noise down at the Orpheum Theater (Second Avenue and St. Marks Place). I asked nicely for seat locations and was told they would not give me the seat locations because, "We want to have the right to change them at the last minute." Duh. Sure they do. That's why the law came about! *Stomp* is being stomped on as we speak.

18

La Club

FLAMINGO EAST

219 Second Avenue between 13th and 14th Streets, 533-2860

There are two vastly different floors here. Downstairs is a steakhouse of sorts and a bar, upstairs is a private party room, used on several nights for partying publicly. (Wednesday is Salon Wednesday, hosted each week with performances by several famed downtown drag queens, starting at 11:00 P.M.)

A great watering hole, kind of dark, often written about as "the Jetsons meet the Flintstones." It's a pretty fashionable crowd and the place is high energy, if that's what you're seeking. Open Monday through Sunday, 11:00 A.M.–3:00 A.M.

MANNY'S CAR WASH

1558 Third Avenue, 369-BLUE

A blues club for dancing and cavorting, this is the Upper East Side's biggest hangout, no contest, featuring some of the best national and regional blues bands. They answer the phones there: "There is no Manny. This is not a car wash." No cover on Sunday, but on all other nights (till 3:30 A.M. on Friday and Saturday and 2:00 A.M. other nights) it's either $3 or $12, depending on who's playing. Quite a sight, worth it for the blues parties where people are wearing shades at night.

ARLENE'S GROCERY
95 Stanton Street, 358-1633

Just like Manny's is not a car wash, this is never gonna be a grocery store. Arlene's is instead one of the best jazz clubs in town! There are live music performances every night, and there is never a cover charge. Celebrity performers of the past have included David Bowie, Lou Reed, Dr. John, a mellowed Joe Jackson, Joan Osborne, and David Byrne. So after a long, frustrating day at the office, call Arlene's, check out the schedule for the evening, and go unwind to some tunes. It's the coolest little venue in town. This year.

ROXY
515 West 18th Street, 645-5156

The most interesting club is one that still does what it said it would do when it started, namely Roxy, which has been in business for around twenty years (a year or two as "10–18," but still Roxy to those in the know). It offers roller skating on Tuesday for a basically okay crowd, and serious disco and dance-hall music on Saturday nights. Saturday is about 80 percent to 20 percent, straight to gay, but it's still a cool crowd, especially terrific to watch and mix with. This is the crowd that for some reason keeps coming back year after year. Which is odd in a city that changes tastes with undergear!

But there's a downside: like every other club in town, the Roxy has a door policy (they call the bouncer a door censor!) and are picky about whom they allow to enter. It's a little silly, considering they charge $10–$15 for admission, $5.50 for beer, and about $10 for anything harder. Don't like the way that sounds? Do what I do when they get elitist, spend your money elsewhere.

NELL'S
246 West 14th Street, 675-1567

What used to be the hottest place in creation is now merely a place for budding musicians. Which is not a bad thing at all!

New bands on Sunday; funky buddha on Monday; techno on Wednesday; the art crowd and a fashion "thing" on Thursday; and what they call international music on Fridays. Saturday—jazz! all weekend long. Nell, meanwhile, is the character from *Rocky Horror Picture Show.* And quite a character is she, for she once opened an uptown Nell's, which closed.

THE KNITTING FACTORY
74 Leonard Street, 219-3055

With a café over to the side, some of the city's best jazz or punk bands, and readings too, the Factory has broken through as the best place to spend an evening. But check out the night's schedule before you go. Sometimes they hold Composers' Forums with jazz trios, duos, and performance artists. Other times it might be a grab bag with local and touring bands. This is a great place to pick up tickets to other shows in the area (see the lobby).

PYRAMID LOUNGE
101 Avenue A, 420-1590

Pyramid, winding its way back after being closed down by the city for an illegal second bar, will reopen sometime in '98 with the same motif: About fifteen years ago, Pyramid arrived and installed a bar, a disco room, a movie screen, and a cellar for sitting and drinking. Fine. Then ads touted the "World Famous Pyramid," mainly because tourists had made it their night haunt. It's authentic East Village, but the best part of the Pyramid is hardly the weekend jamboree. Laid-back weekdays will have you dancing to a funky spin with a Bass Ale in one hand.

On the other hand, most people attend because the Pyramid has drag shows after midnight on Sundays, which are always entertaining. The DJ plays Prince, the Archies, and Springsteen in a single set.

ELEMENT ZERO
215 East 10th Street, 780-9855; http://www.elementzero.com

Yes, they even have a Web site. Isn't technology magnificent? Speaking of, this club, with its comfy couches and walls adorned with artwork from local starving artists, specializes in American and European-style serious electronica (i.e., drums-n-bass) on Saturday nights, where the party is called "Elevator." Usually no cover, but there is a one-drink minimum. Young, sorta-hip crowd, nice if you go for that sort.

S.O.B.'S (SOUNDS OF BRAZIL)
204 Varick Street, 243-4940

Some of the best Latin sounds in the city come from S.O.B.'s, a name that means what it sounds like but actually stands for Sounds of Brazil. It's not all sounds from Rio—they also come from Buenos Aires and Long Island City, and places in between.

This is the place to go for shake-down music. Where else can you hear berimbau, cuica, Carnaval drums, and even Average White Band, in the course of one month? The cover is steep, but comfort minus attitude is quite an equation. Bahian cuisine is a wow—including cream sauces and Brazil's national dish, the scrumptious feijoada. Opens at 8:00 P.M., cover is $15–$20, and often more.

SIDEBAR SPECIAL Learn To Dance—There's No Excuse

SUMMER DANCE EVENTS

Big Apple Tango Weekend
Workshops and performances all over the city; first weekend in August, 245-5200.

Forever Tango
June through August at the Walter Kerr Theater, 218 West 48th Street, 239-6300.

Hit and Run Tango
At the Bethesda Fountain in Central Park, every Saturday from 5:00 P.M. untily dark.

Midsummer Night Swing
At Lincoln Center Plaza, 721-6500.

LESSONS AND PRACTICE

Dance Manhattan
Classes in most forms of dance including tango; 39 West 19th Street, 807-0802.

Dance New York
Tango and Latin dance classes; 237 West 54th Street, 677-9314.

DanceSport
Classes and practice sessions weekly; 1845 Broadway, 307-1111.

Djoniba Dance & Drum Centre
Afro-Cuban, salsa, mambo; 37 East 18th Street, 477-3464.

Fred Astaire Dance Studio
Bolero, tango, salsa, samba, ballroom dancing; 207–29 Northern Boulevard, Bayside, 718-225-1980.

Los Milongueros
For men only on Tuesdays; 440 Lafayette Street, fourth floor, 866-5827.

Sandra Cameron Dance Center
Tango, Latin salons, and workshops; 20 Cooper Square, 674-0505.

Stepping Out
Classes in Latin, tango, ballroom, many varieties; 1780 Broadway, 245-5200.

HANGOUTS (OFTEN WITH A TEACHER WILLING TO HELP, AS IN MY FAIR LADY)

Bistro Latino
Latin dancing Friday and Saturday, tango class Wednesday, samba night Thursday; 1711 Broadway, 956-1000.

Il Campinello
Thursday night tango classes; 136 West 31st Street, 695-6111.

La Belle Epoque
Tango first and third Fridays of the month; 827 Broadway, 254-6436.

S.O.B.'s (Sounds of Brazil)
Tango on Sunday, salsa on Monday; 200 Varick Street, 243-4940. As discussed in the chapter: best Latin romp.

Latin Quarter
Big bands, big dance floor; 2551 Broadway, 864-7600.

Les Poulets
Salsa and merengue Wednesday through Sunday; 16 West 22nd Street, 229-2000.

Broadway II
Salsa bands Friday and Saturday; 2700 Queens Plaza South, 718-937-7111.

Bayamo
Salsa Tuesdays; 704 Broadway, 475-5151.

El Flamingo
Salsa Sunday evenings; 547 West 21st Street, 243-2121.

Tango Hotline

Recorded listing of events, classes, etc. Updated daily; 718-35TANGO.

The above information was contributed, happily, by Suki John. John is a dance and politics writer for the *Village Voice*.

In addition, here is what the people from Native's Guide's Forum have to recommend to us:

- Try magazines like *Ballroom Review,* available at Hudson News (753 Broadway, 674-6655), or the *New York Press* to find lots of listings of dance events.
- **RAINBOW ROOM** (30 Rockefeller Plaza, 632-5000). Tango and ballroom every night; all couples welcome.
- **WELLS RESTAURANT** (2246–49 Adam Clayton Powell Blvd. at 132nd Street, 234-0700). A fancy-schmancy, old-fashioned place.
- **LOUISIANA COMMUNITY BAR AND GRILL** (622 Broadway at Bleecker Street, 460-9633). The newfangled dance hall.
- **SWING 46 JAZZ CLUB** (349 West 46th Street, 262-9554).
- **GREATEST BAR ON EARTH** (in name only), at One World Trade Center, Windows on the World, 524-7011.
- **ROSELAND BALLROOM** (239 West 52nd Street, 247-0200). An endangered species, hoping to hang on as long as possible. Old-fashioned.
- **SUPPER CLUB RESTAURANT** (240 West 47th Street, 921-1940). Seventeen-piece swing band on Friday and Saturday nights.

WEBSTER HALL

125 East 11th Street at Third Avenue, 353-1600;

http://www.webster-hall.com

Webster Hall (in the space where The Ritz stood for years) is one of the most popular clubs in the city, if not *the* most popular. I have to say that the crowd is tacky. And yet still this huge club offers four different dance floors with four different DJs, spinning everything from the golden oldies of the 1950s to techno ("it's bloody techno, dahling") music. You will see it all here, from preppy college students to drag queens to Super Guidos. Cover varies depending on the night and show (call for schedule information).

Sometimes cover gets steep, but if you have Internet access, visit the club's Web site, where you can sign up on the guest list for that evening and pay as little as $5 to get in the door. It's a cool way to seem like you know everyone/everything. And yet, again I must caution you that drinks are expensive; but most come to dance, not drink.

Open only on Thursday, Friday, and Saturday, this club actually has a dress code (nothing major, just no sneakers, torn jeans, or baseball hats), so make sure you look halfway presentable!

Last note: anyone with brains would open an Advil stand and make a fortune; the rooms are just totally noisy!

FLOATING NIGHTCLUBS, AN EXPLANATION

Clubs sometimes pop up with names like Payday, Milky Way, $100,000 Bar, and the Hotel Amazon (notice many are named for candy!), never warn you about their location, and usually only stick around for, at most, two weekends. You just have to "know," says a former publisher of a now-defunct downtown-based magazine. This man, who was responsible for one or more of these events, explains that because securing a liquor license is not always a priority, he prefers anonymity.

At these clubs, which are as rare as $2 bills, music is hot—with hip-hop played for crowds who schmooze, network, dance, drink, and never get rowdy. If you are anxious to see one of these floating clubs in action, go to some East Village, Soho, or Noho boutique and look by the cash register for "invitations" that may or may not get you admitted. Try Tower Records' locations, HMV Records, Disc-O-Rama in the Village, or your video store to find invites. Or Astor Place Haircutters in the Village.

One place that keeps opening up and then closing again, but is a floating nightclub of sorts, is **THE SPACE** (555 West 33rd Street, 947-0400) and it is in the floating category because it keeps changing hands and nobody can tell what it is from day to day. Once called Octagon, this is the one place where dancing in a large cavern (and even going after work) can be okay, but it is pretty much a place for people over forty who can handle the Advil requirements of dancing in a place that has no escape hatch—it is loud everywhere. And the music isn't half-bad.

WHERE ELSE TO GO

This is a list of places that cannot be wholeheartedly recommended, but I add here just so you know I know them:

Nightclubbing in New York is no longer a divided scene, with "gay nights" and "straight nights." Partiers of all orientations can check into clubs all nights of the week. **EDELWEISS** (629-1021) is at 23 West 39th Street, but no longer the great transvestite-gender bender wonderhouse it once was. They moved it to a famous 20th Street club route, but the place got vandalized *before* it officially opened. Call to be sure that they haven't moved again. If you're on the lookout for a good show (drag), this $5–$10 hangout is your best bet. On Fridays and Saturdays it's half price for couples. Aw, it's family values. Also try Escuelita—see below.

The constantly changing **GROOVE** (565 West 23rd Street; $2–$7) opens at 10:00 P.M. and features go-go dancers. Not much else. A large dance space. Mostly happening on Monday nights.

Salon Wednesday is a hot thing at the previously mentioned **FLAMINGO EAST** (219 Second Avenue, 533-2860), where soul aficionados jam with a great DJ and many of the most inspiring drag queens you've ever met. Free. These are nights you drink, sweat, and never regret.

LA NUEVA ESCUELITA (301 West 39th Street, 631-0588), which never had a phone number until recently, is a dark place in the midst of the Times Square scene, with boys, some girls, some "mixed-scene" (I'll let you figure it out on your own), a floor show, and a helluva sound system in the dance hall. You can dance if you want, but I usually choose the show. (Hint: On Saturdays around 2:00 A.M., this place kicks.)

Gay and lesbian nights at **COLUMBIA UNIVERSITY DANCES** (Earl Hall, 116th

Street and Broadway, 629-1989), the third Saturday of each month, are titled "SamE BuT DifferenT." Admission is $5. Mix of students, wallflow-
ers, pretty boys, and sexy gals. Sort of a gay Junior Prom. . . .
SOUND FACTORY (460 West 46th Street, 489-0001) is a hellhole of
house music and sweaty bodies. No liquor, but then again, they
open at 3:00 A.M. People *pay* about $20 as cover charge because the scene is
an asset worth paying for. Means it's popular*. . . . **SYSTEM** (76 East 13th
Street) is a club open on weekend nights, quite pretty, but steaming up as
one helluva hot club on Sunday nights for gay men. Nearly a million dollars
in renovations from the days when this was Cat Club make this, at least,
quite gorgeous.

EXTRA: MORE CLUBS IN NEW YORK

A lot of clubs think they're hot, but may only be for fifteen minutes. Here's
a look at some of the ones we imagine will still be here in mid-1998. Hope-
fully. Keep in mind that some bars—including a few mentioned just ahead
in Chapter 19—think of themselves as clubs (i.e., music spaces). But for the
purposes of this sidebar, let's talk about real music.

Dewar's Straight No Chaser (whatever that means) presents parties at the
SUPPER CLUB on Tuesdays (240 West 47th Street). However, Supper Club is
no extravagant hangout; since the club was sold, you never can tell what will
be happening there! Cover is $12. The place's bouncers are people with egos
the size of Mt. Everest.

Just on the safe side, let me say that if you fear being turned away at the
door at any of these so-called experimental nightclubs, get a bunch of invites
from places that are packed with "early-twenties types," such as **ASTOR PLACE
HAIRCUTTERS,** Astor Place and Broadway. This place was discussed in Chapter 16—haircuts, music, good-looking daytime crowds, free invites, and my
friend Jay, the haircutter—from Russia with love.

It's a phenom, but Tuesday night is still best at **JACKIE 60** after nearly a
decade. It's a house party, and DJ Tedsmooth offers "Funk Hut" all the

---

* The Sound Factory has membership cards available at most area music stores for reduced
entry; it's worth it to get one. If you can dance.

livelong night. Nice club, weird vibe. At 432 West 14th Street, all the way west at Washington Street. (See other uses for this club space later in this section.)

CHINA CLUB is still open, at 2130 Broadway (at 74th Street) and, on Thursdays, Prestige Promotions presents the night of absolute dweebs, which I say you should check out once. Their invite reads, "No hats, no sneakers, no Timberlands, no baggy jeans, no large earrings, no bulky gold, no exceptions." And I'm sure no fun, unless you go to make fun of this place. Which I'd do.

Giant Step Thursdays is the $10 dance night at the club we've seen open and close constantly, **BANK** (225 East Houston, 714-8001). The management asks you to call first for any details. Times and places are known to change. This is close to the **MERCURY LOUNGE,** near the corner of Stanton and Houston (260-4700), a great, albeit tiny-as-heck, and insanely dark club that hosts just about every type of music people pay to hear.

Here now the rest . . .

The point of this section is to allow you a taste of the places, in certain neighborhoods, with the best selection of monickers! If you want to go and get yourself some tunes, these are the experimental spaces. PS: These are "B" clubs, not to be confused with mainstays in the neighborhoods or others in this section.

Avenue A Sushi

103 Avenue A between 6th and 7th Streets, 982-8109. Monday–Sunday, 5:00 P.M.–2:00 A.M. A very nice place for a plate of cold fish—some bands, some nights.

Bar d'O

29 Bedford Street at Houston Street and Sixth Avenue, 627-1580. Sunday–Thursday, 7:00 P.M.–3:00 A.M.; Friday–Saturday, 7:00 P.M.–4:00 A.M. Very drag-oriented, cute crowd too (mixed, always). The show is on weekends and includes legends (e.g., dragster Joey Arias).

Bar 6

502 Sixth Avenue between 12th and 13th Streets, 645-2439. Monday–Sunday, 12:00 P.M.–3:00 A.M. Only Sundays are really hot here—and they schedule the DJ spinning "Nu-Soul" yet. The food, however, is exceptional, and the crowd rocks. Try the couscous and shrimp. Then dance.

bOb

235 Eldridge Street between Houston and Stanton Streets, 777-0588. Monday–Sunday, 7:00 P.M.–4:00 A.M. This place cracks us up—what a name and how they spell it out, too.

Botanica

47 Houston Street between Mott and Mulberry Streets, 343-7251. Monday–Friday, 5:00 P.M.–4:00 A.M.; Saturday–Sunday, 6:00 P.M.–4:00 A.M.

Carbon

605 West 55th Street between Eleventh and Twelfth Avenues, 582-8282. Thursday, Friday, 10:00 P.M.–4:00 A.M.; Saturday, 10:00 P.M.–5:00 A.M. A copy, natch.

Chaos

23 Watts Street between West Broadway and Thompson Street, 925-8966. Monday–Sunday, 5:00 P.M.–4:00 A.M. None I could see—late-night calm crowd.

Cheetah

12 West 21st Street between Fifth and Sixth Avenues, 206-7770. Monday–Saturday, 9:30 P.M.–4:00 A.M. Ee-eee. (Had to say that.) A really new bar/club with many experiences, changing nightly. This block, meanwhile, is and has been since the late '70s, the street with the most nightclubs that change!

Circa

103 Second Avenue at 6th Street, 777-4120. Monday–Thursday, 6:00 P.M.–midnight; Friday, 6:00 P.M.–1:00 A.M.; Saturday–Sunday, 5:00 P.M.–4:00 A.M. The only club-cum-bar-cum-lounge area I have seen with a name that has naught to do with its surroundings (i.e., circa *what?*).

Coney Island High

15 St. Marks Place between Second and Third Avenues, 674-7959. Monday–Sunday, 5:00 P.M.–4:00 A.M. Once Boy Bar, then a cruisey gay place, and now a mixed club where rockers go to hang out and veg.

The Cooler

416 West 14th Street at Ninth Avenue, 645-5189 or 229-0785—also a fax. Monday–Thursday, 8:00 P.M.–4:00 A.M.; Friday–Saturday, 9:00 P.M.–4:00 A.M. Another one of those west-west 14th Street dives, a name a night. Lots of music—stop by. Loud.

Decade

1117 First Avenue at 61st Street, 835-5979. Tuesday–Friday, 6:00 P.M.–2:00 A.M. From what I could see—and my friend at the *New York Times* said it quite aptly—"this is a place that refuses to call itself a club." It's a club. Just a club. Still, it wants to be a salon. Figures.

Dusk of London

147 West 24th Street between Sixth and Seventh Avenues, 924-4490. Monday–Wednesday, 5:00 P.M.–2:00 A.M.; Thursday–Saturday 7:00 P.M.–2:00 A.M. One of the prettiest new bars—lots of great 'tenders, some celebs, a nice couch-filled congregation center—and a gimmick: Buy a bottle, they'll tag it and *hold* the thing for you every single gosh-darn night. (*Veddy* British.) (Also "cheap" if you think of using it during six or seven visits!)

Fat Boy

409 West 14th Street between Ninth and Tenth Avenues, 367-9054. Wednesday–Sunday, 11:00 A.M.–3:00 A.M. As in frat boy.

Hell
59 Ganesvoort Street between Greenwich and Washington Streets, 727-1666. Monday–Sunday, 7:00 P.M.–4:00 A.M. A really cool gay bar with a lot of dressed (i.e., costumed) men—note we said men and not boys. Interestingly, *women* are here, too. Odd for downtown. (And nice chairs.)

In Da Village, see the newest "gay scene" bar—**JUNGLE,** at 12th and West Streets. Very chic, for now.

Jet Lounge
286 Spring Street between Varick and Husdon Streets, 675-2277. Tuesday–Saturday, 9:00 P.M.–4:00 A.M. As in Bennie and the . . .

Life/The Ki Club
158 Bleecker Street at Thompson Street, 420-1999. Hours vary. A very hip club now, because so little is left in the West Village. Eeeevryone plays here, it seems.

Limelight
Sixth Avenue and 21st Street, 807-7850 Open real late, kids. Once a church, then a drug rehab center. Then a club. Back again. Mazeltov.

Liquidity/Black Star
92 Second Avenue between 5th and 6th Streets, 254-4747. Monday–Sunday, 5:00 P.M.–4:00 A.M. Not to be confused with Liquids, next, and Liquid, from Miami, which is scheduled to open in New York soon (Ingrid, Madonna's ex-'s place).

Liquids
266 East 10th Street between Avenue A and First Avenue, 677-1717. Monday–Sunday, 7:00 P.M.–4:00 A.M. Who can figure? The scene here changes and changes. Also, nearby, is the trendy nondescript **RIVERTOWN LOUNGE** (187 Orchard Street, 388-1288). Now what's so crazy about this is you make your own Bloody Mary's every Sunday. Mmm—gooooood.

Lounge

188 Avenue A at 12th Street, 777-6254. Thursday–Saturday, 11:00 P.M.–4:00 A.M. A nondescript place with a nondescript name, fer sher.

Mantra

28 East 23rd Street between Madison Avenue and Park Avenue South, 254-6117. Hours vary. Newcomer to the area, where places like Live Bait serve beer to underaged (to me) drinkers. "Too soon to tell" is *my* mantra.

Meow Mix

269 Houston Street at Suffolk Street, 254-0688. Tuesday–Sunday, 8:00 P.M.–4:00 A.M. Hot lezzy club that gets mixed crowds and accepts us all. *Very* pop-u-lar. Featured in *Chasing Amy,* in a fun light.

Metronome

915 Broadway at 21st Street, 505-7400. Hours vary. A big club that is also a restaurant, but mostly a gents and ladies pickup place.

Mother

432 West 14th Street at Washington Street, 366-5680. Hours vary. Not my mother, meanwhile. A very dark place.

Motor City Bar

127 Ludlow Street between Rivington and Delancey Streets, 358-1595. Seven days a week, 4:00 P.M.–4:00 A.M. Just like Detroit, only classier. (Oooh.) No special events, no Supremes. Nothing. Oh: Liquor.

Mystic

217 West 85th Street between Broadway and Amsterdam Avenue, 874-6241. Thursday, 10:00 P.M.–3:00 A.M.; Friday–Saturday, 11:00 P.M.–4:00 A.M. An Upper West Side (new) mainstay. Guest DJs and food (separately).

New Music Cafe

380 Canal Street at West Broadway, 941-1019. Monday–Sunday, doors open at 9:00 P.M. Closing times vary. A very nice place, mentioned else-

where in the book; reminiscent of the old Siné in the East Village. Lots of new, earth/world music and chanting going on.

Nowbar
22 Seventh Avenue at Leroy Street, 293-0323. Hours vary. See the club section. Owned by Mason Reese of bologna sandwich fame. A sense of self-importance looms over the door, yet the inside is shamelessly upbeat. But at least his sandwich had a "name."

NV
289 Spring Street at Hudson Street, 929-NVNV. Wednesday–Friday, 4:30 P.M.–4:00 A.M.; Saturday, 8:00 P.M.–4:00 A.M. No vay. (Grungy garage band bar with a lot of napkins that say "NV.")

New York City Jukebox/Voodoo Lounge
304 East 39th Street at Second Avenue, 685-1556. Hours vary. Not a better or more exciting place for blocks, but you are in a sort of no man's land for music (lots of Irish places, including a few bars where the folks here *swear* Sinead O'Connor hangs.)

Opera
539 West 21st Street between Tenth and Eleventh Avenues, 229-1618. Hours vary. A nice looking crowd, music varies.

Opium Den
29 East 3rd Street between Bowery and Second Avenue, 505-7344. Monday–Sunday, 8:00 P.M.–4:00 A.M. Not what you think.

Planet 28/Clubhouse
215 West 28th Street between Seventh and Eighth Avenues, 726-8820. Hours vary. I keep walking by this place hoping to see it open; never have. Can you say, "Waste your time"?

Plush
431 West 14th Street between Ninth Avenue and Washington Street, 367-7035. Hours vary. Very nice-looking space, no music as far as I can see.

Pulse

226 East 54th Street between Second and Third Avenues, 688-5577. Hours vary. So far, the attitude is happenin' . . . Check the pulse. (I should charge them for that slogan.)

Rebar

127 Eighth Avenue at 16th Street, 627-1680. Monday–Saturday, 8:00 P.M.–4:00 A.M. A formerly you-can't-touch-this dive that is now, well, a dive. (Comedy on Mondays, as mentioned in Chapter 17.)

XVI

16 First Avenue between 1st and 2nd Streets, 260-1549. Hours vary. So, 'splain that name.

Spoon

12 Avenue A between Houston and 2nd Streets, 477-9050. Monday–Friday, 4:00 P.M.–4:00 A.M.; Saturday–Sunday, 7:00 P.M.–4:00 A.M. No spooning going on at this tiny joint; great neck of woods for bar hopping.

Spy

101 Greene Street between Prince and Spring Streets, 343-9000. Monday–Sunday, 5:00 P.M.–4:00 A.M. So hip it hurts. (See "What Would Happen If . . . ?" sidebar on page 274.)

Thirteen

35 East 13th Street between Broadway and University Place, 979-6677. Tuesday–Saturday, 10:00 P.M.–4:00 A.M. A place with no identity.

Twilo

530 West 27th Street between Tenth and Eleventh Avenues, 268-1600. Hours vary. This is where the gay boys go to party on the weekends, so we are told; it's rumored to be the new "Liquid" if all permits come in as planned, named after a superhot Miami space *(right)*.

205 Club

205 Chrystie Street at Stanton Street, 473-5816. Wednesday–Sunday, 9:00 P.M.–4:00 A.M. Very hot. Very new.

2i's

248 West 14th Street between Seventh and Eighth Avenues, 807-1775. Monday, 10:00 P.M.–4:00 A.M.; Tuesday–Saturday, 10:00 P.M.–4:00 A.M. It remains (also) to be seen.

Vain

9 Avenue A off Houston Street, 253-1462. Monday–Sunday, 6:00 P.M.–4:00 A.M. As in, you're so.

Velvet

167 Avenue A between 10th and 11th Streets, 475-2172. Monday–Sunday, 6:00 P.M.–4:00 A.M. Ropes.

Venue

505 Columbus Avenue between 84th and 85th Streets, 579-9463. Monday–Sunday, 7:00 P.M.–4:00 A.M. I like the idea of a great club on Columbus but have yet to be swayed.

Void

16 Mercer Street at Canal Street, 941-6492. Wednesday–Thursday, 8:00 P.M.–2:00 A.M.; Friday–Saturday, 8:00 P.M.–3:00 A.M. Hip place for people who pose. A very cool DJ.

Wax

113 Mercer Street between Spring and Prince Streets, 226-6082. Hours vary. This is one of those places, somewhat like Void, that is so completely trendy that you might as well wait until Wax Two opens— not worth the wait outside, nor the wait at the bar, nor the wait at the bathroom . . .

The Web

40 East 58th Street between Madison and Park Avenues, 308-1546. Sunday–Thursday, 4:30 P.M.–3:00 A.M.; Friday–Saturday, 4:00 P.M.–4:00 A.M. Has no computer connections here, more of a spider thing.

The Wreck Room

116 Macdougal Street between 3rd and 4th Streets, 253-1843. Monday–Sunday, 8:00 P.M.–4:00 A.M. Not the wreck you might imagine me describing. A surprise guest in the West Village.

Z Bar

206 Avenue A between 12th and 13th Streets, 982-9173. Monday–Sunday, 3:00 P.M.–4:00 A.M. Zzzz!

Go to sleep now.

Bars Are Not for Bores

PUB CRAWL ALONG:
AN INTRODUCTION TO BARS IN NEW YORK

The Native's Guide to New York Forum was restless, so we all went out and had a virtual drink. It's amazing what a lot of youngish minds can accomplish while crawling around town. Here is what we found, with a special virtual nod of thanks to "ex Pat."

First, let's get bars that we like out of the way, those with a connection to our various Irish heritages: **MORAN'S** (at the World Financial Center, 250 Vesey Street, 945-2255); **MAC MENAMIN'S** (Fulton Pier 17); **HARBOUR LIGHTS** (Fulton Pier 17, 227-2800); **NORTH STAR** (claims to be English, but is run by Irish people, 93 South Street, 509-6757); and **ROSIE O'GRADY'S** (800 Seventh Avenue, 582-2975).

Just looking at this, you realize that most bars in the city are Irish, like diners are Greek. Most of the time, bars that are not Irish, are yuppie drinking holes. Not bad, just not interesting.

At **JEREMY'S ALE HOUSE** (254 Front Street, 964-3537), if you get too drunk at lunchtime, your neck tie will be snipped off by the staff and nailed up on the wall with the rest of the neckwear reprobates.

Also downtown, and we like them, are the two **HARRY'S,** Harry's at

Hanover Square (1 Hanover Square, 425-3412) and Harry's at the Woolworth Building (233 Broadway, 513-0455). Okay, broker hangouts, sure, but looser than in real life.

Moving north, before you get to the heart of the village, is the **EAR INN** (326 Spring Street, 226-9060). Great for the mad-genius artists who hang there. We'll repeat reasons why it's called the Ear if any of the people here asks. [Ed. note: we didn't ask.]

Let's do it anyway. If you take a good close look at the sign for the Ear, you'll see that it was a Bar once, but with the rounded bits covered over on the neon "B." That was because the original owners wanted to call the place the Bar, but they found that there was a New York City ordinance that wouldn't allow a bar to be called "The" Bar. *Violà!* The Ear.

CHUMLEY'S (86 Bedford Street, 675-4449) is a bit old and collegiate for me, but there is a historical rumor connected with the place. It is said that F. Scott Fitzgerald had sex with someone in one of the booths there.

The next stop would be the Village. **ACME'S** is great with the right company (9 Great Jones Street, 420-1934, the **KNITTING FACTORY** Inc. is just downtown, 74 Leonard Street, 219-3055). One of our favorites—**GOOGIE'S** (237 Sullivan Street just off 3rd Street, 673-0050)—for the jukebox and the pool table. Nobody can recall if there was sawdust on the floor, but it is that kind of a place. **PECULIAR PUB** (145 Bleecker Street, 353-1327) was originally located on West 4th Street, where it was peculiarly titled Peculier [sic] Pub, and is now the site of the **SLAUGHTERED LAMB PUB** (182 West 4th Street, 627-5262), a very eerie bar in my opinion.

Our old hangout from our days at NYU was the **CEDAR TAVERN** (82 University Place, 741-9754), which was (and unknown to me when we schooled) a hangout for many Abstract Expressionists of the '50s and '60s. We didn't find out about this until it was mentioned in the Kurt Vonnegut book *Hocus Pocus*.

When we last left our hero, we were in the Village on our way uptown.

A comment about one last place before we leave the Village: what a disappointment **MCSORLEY'S OLD ALE HOUSE** is (15 East 7th Street just off Bowery, 473-9148), for those who have heard the hype! When I was at NYU, it was a good, cheap place for students to eat and drink. But in the '80s, it became a stopover for yuppies on their way up from Wall Street to their uptown apartments. Gentrification was replacing the soon-to-be-middle class. Do we hate them for it? Nah. Fortunately a lot of those stopovers have stopped.

Once out of the Village, there's pretty sparse drinking until we start to get to midtown. Ho hum. Of course the **OLD TOWN BAR** (45 East 18th Street, 529-6732) has great TV—sports for my buddies, all slobs—and there is **PETE'S TAVERN** (129 East 18th Street and Irving Place, 473-7676). Is it really the oldest bar on earth? Who knows.

Two places that we have discovered on this pub crawl are the **GRAND SALOON** (158 East 23rd Street, 477-6161) and **FITZGERALD'S PUB** (336 Third Avenue, 532-3453). Grand Saloon had live music after the Saint Patrick's Day parade this year and had us up dancing. Even the fat ladies. The problem with this place was that they really didn't now how to do a proper pint of Guinness, so it was just as well we switched to whiskey.

Fitzgerald's opened a few years ago and it is a mecca for the international sport enthusiast. When we were there, they were showing Five Nations Rugby from the week before. It's good to find places like this in New York City, because it validates the fact that it is an International City.

Now there's a place on 56 West 31st Street just off Broadway called **O'REILLY'S PUB** (684-4244; I think, except that it has changed its name a few times since press). And we are not talking about Paddy Reilly's. Again, good food, booze, and atmosphere. Lots of that.

Here we find another guilty pleasure, the **HOULIHAN'S** in the Empire State Building (350 Fifth Avenue, 630-0339). The reason we like this place is if you want a bite to eat, but know you're going to be waiting for the person eating with you, then it's a great place to have a drink and either read your paper or watch the hustle go by outside in the dark streets. When your date arrives, then there's Mexican food downstairs.

And another pause for breath . . .

For the next ten blocks or so, going uptown, there are probably a lot of places that you can go drink, but we went on ahead to **PATRICK CONWAY'S** on 44th Street, just off Vanderbilt (286-1873) just as you walk out of Grand Central Terminal. And just discovered two doors down from Conway's is **ANNIE MOORES BAR & RESTAURANT** (50 East 43rd Street, 986-7826) which, in a head-to-head competition with Conway's, wins hands down. It's much more open and comfortable and the waitresses must have moved from Madigan's to this place when they changed the name.

In Grand Central, downstairs, there's the **OYSTER BAR & RESTAU-RANT.** Ever since they closed down the public toilets in the station, The Oyster Bar seems to be the only place to go to the bathroom, if you're not on the train (490-6650).

The inside bit of it, the part that doesn't look like a diner, is comfortable enough, but it's not a place to stay for more than one drink. But train station bars feel like that. So why should New York be any different? (The Oyster Bar burned down last year and was rebuilt in record time. It's not the same anymore, but it's still there.)

Then, as you move into the '50s, yep, things start to pick up a bit. You'll find that most of the bars on the east side of town are Irish places.

If anyone can remember the movie *Marty* with Ernest Borgnine (the TV show was with Rod Steiger, but both were written by 1950s Native Guy, Paddy Chayefsky), then sit back and listen: Marty—who used to ask his friends, "Wheredyouwannagotonight," only to be told, "Idunnowhere-doyouwannagotonight?"—and his pals used to go downtown to Second and Third Avenues to go to the bars and dance places that were all part of the city mating rituals in the 1950s.

For those who care, **P.J. CLARKE'S** (one of the crew's faves) was the scene (915 Third Avenue at 55th St., 759-1650) for the fabo drinkin' man's movie *The Lost Weekend* . . . way back in the late 1940s. The thing that we like about it the most is that it is the way McSorley's should be. It has the same ancient bathrooms, and a nice leisurely feel to it; and you can always get a quiet bite to eat in the back. We just are not sure if it has sawdust on the floor, but it should.

The 1950s era was filled with German places and Italian places, but they're mostly gone now. We spoke too soon, because all of a sudden you can still find these places, with the original decor, only they've been converted into ethnic social clubs. In the 1980s the Peppermint Lounge existed uptown at East 84th, in a former bar of German nature called the Jagerhaus. But all that's left of that 50s scene are the many Irish places.

Along Second and Third Avenues are places like **KENNEDY'S** (327 West 57th Street, 489-8335) and li'l **KATE KEARNEY'S** (251 East 50th Street between Second and Third Avenues—next to Lutece, 935-2045).

Just to wind up the Irish places in this part of town, there's **O'FLANAGANS ALE HOUSE** (1591 Second Avenue, 472-2800); it used to be just Flannigan's. (Is that a marketing decision?) Great for dancing and drinking and the food is sort of good. The best pint of Guinness can be found in **TOMMY MAKEMS-IRISH PAVILION** at 130 East 57th Street (759-9040). It's also a good venue for hep live music. We mean hep, cats.

In one last burst of desperation for a drink, we take our last leg up the East Side. It's been a long crawl and we have only a few places left. We've only been in one bar on the Upper West Side, and that's because they all sort of stink—forgive us. We can't remember the name of the place. We were there for a bachelor party years ago, and the only recollection that we have of it is that they had blue drinks that they used to float rubber sharks in. Or maybe that's just us.

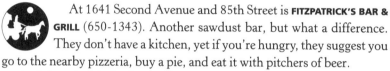 At 1641 Second Avenue and 85th Street is **FITZPATRICK'S BAR & GRILL** (650-1343). Another sawdust bar, but what a difference. They don't have a kitchen, yet if you're hungry, they suggest you go to the nearby pizzeria, buy a pie, and eat it with pitchers of beer.

And they do a hell of a pint of Guinness for this side of the Atlantic. Have you noticed how our group loves Guinness?

Until we walked by, we were unsure if the place is still there, its notoriety seems not to have disappeared since it became famous: **DORIAN'S** was the place to go to drink (450 Seventh Avenue and 82nd Street, 695-7860) when we were underage. Today it's sad space.

Another is **AUSTRALIA THE BAR** on 90th Street and First Avenue, 876-0203. We mention it because we had a great time there at a bachelor party, but we'd say is was a crowded mess otherwise. As Bette Davis remarked in *All About Eve,* "What a dump!"

And lastly, in the East 60s, there's **O'NEILL'S** at 729 Third Avenue (661-3530), which would never say out loud that it was an Irish place. Famous for its Moonburgers, not to be confused with Moondoggie Burgers from the 1960s, we like to sit inside and drink and eat and look out on the corner where Woody Allen and Diane Keaton said a quick hello and goodbye in the last scene of *Annie Hall.* It's just one of those places that gives us the warm fuzzies. (Incidentally, it's Irish.) And to bring the movie people up to date, it is the restaurant where Al Pacino and John Goodman interviewed their suspects in *Sea of Love.*

Well, that's a good survey—and quite a trek. Go out there and attack those bars. Also in *All About Eve* the much-suffering wife character exclaimed: "Fasten your seatbelts. It's going to be a bumpy ride."

Ain't that the truth.

SIDEBAR SPECIAL **Best Places to Play Games**

First a note. You can't play games and drink liquor, legally, in most places in the city. It has to do with the arcane and inane liquor license laws in town, and I won't even begin to tell you how silly they are (e.g., if you have a dance floor, you have to add a license—more money, more politicking, more headaches). So here are the places to just play games. Drink on your own.

If chess is your bag, at **VILLAGE CHESS** (230 Thompson Street, 475-9580), you can play for $1.50 an hour or $2 an hour for clocked chess. Unlike associations that treat chess as an obsession, this old fraternity feels the game should be a hobby. Come early in the day (around noon), if you're anxious to brush up on your skills. The later in the day you arrive, the longer you have to wait. Refreshments are available; no liquor. Open daily from 12:00 P.M. to midnight.

How about some one-eyed jack? Play poker at the **MAYFAIR CLUB** (51 East 25th Street, 779-1750). It's a newfangled-type club with great poker lessons and lots of couples in attendance, which is a nice change—Mayfair used to be men-only. It's an old world atmosphere that asks you to pay a membership fee—still no drinks.

Since times have seemingly brought down the discos, more and more people are seeking intimacy in the game of pool. Try the unbelievably long-staying **HACKERS, HITTERS, AND HOOPS** (123 West 18th Street, 929-7482). Hackers has music, Cokes (no liquor), and the very same smoke levels you would find in a run-of-the-mill disco. Hackers has many bonuses: basketball, batting cages, mini-golf, spaceball, dunk shot, orbotron, ping-pong, and even volleyball. You'd have to spend a few days there before you'd even get slightly bored, but even spending a few hours there will significantly affect your cash flow. **MAM-MOTH BILLIARDS** (114 West 26th Street, 675-2626) also has many of the same games. Lots of great ping-pong, but there is only one workable pool table here, and it is usually surrounded by sharks (the kind of people who look like Paul Newman in *The Hustler*). Incidentally, at last glance the action here was focused on ping-pong!

If the **BILLIARD CLUB** (220 West 19th Street, 206-POOL) is any indication, the smoky pool hall may be a thing of the past. This latest addition to the world of eight-ball sports a neon facade and an oversized awning, while inside it's as plush as a private clubhouse. A coffee bar sells overstuffed sandwiches, and the walls boast moose heads and bearskins. Very high testosterone levels here. Lately, the place is filled with kids or "the element" (referring to people who seem to have an agenda, be it hustling or—gasp!—drinking). Go at your own risk. Open to 3:00 A.M. on Sunday–Thursday, and until 5:00 A.M. on Friday and Saturday.

Or how about a shooting spree? No, I'm not making a crack at crime levels in New York (which the Giuliani administration claims are decreasing all the time), I'm referring to the **WEST SIDE RIFLE AND PISTOL RANGE** (20 West 20th Street, 243-9448). In the 1950s, the city had dozens of shooting galleries (i.e., licensed pistol and rifle firing ranges) on the blocks between West 40th and 50th Streets, as well as at many amusement parks, but most are long since closed. West Side, for your information, is a member of the National Rifle Association ("Guns don't kill people, people kill people") and boasts 3,000 enthusiastic members, including stock brokers, diplomats, security guards, housewives, even grandmothers. There are handguns for practice and a riot shotgun with a short chrome barrel. The owner says shooting is "a sport" and not a defense mechanism. Open Monday–Friday, 9:00 A.M.–10:00 P.M.; Saturday and Sunday, 9:00 A.M.–4:00 P.M. Long live the NRA—not.

BARS ARE NOT FOR BORES

BEST BARS FOR NIGHT TRAVELERS

ART BAR
52 Eighth Avenue, 727-0244

The Art Bar is small; not cramped, but intimate, which makes it ideal for meeting friends after work or going for a drink with a date. The working fireplace, pool tables, and art on walls add to the intimacy.

ARTHUR'S TAVERN
57 Grove Street, one block south of Christopher Street, 675-6879

My most-jaded friend has the hots for this place: a great place for Village denizens to drink gin. The story behind it: In the late 1940s to mid-1950s Arthur's was home to many of bebop's rising stars; even Charlie "Bird" Parker called this home. They feature jazz, blues, and dixieland seven nights a week, always for free. They have been in biz for almost thirty-five years. Sundays and Mondays the music starts at 8:00 P.M.; the rest of the week it gets going at 7:00 P.M.

BAR 89
89 Mercer Street, between Spring and Broome Streets, 274-0989;
fax 274-9284

Talk about trendy! (Okay, let's.) Two floors of tables, the second floor overlooking the first, a bar with lit-up neon bottles, a hip looking twenty-something crowd, and oh, yes, the bathrooms. The coolest thing about Bar 89 is definitely the bathrooms. With large, plexiglass, multi-color doors with light-up "occupied" signs, the bathrooms in this bar/restaurant look like something you would read about in futuristic sci-fi novels. Food is nothing spectacular, more like the diner in every nabe, although I do highly recommend the grilled vegetables, if you're grazing.

BELMONT LOUNGE
117 East 15th Street between Park Avenue South and Irving Place, phone/fax 533-0009

They say that the Belmont Lounge has "the best vibe in N.Y.C.," and that "every drink is poured with love as its main ingredient." They sound good to me. New since the last edition of this guide, the Belmont Lounge opened with a lot of fanfare (celebrities, rock stars, beautiful people, you get the idea). Trendy, hyped, popular, worth a venture.

BOWERY BAR
358 Bowery at 4th Street, 475-2220

Talk about places to be seen—this bar truly takes the cake. You'll find a good mix of yuppies, trendy people, glamour wanna-bes at this bar, which finds itself host very often to celebrities like Robert De Niro. Expensive drinks at plastic lawn-furniture tables with plastic checkered tablecloths may make you wonder why you came, but as soon as some big-name movie star comes in for a drink, you'll know why. It's all about being seen. (See sidebar titled "What Would Happen If . . . ?" beginning on page xxx.)

THE BUBBLE LOUNGE
228 West Broadway between White and Franklin Streets, 431-3433

Want to get rid of money burning a hole in your pocket? But don't feel like buying yet another sports car, co-op, or guidebook? Why not take some friends to the Bubble Lounge? Actually, you can get a champagne cocktail for around eight bucks. Reservations are required to drink. This place is fairly classy, so don't wear jeans. The lower level is great for a small party. Also on the lower level is a small room full of nothing but cigars and humidors. You might feel almost out of your league here, but the service is friendly, and the crowd is not as pretentious as you might imagine. Order the fruit and chocolate fondue for a snack (it's both cheap and good), although you will have to ask for extra strawberries because they seem to almost always be running low (probably because strawberries are champagne's best friend.) Bring a credit card. You never realize how much you spend until the check comes and one of you has to run to the ATM. (Not fun.)

CHUMLEY'S
86 Bedford Street, 675-4449

In the early part of this century, Chumley's was a speakeasy. Today it's NYU's hottest hangout, with ear-splitting levels on the weekends and a beer bar that just won't quit. Don't expect service, don't expect any decent food except a large hamburger. Everyone who ever lived in the neighborhood has drunk here—O. Henry, John Steinbeck, Edna St. Vincent Millay. Chumley's also has a hidden courtyard in back where people congregate in the summer. (You can feel the history that occurred back there.)

If you like sawdust on the floor, this bar's for you. But call for directions—it's in the middle of a street maze and has no sign.

CLEO'S NINTH AVENUE SALOON
656 Ninth Avenue at West 46th Street, 307-1503

A fun drinking hole that calls itself a "mixed neighborhood bar." Cleo's has penny-rolling parties each month, where they ask people to take pennies off the shelf, bring them in, and roll ("Everyone, roll!") for God's Love We Deliver, a local AIDS charity that delivers food to homebound patients. Cleo's will pick up your pennies for you! It's the place where *nobody* knows your name.

CONTINENTAL DIVIDE
25 Third Avenue, 529-6924

A surprise at the edge of the East Village, Continental Divide is a nice, homey Mexican cafe that constantly hosts bands. You can stare at the flying stuffed plesiosaur or catch the regular schedule of loud, quirky music without a cover charge.

CORNER BISTRO
331 West 4th Street, 242-9502; fax 255-9070

An 1827 authentic hamburger joint (the oldest in the village) with twenty-minute cookers, this quiet place gets rowdy late at night but miraculously serves food until 3:30 A.M. You know it's a serious bar when the stained glass has beer-mug designs. The *New York Press* called this "the best place to be treated like shit," but Village regulars—or people who don't give the bartender a hard time—can have a grand old hour at the bar eavesdropping on the banter.

How untrendy is the Corner? The late Stan Getz's "Chocolate Sunday" is the most requested song on the ancient jukebox. Since I wrote about them as a great bar, they have written to say that for nearly thirty years, they've served "the best hamburgers you can find" and that *New York* magazine named their's the best hamburger in New York.

CROSSROADS
128 West Houston Street, 674-4080

Relaxed and friendly, with cool blues and pool. No fighting allowed, they told me. They have requested I not put them in the trendy bar section. Do you see a trendy bar section here? I don't *think* so.

DEW DROP INN
57 Greenwich Avenue on the corner of Perry Street, 924-8055

A village institution for over thirteen years now, Dew Drop specializes in crowded after work do's—with Elvis busts at every turn. In the back, Elvis at table level is pure optical illusion. Is he sitting or what? According to Dew's own staff, "We serve the most mediocre BBQ in Manhattan. Our jukebox has the most mediocre country-western music around. Funky, fattening, and fabulous!" But one thing is sure: Dew Drop Dead is an uncanny drink nobody who works here can figure out. Try one of their 16-oz. mason-jar drinks. The bar is currently under renovation, as well as the menu, which now includes dishes like Mom's Meatloaf and chili dogs. Hours are 11:30 A.M. to 4 A.M.

What Would Happen If You Opened a Really Hot Restaurant and Nobody Showed Up?

So I showed up a little early—perhaps four days early—which makes it a Tuesday night. I was going to Balthazar, the fabulous restaurant that Keith McNally (the younger sibling of the famous Brian McNally) had opened in Soho (80 Spring Street, 965-1414).

I had memories, devalued ones at that, of a place that Brian—who made lots of places famous, like 44 at the Royalton—had made famous, particularly 125 Wooster with the unlisted number.

Not one to accept any sort of derogatory behavior toward New Yorkers, I did not include this then "hothothot" restaurant in *Native's Guide,* second edition. After all, it was 1990, the "me decade" was over; people had to be tiring of the elitist attitude. They soon wouldn't be bothered standing on line to get in the door, even if Bianca Jagger was standing with them . . . or rolling past them.

Strike one. Wooster changed hands, and died a heavenly quick death.

So, back to my story. I go to Balthazar on a Tuesday. *Paper* magazine had called this restaurant, "The place where gods are conceived, contracts are signed, and peace settlements are negotiated." At the onset the minimum wait was twenty minutes at the bar, and on this night, well, the place was EMPTY.

"Do you have a reservation?" the maître d' asks me.

"Do you see any people here?" I reply. The place was dead, and we're talking about *the* restaurant of 1997. There I am at the entryway, sitting with my pad and beginning to take notes, which of course the maître d' notices immediately. He angrily seats me, but I get no waiter. I get no bread. I get no headway with the waiter. I am completely at my wit's end. As far as I know at this point, this place is only busy on the week-ends.

So, why am I being made to wait?

I think I know why.

Strike two for the McNally Brothers.

I got up, paid the bill, and went to visit more allegedly "hot" places that I am starting to believe don't exist anymore. Brian McNally was successful with Restaurant 44 at the Royalton, and a few other restaurant-like inventions he opened in the 1980s. But I really don't think anybody cares to be treated snobbishly anymore. I went for a walk.

First it was off to Pravda, a Soho bar owned by Keith Mc-Nally, with what I would call "hounds" at the door who thor-oughly check you out before you can enter, even if it is empty inside. As you might imagine, inside were a few models, a few gawkers, but again, it was a Tuesday night. This is supposed to be *the* hottest hangout for the literary crowd. I guess they all had manuscripts due.

While still in Soho, I tallied over to Chaos. Chaos was dark, a little grungy, and had only six people in it. I think my point is well-proven.

Sort of stuck in Soho, I hightailed it over to Spy. Spy, in a word, is really dark. At this point Soho was starting to annoy me. All these groovy watering holes, and where was everyone? I had nothing all evening to take notes on, and the bartender was yawning. He appeared (and I can't be positive because it was so very dark and musty in there) to be working on his re-sumé.

When I got around to the ultimately fame-oriented Bowery Bar, I ran into Danny Bonaduce from "The Partridge Family." I assessed the situation at the Bowery Bar: Danny, no patrons of any repute, and me. Bowery had a friendly looking atmos-phere, a few blinis at the bar top (which was dirty, by the way), and the people who worked there all had their arms folded in this serious pose.

BARS ARE NOT FOR BORES

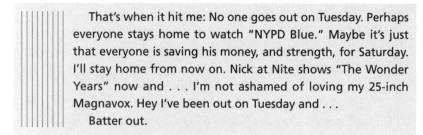

That's when it hit me: No one goes out on Tuesday. Perhaps everyone stays home to watch "NYPD Blue." Maybe it's just that everyone is saving his money, and strength, for Saturday. I'll stay home from now on. Nick at Nite shows "The Wonder Years" now and . . . I'm not ashamed of loving my 25-inch Magnavox. Hey I've been out on Tuesday and . . .

Batter out.

DIVE BAR

732 Amsterdam, 749-4358

Some of the best chicken wings in New York. An owner told me, "the most dive-oriented bar around." Some of the coolest bartenders and indubitably a reasonable place to eat on the West Side.

DOWN THE HATCH

179 West 4th Street between Sixth and Seventh Avenues, 627-9747; fax 647-7670

Management here is proud that this is one of the few bars in the area that does not cater to tourist crowds. They actually dislike them, poor slobs. Down The Hatch is like a hometown bar (you know, the bars you went to before you came to the city). Reasonable prices, and happy hour is 5:00 P.M.–7:00 P.M. on weekdays, when all drinks are half price. Cheers . . .

 ### DOWNTIME BAR

251 West 30th Street between Seventh and Eighth Avenues, 695-2747

Every night four different bands perform live; songwriters from 5:30 to 7:30 every Thursday. There are three floors of activities, including sandbox dance parties. Saturday's dance floor is alive with "gothic industrial and techno"—cool. But the bar, the mixing (people you encounter when drinking), and the combination of those two is what counts here. Their slogan is: "Right by Penn Station, so you never know whom you'll meet!" (PS: Many new nights of music—changing almost daily!) If you want your ears filled with guitar, here's the ticket to chords of noise . . .

THE GIN MILL

442 Amsterdam Avenue between 81st and 82nd Streets, 580-9080;

fax 580-1830

On Saturdays and Sundays between 1:00 P.M. and 6:00 P.M., you can pay
$12 a head and get all-you-can-eat buffalo wings and all-you-can-drink
beer. This bar also has a beautiful private party room to rent out. Live bands
play at the Mill every Wednesday night. And they have a great summer
feature—authentic outdoor bar seating, an endangered species in Manhattan, and one I wish to proliferate.

GOLD BAR

345 East 9th Street, 505-8270

There are some mixed bars in this area, such as the ultra-trendy Tenth Street
Lounge on 10th Street between First and Second Avenues. Yet Gold Bar is
my favorite: The decor is gold, the place is run by friendly German folk, and
the floor is raised above a small storage room you can peek down into. Barmaids serve real Dinkelbokker beer in large German glasses and you can talk
to some interesting no-nonsense people who all dress in black. No cover,
drinks are not cheap, *das es der kulture.* A lesbian crowd for some inexplic-
able reason (see Chapter 20, "Gay And Lesbian New York," for more).

GRAND CENTRAL STATION'S OYSTER BAR—NOT EXACTLY

SMALL TALK

At Grand Central's lower level, find the famed Oyster Bar (490-6650) at the
back of a large, seeming waste of space. If you whisper into one of the corners of the room, a person facing the wall in an opposite corner of this room
can hear you.

I kid you not.

HOTEL ROYALTON'S TINY BAR

44 West 44th Street, 869-4400

When you walk into the lobby, make an immediate right, head up the path,
and check into the tiny bar-in-the-round hidden there. It's a near-perfect

replica of a famous bar in the middle of Tokyo's Roppongi section, and it was just reopened under heavy "secrecy."

Not unexpectedly, the Royalton refuses to let the word out! Yet another example of the attitude found at this tiny art deco palace, meant for people who like plush lobby carpeting, metal seats shaped like giant steer horns, and $4 tea.

HUDSON BAR & BOOKS

636 Hudson Street at Charles Street, 229-2642

This beautiful place offers British food and drink and atmosphere . . . and books to boot. You can read, you can browse, you can meet well-read men and women. Also located uptown on Beekman Place (889 First Avenue, 980-9314), where the concept has been gussied up. There are a few others like it—same firm—that are mainly cigar bars for the pseudo-rich.

JAKE'S DILEMMA

430 Amsterdam Avenue, 580-0556. fax 579-2159

For the beer fan, Jake's has 14 different beers on tap and over 40 more kinds in bottles. Open everyday from 5:00 P.M. to 4:00 A.M., it has all the amenities of a regular bar—private party room, pool tables, dart boards, foosball tables, and a DJ. Go there right after work—between 5:00 P.M. and 8:00 P.M., everything is half-price. Once Adam Sandler ("The Hanukkah Song") stopped in this bar to film a quick piece with *Entertainment Tonight*.

 ## JOE ALLEN'S

326 West 46th Street, 581-6464

Joe Allen's is the perfect spot to have a drink in the theater district. The place is always abuzz with dramatic talk, and nobody seems to care about anything but theater. To get a table, you must reserve early in the day. Otherwise, schmooze at the bar. After theater, the joint is jumping. Open till 3:00 A.M. (unusual for this neck o' the woods).

KGB BAR

85 East 4th Street between Bowery and Second Avenue, 505-3360

Decorated in true quasi-Communist charm, the KGB Bar looks like a bar you'd find in parts of the former Soviet Union. The size (or lack of it) actually adds to the charm. It's a good place to meet a couple of friends for a drink if you're down in that area, and the drinks are nice and strong. However, it's up a flight of old stairs on the second floor, so don't get too drunk or you'll break your neck trying to get out at the night's end.

LICKETY SPLIT
2361 Powell Boulevard, or 138th Street and Seventh Avenue
283-9093

Harlem's grungiest bar from the outside is truly a find once you get past the initial stares given outsiders or non-regulars. When the thaw sets in, you can enjoy backroom live jazz and blues. Except on Sundays, the place regularly hops, 12:00 P.M.–3:30 A.M. (and often much later).

Lickety is on a former hot corner for blues bars. Those that represented music of several eras—the Red Rooster, Jock's, and Kenny's Lounge—have all bitten the dust. Careful consideration of the party habits of its customers, who want good music and great jam sessions, has kept this one going since the mid-1970s.

MANHATTAN CHILI COMPANY
1500 Broadway, 730-8666

"Wish I had time for one more bowl of chili," were the last words of famed cowboy Kit Carson, who never ate here. Manhattan Chili used to be in the Village but economics made them move to touristy midtown, where it is always a challenge to find good food, never mind chili.

Great recipes here, the Real McCoy is "no tomato, no beans, no bull," and it's fiery, delicious.

They also serve a helluva goofy drink here that is not for everyone, folks. It's called a "Blueberry Marge" and has nothing to do with the tall-blue-haired lady from *The Simpsons.* It's a blueberry margarita—all the regular ingredients except the lime; instead they throw in blueberry preserves. This nouveau drink takes guts.

The place has changed since those downtown days—once they had a fabulous trellised garden that was dark and eerie and a bit wild. Now they advertise "Child friendly." The times.

CAFÉ INFERNO

165 Eighth Avenue, 989-2330

Café Inferno is the other side of the coin from its next-door neighbor, Man Ray. This Italian specialty restaurant—once Tiziano—has some extraordinary appetizers, in addition to an awning of a naked woman in neon! While they were building, people passed by muttering, "Put your name on a sign somewhere." Six months later they had more than a name. Years later, another name—and a great rep.

MAN RAY BISTRO

169 Eighth Avenue, 627-4220

The restaurant that was once L'Express is now Man Ray, a simple food spot renowned for salads and seafood; it's teeming with Chelsea's better-dressed. (Its stairway to the bathroom is reportedly a remnant of the Eiffel Tower!) No freebies at Man Ray. They don't offer you more than a $5 bar drink, unless you sit down for a $20-plus-wine meal.

MCALEER'S PUB

425 Amsterdam Avenue, 362-7867

It's really a run-of-the-mill bar: weekly shot specials (including jello shots), specials on beer pitchers, very low-key surroundings and down to earth staff, almost the kind of place you frequented in college. The *New York Post* said McAleer's is, "One of the top places to meet people in New York."

MERC BAR

151 Mercer between Houston and Prince Streets, 966-2727

One of my friend's friends said to me that this is one of the trendiest bars in New York. It's not a bar that you would even notice while you were walking by it unless you were looking for it. With just a few floor-to-ceiling windows and a door out front, it looks very small and unimpressive. Merc Bar *is* very small, but it is impressive nonetheless. Lots of couches and cushy chairs, excellent and moderately priced drinks. The people there are twenty to thirty, or thereabouts, some Yuppies, mixed crowds. Usually very full, so if you want to snag a couch with some friends in front of the windows and people-watch, get there early. And pose like the rest.

TWO CHELSEA BARS, HYPED & TRENDY
Merchants: 17th Street at Seventh Avenue, 366-7267
Chicago B.L.U.E.S.: 13th Street at Eighth Avenue, 924-9755

Barkeep Ismael Merchant runs these two, the first for drinking down in the basement, with a fireplace, comfy couches and some nice salads. It's the B.L.U.E.S. bar, with cover charges of $5 and $7, a not-too popular late-comer to the bar market. You can hear the blues in the dark—however, this is an endangered *space:* five bar-cum-restaurants have attempted business right here in the last ten years. Merchants is also at 525 Columbus Avenue (86th Street) and 1125 First Avenue (62nd Street).

MONTERO BAR AND GRILL
73 Atlantic Avenue, in Red Hook, Brooklyn, 718-624-9799

The bar of Pepe Montero is mentioned here because since 1947 this place has been the most consistent tavern on record. Same jukebox, same stools, same photos on the same walls, and forty wooden Indian head models! The barmaids are, they say, "nice girls with legs." Maritime memorabilia and no two-for-one. Walk in, and I guarantee the first thing someone says is "Hey-howyoudoin?" Stay for a cold brew. Or is that "brewsky"?

MORAN'S
250 Vesey Street, 945-2255

This is a favorite summer watering hole among the Wall Street and Trade Center crowd for the past several years, sandwiched between the World Financial Center's towers. Some come to admire the view of the water and the boats tied up near the Hudson River Yacht club . . . others come to discuss their investments. While there are two other locations of Moran's Bar and Grill, at 103 Washington Street (the meat market district) and at 146 10th Avenue (farther uptown), the Vesey location is the one everyone remembers.

MO'S CARIBBEAN BAR AND GRILL
1454 Second Avenue, 650-0561; fax 288-0065

One of the most friendly and relaxed bars in all of New York, Mo's is a cross between American and Caribbean food and drink. Here there is everything you go to a bar for: a big sports bar with satellite hookups; live reggae bands featured every Tuesday; and Mondays mean lobster madness, when a lobster is only $6 (this is of course the busiest day of the week!). Happy Hour happens seven days a week here, where drink prices are half-off. Open 4:00 P.M.–4:00 A.M., Monday through Friday; and 11:30 A.M.–4:00 A.M. on the weekends. By the way, check out "Free Movie Night" on Sundays! It's a gas.

NANCY WHISKEY PUB
1 Lispenard Street, 226-9943

If you are not a drinker, but aspire to be one, learn the basic steps at this ages-old, way-downtown stopover. Most serious drinking emporia are stocked with guzzlers and shot-downers who are not happy to see amateurs (read not-a-regular). Nancy Whiskey, as the name implies, brings together oldsters and youngsters (not under 21 please) to make drinking the art form it deserves to be. Their home base is a hidden Tribeca street where you might catch the experts going at it. There's no chitchat here, except for, "How about another one?"

O'FLAHERTY'S ALE HOUSE
334 West 46th Street between Eighth and Ninth Avenues, 581-9366

This is the place where everyone may very well know your name. It's not big; decor looks like a cross between a bar, a coffee house, and someone's living room; lots of original art work on the walls from local artists; but what you really come to O'Flats (as the regulars refer to it) for is the people. The wait staff and the regulars here are very friendly and outgoing, and before you know it, you'll get sucked into the O'Flaherty's crowd. On any given night the joint bustles, sometimes with the occasional celebrity (or soap opera actor—I'm not sure if this counts as a celebrity or not).

The prices are very reasonable, another reason why this bar is so attractive. The live music is usually good with rare exceptions, and the tables outside in the back are a relaxing place to unwind with friends.

Meanwhile, as the intro to this chapter suggests, Irish bars are the way to go . . . "if" you are drinking!

OLD TOWN BAR AND RESTAURANT
45 East 18th Street, 529-6732

A circa 1892 tavern with a 600-foot mahogany bar; high, bevelled mirrors; and a 200-foot-high tin ceiling. (Huge urinals, the high kind.) All the facets of a classic old New York bar, and kind of a cliché. Was featured for years in the opening of the old David Letterman Show, though not anymore! It is periodically featured in *Mad About You*. (Must be under contract with NBC.)

For longevity alone, it's worth it to see the old place. The "Old Town" sign is quite beautiful in its neon simplicity. My pensive editor likes the quiet second floor (see "Pub Crawl Along" on page 265).

ORSO
322 West 46th Street, 489-7212

In addition to being one of the most consistently good Italian restaurants on the island, Orso has a comfortable, albeit small, bar area where you can smell the tiny pizzas and anchovied delicacies from the kitchen. A well-kept secret—before *New York* magazine raved!

PEACOCK ALLEY, WALDORF ASTORIA HOTEL
301 Park Avenue, 355-3000

The restaurant gets its name from the original Waldorf, when there was an alley there called Peacock Alley that made the Waldorf and the Astoria Hotels on 33rd Street appear connected. People used to promenade "like peacocks" in their finery, and thus the walkway was dubbed by an intelligent reporter.

PECULIAR PUB
145 Bleecker Street, 353-1327

As mentioned above, Peculiar boasts more bottled and tap beer than any pub, bar, restaurant, or café in the metro area. What's more, you can eat burgers and talk to the regulars, even get rowdy.

Nothing lets up here until 1:00 A.M. While beer is the main attraction, especially good draught beer, there are dart boards and a decent jukebox, too, but no dance floor. The management says Jagermeister Liqueur is the house brew, but Peculiar-ites say the Turkish beer Efes is intense. Or maybe there is nothing like an unimported Christian Moerlein Dark from Cincinnati, Ohio.

PEDRO'S
301 East 91st Street, 831-1788

There is a fabulous Monday night "buckets" held here; Thursday night it's Jagermeister night, for a few bucks. Typical happy hour. Pints for $2.50 each Friday. And of course, all the Upper East Side's famous beers: Miller Genuine Draft, Miller Lite, and Coors Light, better known as the beer of chumps. However, I mention this place because it is a tiny bar with a friendly and relaxed atmosphere, all ages and types like students, professionals, and in-betweens.

Pedro's allows bar and small-table patrons to order any food they want from take-out places, and bring it into the bar! Check out the wallpaper filled with Mexican lottery tix and bullfight posters. And one wall that has a bra and panty collection, just like a boys bar uptown (college boys, that is)—very down to earth! (Irony included in the last sentence, kids.)

PETE'S TAVERN
129 East 18th Street, 473-7676; fax 979-9368

I couldn't do this section without warning people not to miss the barbecued chicken wings at Pete's, the ancient drinkery in Gramercy Park, with its grand (mostly folkloric) and extra-Yuppie regular population. Go there once and do some heavy thinking, I mean, drinking, with the crowds. The bar attracts people from all over the world, as it tries so hard to keep the ancient flavor (founded 1864) intact. This is one of New York's famed "original bars," so make sure to note the tin ceiling and the rosewood bar. O. Henry penned "Gift of the Magi" here.

Food! Pasta Night is Monday; prime rib dinner is only $12.95 on Tuesday; Wednesday is Seafood Cornucopia Night; prix fixe 5-course dinner for $19.95 on the weekends.

PUFFY'S TAVERN

81 Hudson Street, 766-9159

Celebrities from Tribeca and all those noncelebrities that make bars such fun. It's the oldest tavern in the area (circa 1945), and they say it's a local hangout for artists, models, and film starlets.

SKI BAR

1825 Second Avenue between 94th and 95th Streets, 369-9635

Here's a bar that calls itself "the number one place in New York." When asked what occurs there, owner Ali Sama told me that this is totally no-frills: "The Ski Bar Is the Special Event." It's usually a young crowd here. The answering machine says, "Ski hard, but don't drink and drive." I'll try to keep that in mind.

THE SPORTING CLUB

99 Hudson Street, 219-0900

Probably the best sports bar in a town where sports bars are usually filed under "Y" for yahoo. Here men and women cavort together and turn the art of spectator sports into casual camaraderie. A lot of women spend time here; management thinks it's a "Can't beat 'em, then join 'em" attitude. Monday nights, when the action heats up on television, this is the place to let off serious steam.

They have decent food, too, except their menu is a bit sophomoric: "Food Warmups," "In the Bullpen," "Home Stretch," and "The 19th Hole." Pick an unrowdy time to come or face all the screaming fans, the variety that doesn't calm down for a second.

Rated #1 sports bar in New York by *USA Today,* the place has four satellite dishes. It is unofficial alumni headquarters for Michigan, Duke, Colorado, Florida, Virginia, Texas, and many more.

 **TEMPLE BAR**

332 Lafayette Street, 925-4242

Very pretentious and gorgeous bar with great peanuts (the only thing you can afford) and $10 martinis.

TERRA BLUES
149 Bleecker Street, 777-7776

In a city that seems so happy, there are plenty of places with live blues all the time. Terra is known for acoustic blues. Their own house band is considered to be top-notch, and Terra tells me, "We are very critical in our selection process. . . . In the past Edgar Winter, Johnny Copland, Matt "Guitar" Murphy, and so many others have played here, even when they became famous!"

Sounds good to me, so check out the very intimate atmosphere. The walls are covered with pictures—who *was* who of the past performing artists. Painted sculptures are fun to look at. Cover charge is slight, crowd is not.

CHAPTER 20

Gay and Lesbian New York

GAY NEW YORK SPECIALTIES

 EIGHTEENTH & EIGHTH
Corner of 18th Street and Eighth Avenue, 242-5000
The corner of 18th and Eighth is allegedly the focus of gay life and worth
mentioning. (Which is why I mention it twice!) This is the place where gay
men hang out on weekends and sometimes during the week: decent food at
a bargain price, lots and lots of faces from the area, and of course, coffee (two
types). Why, it's a coffee shop. Open early, till midnight, not found in this
book's earnest Food chapters. It's not about food, is it? In these parts, *ever*.

HOMO XTRA
A weekly guide to clubs, bars, theater, cultural events and other goings-on
for gay men in New York. A few listings for lesbians but mostly men-stuff.*
Lots of news about sex clubs, lots of "dish." Ongoing sagas, inside news,
and its own soap opera. Around since September 1991. Available for free at

* A "her" version—seemingly shortlived—is now on the newsstands.

GAY AND LESBIAN NEW YORK

287

bars and clubs and for sale at gay bookstores for $1.50. Also available—
Next and *Twist,* two more dishy rags (free in bars, shops).

QUEER CULTURE

A regular assemblage of gay performers that occurs in early June. Hundreds of shows participate at eighteen participating theaters. A summer
fest, the official name for this montage is "Hot! The Annual New York Celebration of Gay Culture." Check for listings in local gay bars and da *Village
Voice* (it's now free!).

PRIDE DAY ("GAY NEW YEAR'S")
Information: 807-7433

Just like Chinese or Jewish New Year's, gay and lesbian culture has a holiday, a Pride Day, the last Sunday of June, where gay and hetero people
celebrate freedom through the downtown streets of Manhattan, commemorating the Stonewall Riots of 1969 that helped liberate gays and lesbians
from police brutality. There is a loud and colorful march, a day-long cir-
cus/fair at Christopher Street in the Village, and finally a dance at 4:00 P.M.
on the piers off the West Side Highway.

LESBIAN HERSTORY ARCHIVES
484 14th Street, Park Slope, 718-768-3953

The Lesbian Herstory Archives has been around since 1976, and its goal is
to provide a place where lesbians can preserve their "herstory" and where
all lesbian lives are welcome, regardless of race or class.

   With over 10,000 volumes, 12,000 photographs, 1,400 periodicals, special collections, and organizational files, the archives is the largest lesbian
archives in the world and is located in a newly renovated brownstone in
Park Slope, Brooklyn. Great research source and community facility.

OFFICE OF GAY AND LESBIAN HEALTH CONCERNS
125 Worth Street, 788-4310

A part of the New York City Department of Health, this agency provides
health-related information to the lesbian and gay communities in New York,
with a particular focus on AIDS issues. It has an extensive library of materials, an excellent source. (See Chapter 23 for gay resources.)

RAYMOND DRAGON
200 West 18th Street, 727-0368

The clothing store of the A-list set. Here's the place to buy slinky T-shirts and trinkets to dress up a gym body. If you haven't got one, then don't shop here. "We specialize in sewing knit fabrics which fit close to the body," says the manager. And of course, semi-annual sales of the required uniforms of the last season.

SIDEBAR SPECIAL **Lesbian and Gay Community Services Center**

208 West 13th Street, 620-7310

This is it. The Center is a real mecca for many political, social, and entertainment-oriented activities. Gays and lesbians, and just generally In The Know types, call on the center regularly. It's home to social service groups and organizations, provides meeting space for over 250 gay and lesbian registered groups in the city, hosts numerous social events every week, and serves as a clearinghouse for information about what is going on in the community. Six anchor tenants have their offices at the Center: Coalition for Gay and Lesbian Rights, Community Health Project, Lesbian Switchboard, Metropolitan Community Church/NY, NYC Gay and Lesbian Anti-Violence Project, and Senior Action in a Gay Environment (SAGE). Also houses the Pat Parker and Vito Russo Center Library.

A must-stop-by, the people at the front desk are helpful, the bulletin boards are packed with interesting information, and there are always people bopping around. For the new in town, there are tons of flyers announcing upcoming events and group meetings. According to director Richard Burns, "The Lesbian and Gay Community Services Center exists to facilitate emerging gay and lesbian empowerment."

This lesbian and gay safe hub came about after some difficult negotiations with the city, which had problems with the idea of selling the former Food and Maritime Trades High School to queers. They did, for $1.5 million, with the city providing a market-rate mortgage. At the time, even leaders in the gay community were skeptical about the deal being closed, but eventually $200,000 was raised and the Center happened.

There is currently a $10-million capital campaign fund underway to support a complete reconstruction and expansion of the Center. There is reason for it: Some 400 gay, lesbian, and AIDS organizations meet here regularly. A newsletter is mailed to over 25,000 households (get one sent to you by calling 620-7310). In 1985, the Center became temporary home to the Harvey Milk High School, a program of the Hetrick-Martin Institute for the Protection of Lesbian and Gay Youth, which has since moved to 401 West Street (between West 10th and Charles Streets). The Center's prime function is to provide affordable meeting space for gay and lesbian organizations—groups like ACT UP, Queer Nation, and GLAAD were born here. Anyone with an idea can reserve a room for a meeting, as long as it's gay, lesbian, or bisexual in nature, and you collect $2 from each head that attends each meeting. And you clean up after using the space.

The Center also provides many health-related and cultural programs. They include Project Connect, a substance abuse prevention and intervention program established in 1988; Youth Enrichment Services (YES), a substance abuse and HIV/AIDS education and prevention program for lesbian and gay youth; CenterBridge, the Center's AIDS bereavement project; Orientation on the Road, the Center's outreach program in the outer boroughs; Center ILGA (International Lesbian and Gay Association), which advocates for gay and lesbian political prisoners around the world; Center Kids, the Center's family project; The Pat Parker and Vito Russo Center Library, a gay and lesbian lending library jointly developed with Publishing Triangle; and the National Museum and Archive of Lesbian and Gay History, the Center's own archive and museum.

The beautiful pornography in the Center's third floor bathroom (Remember when?) was installed by Keith Haring but has since sadly been painted over. The Center's Annual Garden Party, held the Monday of Lesbian and Gay Pride Week each year, is the premier fundraising event, the most popular community celebration, and the launch of Pride Week in New York City. Keep in mind that whenever you have a birthday party, you might ask friends to donate money to the Center rather than buy you another stupid tie. "Stonewall 25" has all its meetings here.

How to join: Fill in the membership form, send a minimum of $25 and hopefully more, and help the Center build a new building. Your membership dollars also get you discounts with businesses and professional services around town (mostly around Chelsea and the Village).

The Center is located at 208 West 13th Street. Drop by and see what's up. Or call—at all times—620-7310.

And for you media buffs: At the Center you can pick up a copy of *Center Voice,* the Lesbian and Gay Community Service Center's monthly newsletter.

GAY BARS AND LESBIAN BARS

SPLASH BAR
50 West 17th Street, 691-0073

Located on Chelsea's "boardwalk," the street where Chelsea Gym and Video Blitz co-exist, this place has one terrific thing going for it—the boys that adorn its brightly-painted walls . . . and now a dark tower floor for dancing "and" . . .

PS: Uncle Charlie's, New York's grand dame of gay bars, lost the war (i.e., closed) to this place.

HENRIETTA HUDSON
438 Hudson Street at Barrow Street, 924-3347

This lesbian bar is small and not especially friendly. However, there's a jukebox (how much Cyndi Lauper can these girls listen to?) that turns this into a networking mainstay for *femme* cruising.

THE WORKS
428 Columbus Avenue, 799-7365

The Guppiest of gay bars, there are some incredible floor shows here—and that's the crowd. Some decent DJs and the best and most original music videos shown each night. Fridays and Saturdays, buy $1 margaritas for strangers. You'll often have to wait to get into their insanely popular Beer Blast Sunday nights!

JULIE'S
204 East 58th Street, 688-1294

A very pretty bar that opens late in the afternoon and caters to women who want to have fun with their peers, and that includes peers of all ages. The management is so laid back that depending on how busy it is, they will close whenever they feel it's necessary—or stay open all night long.

NEW ON THE GAY/MIXED SCENE

Since most clubs are either gay or mixed—or stupid—I will mention a few of my favorites that you should check out once: A usually gay club called **SOUND FACTORY BAR** (460 West 46th Street between Eleventh and Twelfth Avenues) also has "hot house parties" at 1:00 A.M. sharp on Wednesday nights for $10. The crowd really moves, really dances, and is not interested in a scene at the door . . . **DAZZLE** (on 23rd Street and Eleventh Avenue) is unproven, but run by Lee Chappel, and is the decidedly hip club for boys and girls. The lounge is known as Mixed Nuts, you figure it out. Then there's BeavHer* at the bar **DON HILL** (511 Greenwich Street, 334-1390), the nightclub for women on Thursdays—an early night and a fun night for the men who want to come and gawk. Fridays at Don Hill are everything goes with Squeezebox, which my friends insist is the

---

* Gotta love that name!

only "really fabulous" music night. Personally, I think that Don Hill is a pretty bar. And Don seems like a nice guy. There's hardcore punk on Tuesdays, called Kamikaze Escort Service. Uh-huh . . . **EL FLAMINGO** (547 West 21st Street) allows exhibitionists, voyeurs, and our friends to coexist in a "-non-polarized atmosphere, very much like the one in South Beach [Miami]," the promoter swears up and down. Drag, Latin, Muscle, East, West, Boys, Girls, Boys and Girls, West and East, Uptown and Downtown, White, Black, Everyone Else . . . or so he says. . . . Gay and lesbian night at **COLUMBIA UNIVERSITY DANCES** (Earl Hall, 116th Street and Broadway) are titled "SamE BuT DifferenT." Held the third Saturday of each month, admission costs $5. A mix of students, wallflowers, pretty boys, and sexy gals usually shows up. It is sort of a gay Junior Prom. . . . **SYSTEM** (76 East 13th Street) is a club open on weekend nights. It's quite pretty and is steaming up as the hot club on Sunday nights for gay men.

CHELSEA FOR BOYS: GOOD AND BAD (EVERYTHING SEEMS UGLY!)

A few extra gay haunts are here at the end of this chapter, since you have to bring them up or people will wonder, *"What was he thinking?"*

First, **BARACUDA** (275 West 22nd Street, 645-8613), which is the calmest gay bar to be seen—located in Chelsea and featuring a five-hour Happy Time (two for one drinks) and a gimmick every night. Girls, this is your place too. Mixed bars have come to downtown!

Right down the street is the dirty (albeit crowded) day and night spot, **UNICORN** (277 West 22nd Street between Seventh and Eighth Avenues, 924-2921). Unicorn is home to some definitely naughty fun, but it gets boring and—okay, there's a room over to the side for "clean, safe, adult fun," but there are dozens of "cleaner" places in the city, and that's another book. The most boring bar of all time, **ROME** (290 Eighth Avenue, 242-6969), was so hot for a minute in 1995—now it's so unhot it offers "Village Voice Personals Evenings" each Monday. This place is Michelangelo's worst nightmare, but soothe your soul at the gorgeously designed tho' hidden away **ALLEY'S END** (311 West 17th Street, 627-8899), with a nice indoor garden/atrium known to Chelsea men. It's all food here, but the bar is lit just right for fellows on the move!

There's **POP HEAVEN AND HELL** (304 Eighth Avenue between 25th and 26th Streets, 647-8826), which a friend of mine once described (he wasn't gay) as "the gayest place in creation." It seems to be a coffee shop; often, I can only see the waiters' friends hanging out. (They all make lots of noise with each other! A whole new definition of 'affected.') I can only say that each time I walk on by, they have a brand new gimmick advertised in the window. And it isn't pretty. The designer has the shortest attention span I have ever witnessed. And I have witnessed lots.

I have to say that **BIG CUP** (228 Eighth Avenue between 21st and 22nd Streets, 206-0059) is Chelsea's cruisiest spot, since it's run by people who believe a caffeine high is superior to chocolate or booze; the crowd is so young, you want to proof them for curfew limitations! And nearby on 19th Street is **"g"*** (223 West 19th Street, 929-1085), the giant new bar with the juicer in the back. This is the space that merits discussion only because it is the biggest cliché I've ever seen: lots of men standing around—and I mean around—a giant circular bar while a serious bartender serves EIGHT DOLLAR DRINKS and no one dares crack a smile. "To speak is a sin," the Pet Shop Boys once knowingly sang. It's designed so you *have* to be seen when you walk in.

Is it a bar? A giant roller disco? An enlistment center for the army? Who knows? It's **TWIRL** (208 West 23rd Street, 691-7685), and it's in the spot where a dance club annoyed neighbors so much, they enlisted legal help to get rid of it. They failed. Now, they have a place more packed than the last; my feeling: If you ain't got big muscles—you're going to be standing around!

Last, **SERVICE STATION** (137 Eighth Avenue between 16th and 17th Streets, 243-7770), started by demographic-oriented people for men to go get their bodies waxed (yes, waxed, not a typo) and be serviced—by manicurists, masseurs, hairstylists, and psychotherapists (kidding!).

---

* Small "g" like k.d. lang.

ENDING ON A NICE NOTE

It seemed important to end this chapter on an upbeat note: **CAL'S RESTAURANT,** a mainstay hidden away on 55 West 21st Street (929-0740) is a beautiful, albeit not-hot spot with unpretentious cooking and a lunch patronage who swears by it. In a local magazine I saw this: "Calm, spacious Flatiron loft where pretty boys dine." I never knew it to be gay, yet the collection of wait staff—some so good at their job, others slow as molasses—at dinnertime turn Cal's into a boisterous time on the old town.

Appendices and Stuff

◆

21

What Do We Do with the Child?

FAVORITES FOR YOUNG KIDS

"What shall we do with the child?" is a lament that can be happily remedied in this city. Three public playgrounds are perfect for youngsters: **BLEECKER STREET AT HUDSON** has a series of small grounds where village kids play and parents relax on comfy benches (there's a bulletin board with relevant announcements); Central Park's **LEVIN PLAYGROUND,** on Fifth Avenue and East 77th Street, is an Upper East Side kid's dream with swings and dirt mounds; Little Italy's **MULBERRY AND WORTH STREET** corner comes alive mid-Sunday when, city government structures lurking in the background, kids of several nationalities frolic together. It's a shot from a movie. And it is real.

What book on New York would be complete (especially if it says how to have the time of your life) without a few words about **F.A.O. SCHWARTZ** (767 Fifth Avenue, 644-9400), famous for generations and made even more famous when Tom Hanks danced on a large electric piano in the lobby in the 1980s hit film *Big*.

Working model trains, oversized Nintendo games, juggling balls in every imaginable variety, and loads of other toys beg to be pushed, pulled, played with, and best of all . . . learned. This fantasy land recommends that kids of all ages jump into and out of dozens of cars on view in the **GENERAL MOTORS BUILDING** next door to F.A.O. Schwartz at 767 Fifth Avenue.

Get on the mailing lists for readings at various public library branches (243-6876, for downtown Manhattan; 718-478-3042, for Bay Ridge, Brooklyn). The Toy Collection of the **MUSEUM OF THE CITY OF NEW YORK** (103rd Street and Fifth Avenue, 534-1672) is an exceptional stop for all kids. Camp? A summer camp for all ages is at the **92ND STREET "Y"** (415-5600), including several types of camps for extra creative kids.

SIDEBAR SPECIAL **First, A Note from Our Sponsors— A Few Noted Parent Media Helpers for You to Follow**

Of all the city's newspapers, Queens' *Newsday* is the best for kids. *Newsday* offers a daily children's section—a wonder in itself—called "Kidsday." Though I find the tone sometimes patronizing, "Kidsday" does offer quasi-in-depth interviews with and by kids, thoughtful essays about subjects relevant to teens and under, and a colorful and helpful four-pager in the Sunday edition that includes an advice column, children's art activities and other events, and "Kids in the Kitchen" (with try-this-at-home recipes). In the same vein, the *New York Times* presents a column for kids on Friday and one about the movies in the Arts and Leisure section each Sunday. The kids stuff in the *Daily News* is getting better all the time, with "Stuff For Kids" in their expanded Weekend section (Saturday) and a whole bunch of added attractions in the Sunday section on the arts, under the heading "Views You Can Use."

Last impressive word on *Newsday:* You can call the *Newsday* student line at 718-896-6969 and hear excerpts from books (example: *Little Women* category is 3700, so push 3-7-0-0) daily.

Readings and other activities are found in the listings columns of the weeklies, *New York Press* and *Resident,* which publishes several editions in different parts of our city. The *Vil-*

lage Voice has a pullout that delegates a quarter page to kids' stuff. New York Family magazine (744-0309) is a good way to keep informed, and so is Big Apple Parents Paper (533-2277), something I see all the time, expanding and getting bolder in its advice to parents in New York City. Lastly, the $3 Seaport magazine, something that comes out of the South Street Seaport Museum, is chock filled with details about New York history. Also, the kids pages in the various weeklies, Our Town and Manhattan Spirit, are among other good choices for parents.

Kids and parents with "nuthin' to do" can get help on-line, too, at http://www.citysearch.com. See Chapter 22 for more like-minded helpers.

NEW YORK HALL OF SCIENCE
47-01 111th Street, Flushing Meadows, Queens, 718-699-0005; http://www.nyhallsci.org

Devoted to helping children learn about science, this hands-on museum holds over 150 exhibits. Children can learn here from exhibits on rock formation, our daily interaction with microbes, or the anatomy of a hydrogen atom (they have a working 3-D model of one!). Definitely check this one out on a weekend with the kids; it has been newly renovated, and more exhibits have been added to this ever-expanding museum of wonders.

LIBERTY SCIENCE CENTER
Liberty State Park, 251 Phillip Street, Jersey City, New Jersey, 201-200-1000; http://www.lsc.org

So many things to see, so many buttons to press! It makes me wish I were a kid all over again. Liberty Science Center is a true hands-on museum, with both permanent and temporary exhibits and live demonstrations. See a movie about nature in the Kodak Omnimax Theater, with its 8-story domed screen. Your children will never be bored.

NEW YORK UNEARTHED

17 State Street, 748-8628; fax 809-4236

Tucked into a cobbled courtyard this archaeological excavation and museum pieces together New York's past through artifacts found beneath its streets. There is a glass-enclosed laboratory in which real life archaeologists answer questions as they work. The elevator is its main attraction because the video and recording of authentic sounds played in the museum simulates the depths of a dig in progress. Free!

And, because this is a truly distinctive teaching environment, the staff has developed a series of programs, tours, and workshops for school children, special needs groups, and adults. In the spring, there are free Wednesday lunchtime lectures on archaeology for youths (and kids on lunch hour from their Wall Street jobs).

CHILDREN'S MUSEUM OF THE ARTS

Temporarily located at 118 Mercer St., 941-9198; scheduled to open again at 72-78 Spring Street in 1998

A roomy and loft-like space that comes alive with mini-playgrounds whose themes include: "Along The Nile," featuring a 6-foot tall replica of the Temple of Dendur that teaches children about Egyptian culture; "Monet Ball Pond," with brightly colored balls to encourage motor skills; and "Creative Play Area," with arts and crafts for quiet relaxation in a little playhouse on the side. What parent wouldn't love a little of that?

STUDIO MUSEUM

144 West 125th Street, 864-4500; fax 666-5753

The largest museum in Harlem, also the first accredited African-American or Latino fine arts museum in the country, has a monthly puppet-making workshop on Tuesdays and Thursdays (reservations required, since this is big with adults, too). The fee is $25 per (entire) group, maximum thirty people, with whom you create movable toys from cardboard, fasteners, paper, and glue.

The doll-making mini-course is fascinating as well: Artists discuss the history of art and demonstrate construction of sock dolls, nut-head dolls, Zulu dolls, and more. This is hands-on learning for children; fee for the workshop is $18 each, which includes supplies. Museum open Wednesday–Friday, 10:00 A.M.–5:00 P.M.; Saturday–Sunday, 1:00 P.M.–6:00 P.M.; $2 for adults, $1 for children and students.

BROOKLYN CHILDREN'S MUSEUM
145 Brooklyn Avenue, Crown Heights, Brooklyn, 718-735-4400

First you enter through a tunnel, and everything else, too, is kid mania: This place is outfitted with waterwheels, gates, turbines, steam controls, and wow! you can operate it all. A space-age geodesic dome and more than 40,000 authentic ethnological, technological, and historical artifacts; many fun facts for kids of any age.

I once saw an exhibit there called "Home Is Where I Sleep" and it explained to me how much I get done while I sleep. (Also, why I'm afraid of the dark.) It's neat. . . . And lastly, a series of performances: Caribbean and African performers, tap, clog, Irish, swing dancing, and even vaudeville. Call and get a complete schedule; it's easy to get to and a lot more entertaining than the stuffy . . .

CHILDREN'S MUSEUM OF MANHATTAN
212 West 83rd Street, 721-1234

This is the only museum in the city that has a we-want-the-best-for-our-kids committee to decide what kids will like. Young folk seem comfortable here, though, and kids can go on their own. And there's one room (this is neat) where young people produce their own TV shows. In addition, there are fun lectures, special events, and five floors of hands-on exhibitions for kids aged 2 to 10. There is art, storytelling, music, preschool stuff, and even a museum store for kids who *want*. Great half-hour changing program guide for every kid (and guardian) with a short attention span.

But one scheduled lecture, "Learning and the Human Brain," was perplexing; it wasn't for kids. Then again, the museum's "brain section" does include a walk-through, multimedia structure called the Braintarium, with games kids can play *in*. CMOM's outdoor courtyard is brilliant because kids play in the urban treehouse and learn about the four "R's," namely, reduce, reuse, recycle, and rethink. Open Tuesday–Friday, 1:00 P.M.–5:00 P.M.; Saturday–Sunday, 10:00 A.M.–5:00 P.M. Admission $5 for adults and children over 2 (under 2, for free). Seniors, $2.50.

TANNEN'S MAGIC STUDIO
24 West 25th Street, second floor, 929-4500

Magic is learned and you can get it from the sales staff at stores. *This* one-of-a-kind shop is stocked to the rafters with all kinds of magic accessories. Children will love the salesmen-cum-magicians, who demonstrate coin tricks, classic disappearing acts, and lots more. Tannen's is open Monday–Friday, 10:00 A.M.–5:30 P.M.; Saturday 10:00 A.M.–4:00 P.M.

NEW YORK HALL OF SCIENCE/SCIENCE TIPS!
48th Avenue and 111th Street, Flushing Meadows, Queens, 718-699-0005

A public science and technology center, The New York Hall of Science is the city's only hands-on science and technology center featuring 150 exciting exhibits. It simply helps kids learn through push-button exhibits. For example, "Seeing the Light" has children pushing buttons to examine colors through light patterns. Over 100 other hands-on exhibits come equipped with college student/"explainers" who answer questions and offer demonstrations on things like how to make bubbles.

This year's annual event features an exciting combination of three art works that blend art and technology to create kinetic exhibits. And added activity on how light reflects off smooth and rough surfaces was recently introduced for grades 3 to 6. (Writers liked it, too!) This museum never condescends to kids and consistently comes up with new concepts to make sure that future generations care about science and technology. An "electronic bibliography" for computerized browsing is near the first exhibit on quantum theory and atoms. Open Wednesday–Sunday, 10:00 A.M.–5:00 P.M.; $3.50 adults, $2.50 children.

What else? Pull a 400-pound pendulum with nothing but a string and a miniature magnet. Create bubbles big enough to swallow you. Take a peek through a video-microscope to discover a crowded microscopic world living in a single drop of pond water.

CHILDREN'S GARDENING AT NEW YORK BOTANICAL GARDENS
200th Street and Southern Boulevard, Bronx, 718-817-8700

Activities at the Botanical include hands-on gardening for children ages 5 to 16, spring gardening for young kids, and a Garden Volunteers Training Program, all for around $60 for twelve sessions or $30 for six. These courses take place in the children's garden, where kids can reap what they sow and take home plump tomatoes, great-looking flowers, and juicy fruits.

Did you know that the Botanical has a library and Plant Studies Center? Their mission is to promote greater understanding, use, and protection of plants to improve human life. Not only are there books and other printed resources, an herbarium "library" has more than five million plants—pressed, dried, and described for study and preservation. Grounds open Tuesday–Sunday, 10:00 A.M.–6:00 P.M.; cost is $3.50 for adults, $1.25 for children.

FOR KIDS ONLY (FUN AND SKILLS)

DJONIBA DANCE & DRUM CENTRE
37 East 18th Street, 477-3464

"We believe the children are our future and teach them the truth," says Djoniba, owner of the drum/dance/art school that offers ballet, jazz, African dance, and hiphop for kids, ages 3 to 16, and a wide array of karate classes. Financial aid assistance available; classes can also be exchanged for "work at the centre."

ASPHALT GREEN—SUMMER SKILLS CAMP AND MORE
555 East 90th Street, 369-8890

Asphalt Green is a landmark building at East 90th Street that was once an asphalt plant. Now it's an educational, recreational, sports, and environmental youth center. Your kids can enjoy activities galore: basketball, touch football (on the Astro Turf field), and softball; fine arts, graphics, and theater programs; photography classes; and running programs.

"Sea Scouting" on Explorer Ship 272 teaches sailing, rowing, and powerboating. A spokesperson says, "Class lists are enormous. We've got volleyball, and puppet making—anything we could think of." Best thing is, parents know exactly where their offspring are. Healthy addition: a 74,000 square foot sports and fitness complex with a 648,000 gallon pool (16 feet deep!). Wowee!

CENTER 54
103 West 107th Street, 866-5554

Someone once asked, "What do you do with a 14-year-old on Saturday?" Turn the kid on to the excellent Center 54, run by a community-based organization, the Rheedlen Foundation, at a local supervised junior high. The Center has a gym, weight-lifting program, computers, tutoring, and more.

Center 54 has become a haven for kids with nothing to do, no money to spend, and, crucially, no place to congregate. The rest of the city could use a few more places like this.

CHARAS AFTER-SCHOOL PROGRAM
605 East 9th Street, 982-0627

With a little help from the New York State Council on the Arts, this community group invites kids from the Lower East Side to design and transfer murals on to the building Charas is housed in, as well as other structures in the area known as Alphabet City. Youngsters create designs, mix paint, and do the work; and *they are paid* for their pleasure!

This is not some throwaway project, either. Real artists come and show the kids how to do it; the teens and preteens are, says a spokesperson, "being taught a trade." How much do they make? "Depending on how ambitious they are," $25–$35 per session.

HALLOWEEN HOLIDAY

The West Village dresses up Sixth Avenue and the crowds are ferocious—but without monsters. For those who prefer a less hectic atmosphere, THEATER FOR THE NEW CITY (254-1109) has a cool party that's not as tumultuous as its Western counterpart.

Parks, libraries, and societies go all out: first, with All Hallows stories, (they usually frighten adults, but you're not invited anyway) at the ST. AGNES LIBRARY (877-4380); second, a haunted Halloween tour at the RAMBLES IN CENTRAL PARK (722-0210), which is forever haunted, according to legend. Maybe you're into the idea of a "Grave Party" and crave face painting, storytelling, and rock and roll? This can all be found at the BROOKLYN CHILDREN'S MUSEUM (718-735-4400). There are dozens of children disguised as goblins at the **BROOKLYN YWCA** (718-875-1190). (All events are priced $3 and under.)

WHOLE FAMILY OUTINGS

THEATERWORKS, USA
890 Broadway, 647-1100

Billed as "America's foremost theater company for young and family audiences," Theaterworks is in residence at the same theater that takes chances with many great American playwrights, namely the Promenade (Broadway and 76th Street), which took a chance on the great Pulitzer Prize–winning work by Edward Albee, *Three Tall Women,* when no Broadway producer would. Theaterworks puts on seven musicals a year, and offers ten blocks of adult/kid tickets for a reasonable price. Their season's October–March. New shows have included *Where's Waldo?* and *Curious George.*

Their traveling company visits 49 states and has entertained 2.5 million people. Single tickets are $17, children under five are not admitted.

THEATER SPECIALS FOR CHILDREN

TADA! (120 West 28th Street, 627-1732; fax 243-6736; e-mail tada@ziplink.net; http://www.tadatheater.com) produces a variety of kids shows. All have messages for the young set. Schedules change constantly. . . . **ON STAGE CHILDREN** (50 West 97th Street, 666-1716) revives classics in a cute forum. *The Alice In Wonderland Game* is an example of a newfangled classic. . . . **THEATER OF THE OPEN EYE** (270 West 89th Street, 769-4141) offers "innovative interpretations" of classics. Their productions are truly breaths of fresh air. . . . Twenty-four years and still going strong, **LITTLE PEOPLE'S THEATER COMPANY** (39 Grove Street, 765-9540) performs weekend fairy tales for about seven bucks. . . . **DON QUIXOTE EXPERIMENTAL CHILDREN'S THEATER** (250 West 65th

Street, 496-8009) offers cross-cultural entertainment and a bridge of many ethnic gaps. . . . Lastly, the **PAPER BAG PLAYERS** (Kaye Playhouse on 68th Street between Park and Lexington Avenues, 362-0431; fax 650-3919) is the world's best and funniest theater for children, they tell me. And I believe them because the shows are so creative. This year the program—about garbage in the modern age—was called *"Rubbish!" She Cried.* The show combines dance, theater, music, comedy, and audience participation for ages 4 to 9. The last issue of the yearly *Teacher's Guide* featured a playlet about recycling titled *A Neat Trick,* which acted as a classroom companion to *"Rubbish!"* (Ticket inquiries, 772-4448.)

SPECIAL CONCERTS AT LITTLE ORCHESTRA SOCIETY
220 West 42nd Street, eighteenth floor, 704-2100; fax 921-2874

Avery Fisher Hall, Lincoln Center, Sylvia and Danny Kaye Playhouse at Hunter College, Florence Guild Hall: Since 1949, kids have been given special concerts at the big halls in Manhattan—waltzes, polkas, Mozart, Gershwin, piccolos, tubas, and more. Five-show subscriptions to all types, around $50, and single tickets, $15.

THE ART CENTER AT "Y"/FAMILY MUSIK SERIES
Center information: 415-5562; theater: 996-1100

The Arts Center offers classes in fine arts, ceramics, and jewelry making for children, teens, and adults. All age levels, all types imaginations. Also, invites children to see shows like the recent musical adaptation of Dr. Seuss's *Green Eggs & Ham;* costs $60 for a series combination of adult/child or $10 per seat.

HENRY STREET SETTLEMENT SERIES
466 Grand Street, 598-0400

An interesting family series takes place at this racially mixed settlement on the Lower East Side (near several good kid romping grounds). First, parents can take their children to a Chinese

Folk Arts Festival around the Chinese New Year. These evenings of dance and song demonstrate "similarities between many cultures," among them Jewish, black, and Chinese. Then, each year, twenty-three children and a pianist present one story in song (a recent one was about kids who make gift-giving law). This is under the auspices of the Arts For Family Series, and it's crucial for families who groove on tunes.

Settlement's "Peformance Panorama" at 2:00 P.M. on weekends has music, stories, and a $3 fee for adults, $2 for kids.

PUPPETS, INC.

Just to be fair to the little people, why not give 'em an afternoon with a puppet—or a dozen? Get out your crayons, for this is only a small sampling of the companies to look into: Barnes & Noble (information: 633-3500) has books and puppeteers who show at all their major locations. In Central Park, the Swedish Cottage Marionette Theater (information: 998-9093) puts on a special puppet extravaganza—reservations required. . . . Macy's Puppet Theater (information: 695-4400) comes alive at Christmas. . . . A seasonal New York Puppet Festival is held at the Museum of the City of New York (information: 534-1672). Overheard there, "Wow, Mom, that monster's humongous!"

For more information on staying informed, see "Staying Informed" sidebar later in this book.

I WANT TO TELL YOU . . .

The stuffed giants at the American Museum of Natural History (769-5100; fax 769-5006) get very dusty and have to be cleaned by a special Elephant Vacuumer! Yes, a special machine with an electrical lift (extensions too!) takes a whole day to make those elephants remember better! Cal and you can watch as the seven African elephants are cleaned: A Q-tip dipped in alcohol wipes the glass eyes to give them a nice life-like sheen. It's a fun experience for a kid who isn't already into cleaning . . .

CHAPTER

22

Cyber Situation

Note: Here is a good sample of the many places to go on the Internet with a well-equipped browser. (I recommend Netscape Communicator, since Netscape is the original browser company. Use at least a "28.8 speed" and get plug-ins like Java, Real Player, and AudioNet.)

Plug away: For updates on Web sites and links, and new information found for *Native's Guide* users, see our Web site—http://www.yeahwhat ever.com—which promises no advertising whatsoever, except for the occasional mention of my media company, RLM.

PAPERMAG

http://www.papermag.com

This is a funky magazine with a downtown flavor! In 1984, *Paper* magazine started out as a foldout magazine, and ten years later, they launched an interactive *Paper* magazine, spreading eternal and cool hipness around the globe. *Paper* magazine interactive is a great guide for those new to the city, tourists and of course natives! They have always been known to keep their finger on the pulse of what's happening today. It's updated daily, and you can find out information on the latest runway shows in Paris and New York, club life, and "community" and cultural events.

DIGITAL CITY

http://www.digitalcity.com/

"Learn More, Do More"

Pick a city, any city. Digital network of community-based sites that blends useful information with expert opinion and personalized content to help you get more out of your community. Digital City features a series of helpful products within the site: The Digital City WebGuide, a local links service and search engine that combines expert reviews, handy categories, White and Yellow Pages, and a 7-day events calendar to help you turn the Internet into a tool for better living.

LIVE SHOTS

http://romdog.com/bridge/live.html

If you like to live vicariously and virtually, then here's a site for you! This site features live shots from different landmarks of New York, such as the Empire State Building, Rockefeller Center, and Bryant Park. These sites are live—they change every three minutes.

 SIDEWALK

http://newyork.sidewalk.com

Sidewalk is the kind of Web site that stays on your mind all day long. Why? Because they are advertising on everything from billboards to coffee cups, bearing circles much like a bulls-eye bearing letters like "a," "p," "m," and "r." No, this isn't the Mass Transit's way of sending subliminal messages, these are the categories on Sidewalk's Web site: a for arts and music, p for places to go, m for movies, and r for restaurants, and x for sex (kidding). This is a great site, which lets the user customize Sidewalk for the greatest utility. This site digs up the most interesting facts about New York, featuring up-to-the-minute hot spots, activities, and events.

THE INSIDER

http://www.theinsider.com/NYC/index.html

The number of New York City Web sites is growing, and the competition is probably getting a little stiff too, but variety is good. Unlike other New York City Web sites, this one has a daily survival guide for natives and newcomers, such as: 4 Ways to Find a No-Fee Apartment, 7 Tips for Traveling with your Laptop Computer, Alternate Side of the Street Parking Rules, and Coffee Bar Primer. They also provide a daily tip and a link to many Manhattan "e-zines," which for all intents and purposes we'll call http://www.theinsider.com/NYC/links/link3.htm.

ALLNY
http://www.allny.com/

This site is a bit over the edge, since there's almost everything you could ever want here, but why so many categories is a mystery. It teeters between business and personal, as they have resources on internships, personals, and classifieds. Allny also includes a pet's page, so even the family dog won't feel left out; here you'll find listings on pet services, pet stores, and a pet lawyer page; http://www.allny.com/pets.html. And not to worry when Rover is in serious danger, since they have 24-hour emergency service resources on this site.

ECHO
http://www.echonyc.com/cgi-bin/spiral.cgi

Claimed as the virtual salon of New York City, Echo (East Coast Hang Out) was the first virtual community to take hold in New York City. Run by Stacy Horn, she made it the happening place for New York. Before there was a "Silicon Alley," before the World Wide Web, before *Wired*, Echo was home to a small but vibrant collective of people who shared common passions for reading, writing, and conversation.

ZAGAT SURVEY
http://www.pathfinder.com

This is Time Warner's site, a very comprehensive guide on many things as wide-ranging as sports and news. Here you can access the Zagat Survey, a listing of top restaurants from America's Premier Dining Guide. For the New York entries, you can find over a hundred restaurants from A to Z, and they are all worth going to. I'm not endorsing *Zagat's*, but a restaurant is worth a search, surely.

CYBER SITUATION

CITYSEARCH.
http://www.citysearchnyc.com/nyc/

Backed with a powerful search engine, City Search has a top pick of the day, featuring art exhibits, festivals, and many more events/happenings often overlooked. Citysearch also has a "clickable" map of the inner and outer boroughs of New York City. The great thing about this site is it tallies up all the events and locations on its site, so you know how many things you are choosing; that's what I call smart marketing. . . . Also on the same subjects are the brand new site, still untitled at press deadline, on the www.nytimes.com page. . . . MOST NEW YORK by my favorite newspaper called the *Daily News* is at: http://www.mostnewyork.com/MOST/HOME.HTM. It's the *News'* site for sure, but it is most confusing. So many categories and too much silly and/or trivial information on celebrity business. I really don't care about the supermodels, forgive me Vendela. . . . Also www.nypostonline.com, which is pretty groovy if you're interested in New York off-line tidbits. And the latest and greatest hits of the papparazzi, the latest *scandale du jour,* and 'cultcha news' in New York and surrounding burbs.

REAL CITY
http://www.realcitynyc.com

Here's a site that would dispel any word about New Yorkers not being helpful. This site's motto is "New Yorkers helping visitors get the most out of New York." Real City's site asks the visitors questions instead of telling you what or where to go. They do have tips on travel and taxes, and their listing on hotels is the most comprehensive, since you can search for particular hotels.

GOLDEN NYC
http://www.goldennyc.com

Golden is New York City's Downtown Authority, featuring hip and funky happening events for the young. This site is very geared towards nightlife. Golden is so right on the money, as they provide up-to-the-minute cutting-edge scenes like the Lounge bars popping up all over Avenue A. They offer cheap thrills suggestions for $10-a-night outings and how to be AbFab on an entry-level salary. Golden also has a pop-up menu, that gives you a hot or top pick of events/clubs to make you wanna sweat!

NYNOW

http://www.nynow.com/

Looking for love in the wrong places? Well, look no further than **nynow,** as you'll find in their Smitten category a definitive match. This takes away the pain and agony during those lonely Fridays, because New Yorkers who yearn to be in love or those travelers who want to be New Yorkers can find a date, a relationship, or more here. There's more to this site though; it features weather and restaurants. They even have a section called the intelligent shopper, a stop for shoppers who want bargains in a New York minute.

NY DELIVERY

http://www.nydelivery.com

NYdelivery.com is Manhattan's only free full-service on-line ordering system. You don't need to register and you don't need a password! No more hunting for menus. No more incorrect orders. Choose from hundreds of restaurants. Your order will go directly to the restaurant. You will also receive a confirmation of your order to your e-mail address. *Yep—"you have mail."*

WHERE MAGAZINES

http://www.wheremags.com

Published by *Where* magazine, the largest publisher of travel magazines, Where has the basic weather and hotel information, but delivers great textual caveats about the city and its happenings. An interesting feature that no other Web site has is their text search engine; you can look up anything you have an interest in, and it will match it as best as it can. Tip: Be specific and use linking terms like "and" and "or."

RICHNET.ORG

http://richnet.org

Perhaps New York City's "Coolest E-zine" around! Rich Santalesa, the author of this site, was last seen updating Richnet. Its provisions are quite comical as Rich gives credit to his dog Pringles who happened to be doing the coding for his page. Richnet will have contents like "On Our Minds and Modems—Safetylinks Run Amok!" and "Overheard & Seen in NY—666's the Number."

RESIDENT

http://www.resident.com/indexm.html

This site is based on the *Resident* magazine found throughout Manhattan. It presents information on a whole new level, as far as guides are concerned; this site is targeted to residents from the Upper East Side to downtown. There are pieces here for those who like in-depth reports on New York life/local news, as in the redesign of Fifth Avenue and the women's chess championship. With a community-oriented feel, this site is great for those travelers who would like more on great escapes and over-discussed landmarks; site features everything from entertainment/clubs and personals to children's interests.

You may be reading this and thinking, oh great—I don't have a computer. What good is all that? Worries are for naught.

According to experts, the New York Public Library, in the inner as well as the outer borough(s), has committed to providing free Internet access to the public. Each branch includes at least two computers with Internet access—bigger branches have more—with at least one of them reserved for the kiddies.

Having asked an expert, on-line editor John Flinn, I found out more: "What's more," he said, "the public library has reserved considerable funds for providing information electronically."

"NYPL [library] cardholders can dial in [by modem] for access to magazine abstracts and archives once available only on microfilm, and can also electronically check the library stacks to see if a particular book is stocked by a local branch—even whether or not it's currently checked out." (Wish I could do that with my local video store.)

See the Chapter 23 for info on what numbers to dial up.

Of course, New York's fantastic library also maintains an extensive Web site of its own (http://www.nypl.org), with library tips and links to some serious places! But please use the library . . .

Plus: See Rudy Giuliani's second-term Web effort at http://www.ci.nyc.ny.us (New York Mayor's site [NYC-LINK]; e-mail, guiliani@www.ci.nyc.ny.us). The mission of NYC LINK, the official New York City Web site, is to provide the public with quick and easy access to information about New York City agencies, programs, and services. The city's home page also provides, through links to external sites, information about cultural, educational, and recreational activities in this city.

You'll want to see the message from the mayor himself. Take time out to see what's buzzing around in the city chief's head. And if you agree, disagree, or have something to get off your chest, then tell him what you think—send feedback (for e-mail to the mayor, see the above address). Oh yeah, sign the Visitor's Book.

And http://www.users.interport.net/~park/parking.html for parking/cleaning rules/suspension calendar. Talk about a useful site.

And, finally, http://www.ci.nyc.ny.us/html/nypd—for the New York City Police.

Here's back @ you.

CHAPTER 23

Sources to Have and to Hold

In this city we need to know who to call when we want something. Read this list for a quick chuckle and some raised eyebrows.

Most people think of the telephone as a necessary nuisance. In New York City, it's quite an invaluable tool. Also, see Chapter 22, "Cyber Situation," for the Web sites for those on-the-go types who are in need of fast, helpful, no-BS information.

Mailers should remember: the Post Office number is 967-8585. As you start to spend time sending out postcards and getting information back from organizations and establishments, this number will help you to answer all questions about mail and zip codes and make your life a whole lot easier.

LIST OF NATIVE HELPERS

 **ADOPT A BUILDING**
254-5459; fax 533-6490

ALLIANCE OF RESIDENT THEATERS/NEW YORK
989-5257; e-mail artnewyork@aol.com

AMERICAN SOCIETY FOR THE PREVENTION OF CRUELTY TO ANIMALS (ASPCA)
Hotline: 718-272-7200. Headquarters: 876-7700; fax 876-0014; http://www.aspca.org

ARCHITECTURAL LEAGUE
753-1722; fax 486-9173

COPSHOT, A CITIZEN'S GROUP TO STOP COP KILLERS
Hotline: COP-SHOT (267-7468). Director: John Provetto, 718-994-5644; fax 718-994-6927

COURIER FLIGHTS, CHEAPO TRIPS
Now Voyager: 431-1616, fax 334-5243; http://www.nowvoyagertravel.com

Now Voyager has great tips on traveling dirt cheap, but the people who run the place are amazingly rude! If you have never done a courier flight, all you need to know is: Do it! It's cheaper than any Bucket Shop, all you have to forfeit is luggage space, you carry nothing, and you end up traveling to places you only dreamed of going (did anyone say you can go to Hong Kong for only $100?). Endangered due to proposed "tighter restrictions" legislation.

CRIME STOPPERS
Hotline: 557-TIPS

GREENMARKET LOCATOR
477-3220; fax 533-0242

MEDIA NETWORK
501-3841; http://www.medianetwork.org

CITY HELP AND CRISIS/INFORMATION LINES

ALCOHOLICS ANONYMOUS
870-3400; fax 870-3003; http://www.alcoholics-anonymous.org

ARSON HOTLINE
718-694-2109; fax 718-694-2675

BREAST EXAMINATION CENTER OF HARLEM
864-0600; fax 749-1375

AMERICAN CANCER SOCIETY
586-8700; fax 237-3855; http://www.cancer.org
They offer a two-visit mammogram and exam at local hospitals.

CHILD ABUSE HELP LINE
800-422-4453

DENTISTS AFTER-HOURS LINE
679-3966 (strictly recordings of dentist listings)

DOCTORS WHO MAKE HOUSE CALLS
718-745-5900; fax 718-836-1087, 212-971-9692

SIDEBAR SPECIAL **Staying Informed**

What makes New York different from all other cities is that, unlike other places, where you can depend on the kindness of strangers, in this city it is always best to keep abreast of what's going on.

As an author and a media junkie I am going to take you on a tour of the daily newspaper and weekly magazine world, particularly since so many of *them* are endangered beyond belief. As Jefferson remarked sometime a long way back: "Were it left to me to decide whether we should have a government without newspapers, or newspapers without a government, I should not hesitate a moment to choose the latter." Amen.

Since time is of the essence for most information-seekers, choose one day to read up:

ON SUNDAY

In addition to critical pieces and features, the *New York Times'* Arts and Leisure section also provides a guide to current arts in the back. The City section on Sunday is the best place to find out what's really going on, though, I can't tell you how happy I am to see the city getting coverage on things that are not necessarily news—but they're news to the guidebook writers of this town.

The *Times* has an everyday arts section, finally, which means everything I always wanted them to cover, they do. Previously, it was a crap shoot and much of the daily paper was overshadowed by the ahts rather than an idea of what "real people" might be interested in seeing. Drag queens, anyone? (See next sidebar for the results.)

But Sunday—well, these days the arts section and *NYT* magazine have both been covering a great deal of local intriguing theater, film, art openings, and downtown doings. There is hope after all—and that's why the *Times* is keeping up, in fact quite well, more so than ever in its history. So—news junkies can breathe a sigh of relief, and then buy the *Daily News.*

Sunday's *Newsday,* which indeed has the best nightclub section of any newspaper in this lot, and a lot of Sunday's *Daily News,* give some of each section to current occurrences of this town. The *News'* constantly changing Sunday section was a joke last year when it tried to copy a British "spy" technique of the latest escapades of the rich and boring. Now it is a terrific section on trends that are totally off the beaten track—meet friends in the city, get your back fixed quickly, find a place to rest during the day, give up TV for a month, the list goes on.

Once a leisure section, now it's a place to find out what to read on the beach, what the "New New Yorker" newspapers are writing about, what's totally strange in our city, and more of the not-so-same.

Meanwhile there's the not-yet-proven (read unstable) Sunday *New York Post*. For a newspaper that covers so little of the avant-garde (and hardly anything gay, where the dance music scene *takes over*), I was shocked to see a 50-cent rag (25¢ on Sunday) with over a dozen interesting pages of new information I had only seen written about in places like *Paper* mag and on Web sites like http://www.citysearch and available via e-mail as a regular "list-serv" (see Chapter 22 and the sidebar to follow for more details on cyber and "the scoop" on the *Post* . . .).

Wanting desperately to be read by the formerly X generation, this now hip Sunday section—see the essay to follow—has been testing the waters with columns by local "celeb writers" (none of whom have much of a style and all of whom are pretty proud of their knowledge) and people like Sam Pratt, who writes on zip codes—and finds himself discussing where to eat AND where the celebrity sightings are! So, all in all, while the *Post* management could change this into a *National Enquirer* knockoff any day, I say, read this—it's only 50 cents (sometimes 25 cents—hello!) and you can find out the latest bars, know the latest gay happenings, and just locate a place to spend an afternoon sipping iced mochaccino with your feet up! (PS: Untitled Space, the author's favorite hangout,* was discovered in the Sunday *Post*.)

* Untitled, 50 Greene Street, nothing but chairs and coffee—oh, and some paintings. Watch this space!

DAILIES

New York Post, Daily News, and the *Times* seem to cover the same info on the wide releases, but the *Post* often digs a little deeper.

All Friday papers are amazing for culture vultures, and that includes the normally staid *Wall Street Journal* and ("This just in") the newspaper *USA Today.* The *Post* has the New York Women section on Mondays (and often other days), and also an interactive section for cyber buffs on Thursdays. The *Daily News* is trying, really, to cover the arts . . . its coverage of cyber sites is pretty good and appears mostly on Sundays.

The *Times* offers daily reviews, feature articles, and "Critic's Notebooks," hard news that comes out as opinions. You can find out some odd stuff in the *Times* by reading:

- "About New York"—a column on people and places that are quite new or novel in concept.
- "Metro Matters"—a column on problems/challenges specifically related to New Yorkers.
- Metropolitan section's front page index and second page gossip column—new—with some great tidbits you wouldn't expect to read in the *Times.* (Includes "Metropolitan Diary" on Mondays.)
- Style sections on Thursday and Sunday—replete with some items that will make you laugh about new fashions and returning ones. Read Frank DeCaro.

- Frank Rich's Op-Ed column, which is national in scope but always somehow comes back to New York as source material.
- The tiny little ads on the front page, along the lower edge, which are paid for, and are being used as ads for new products or arts and entertainment vehicles. Sometimes they read like a serial!

• The Saturday paper. Because it's not the most read edition, the most offbeat articles that didn't make the cut during the week get placed in this stalwart edition.

For kids, even though it's Queens, remember that of all the city's newspapers, *Newsday* is the best to kids. *Newsday* offers a daily children's section that's a wonder in itself called Kidsday. Though I find the tone sometimes patronizing, "Kidsday" does offer quasi-in-depth interviews with and by kids, thoughtful essays about subjects relevant to teens and under, a colorful and helpful Sunday four-pager that includes an advice column, and "Kids In The Kitchen" (a do-try-this-at-home variety). At press time *Newsday* was being unveiled as "an alternative" paper in Manhattan, but their base of coverage is still Queens.

Newsday has Sunday coverage of events for kids and presents children's arts activities, in the same vein as the *New York Times,* who present a column for kids on Friday and one about the movies in the Arts and Leisure section each Sunday. The kids stuff in the *Daily News* is getting better all the time, with "Stuff For Kids" in their expanded weekend section (Saturday) and a whole bunch of added attractions in the Sunday "Extra" section on the arts, under the heading "Views You Can Use." Yeah, it's not original but it's bulky.

Now . . . here's a look at regularly scheduled papers, magazines and leaflets.

FREE ONES

Every paper wants to be your main informant. Some papers are even free because advertisers pay big money for space. Among the city's best informants are *Manhattan Spirit, Downtown Express, Our Town, Chelsea-Clinton News,* the fat and ever-growing *New York Press,* and my favorite, *Leaflet,* the parks and recreation guide available (free) at the Arsenal in Central Park. As for this list, here are some tips: (1) see the *Ex-*

press magazine's changing on-line columnist, who knows from what he/she speaks; (2) make sure to read the back pages of the *New York Press* for listings of totally unique readings and band gigs; and for its back page, which has ads like Thursday Afternoon Fetish Fest at the Vault, call 255-6758 for information; (3) read the column called "News Of The Weird" (nationally renowned) in *Manhattan Spirit;* and look through the ads. Most of those ads offer discounts to something, and you know that can't be bad! *Spirit* is a good read, every so often they even do Manhattan Pride, a gay section, and they have a phone line (718-518-6363) for brief "Letters To The Editor." Which is what a democracy is about.

I should mention the *Village Voice,* which no one reads but still—it's free. Dance coverage here is unique, and while its listings are usually accurate, there are so many more of them here (though the *New York Press* is coming in a close second) than most; "Savage Love," the column on sex by Dan Savage (find it way in the back in the Classifieds—it's a hoot). See page 326 for more on this.

WEEKLIES AND MONTHLIES

New York magazine has a fantastic theater critic, John Simon, and a section called "Gotham" that attempts to track down the new and exciting, and usually does, though often after-the-fact.

Also, you can find a lot about this city and especially of late—in the back pages of *New York,* which look much nicer since it's "re-do" of 1996.

For the first time since *Cue* magazine was purchased by Mr. Rupert Murdoch, and brought into the pages of *New York* magazine in the 1980s, they have included pull-outs on interesting facts about the city, and all the new coffee shops/restaurants/clubs/etc., complete with pics.

However, I was surprised to see the new editrix go for "I

had to break a man," attributed to officer Justin Volpe of the NYPD, on the cover of *New York* on September 22, 1997. But, while it seemed as though Volpe was an admitted brutalizer, the story said otherwise. It was a shoddy turn—very sensational.

There is lot of input on readings and small museums. Why, thankfully, since the third edition of *Native's Guide,* this small museum thing has gotten so popular that even Channel 13 (PBS in New York) has put their conservative funding toward a show called "City Arts" on some of the lesser-known institutions.

A free magazine that comes up in many of my recent conversations is called *Museums New York,* put out by a for-profit company that wants to bring back some upscale "momentum" to New York's magazine world. (Available on newsstands for $3.95, but free at institutions.)

MNY, which continues to grow and has by some accounts made some m-ney in its three-year existence, is being given out at galleries, museums large and small, and cultural/tourist institutions around town; the only problem with such a magazine is that the ads are hard to tell from the articles, which can be deceiving. Since many museums have stores handy now, the advertising for such gift shops seem to be *MNY*'s most obvious source of income. However, articles on the American Craft Museum's *Making of a Quilt* series are worthwhile reading—and the quilt preparation technique from last summer was most assuredly more intriguing than any *New York Times* museum coverage of late. Its coverage of classes for kids and their guardians is especially timely, useful, and again the type of reporting not found in daily papers.

The aforementioned *Village Voice* is not that exciting, either, but it certainly has opinions up the wazoo, "Sexerati" Dan Savage ("Savage Love"), and a few good media columnists, not to mention Michael Musto, the club and gossip maven, who has a way with the word on every known subject. Its listings are now free—and are worthy adversaries to the myriad of freebies that list subjects. The *Voice*'s trusty critics have, in many cases, been toiling in their respective areas for years, while the nearest competitor, *New York Press* picks people who seem to just write what they know from hoisting references (i.e., what they've read)—they show off that habit incessantly.

The *New York Observer,* an uptown-based sheet on everything you can think of, really digs deep into what is going on in the New York media scene: Columnists, especially a terrific media columnist; regular feature writers; events listings; once-held-back movie critic Andrew Sarris, formerly of the *Village Voice;* an Arts Digest; this thing called "Transom" that is supposed to be all gossip; the "8-Day Week" which is an events listing that constantly cracks me up; and even a shopping columnist! What more could you need? Okay, there's even a Real Estate section that makes sense and a front-of-the-book NEW YORK SCENE that has fun stories on ultimately weird N.Y.C.-ites.

Also, Rex Reed, still a good and often frisky columnist, although a little dainty; a court columnist; oh, the list goes on; and they even sponsor 777-ARTS, a phone number with information on what's happening at Phillips and other cool galleries/auction houses around town. This service is free!

The slightly-discussed, culty *Paper* magazine, which has a very small reader base, is fun to read, contains listings that are helpful, and is stylish in its approach. Recently it has become very journal oriented and seems to be pop-ish in its approach to music (it will also cover people in jail, quasi-famous people, people with an "ax" to grind, people like the Fugees, and of all things, an article called, "John Tesh Is Cool").

No. The reason to buy *Paper* ("the grooviest magazine with the coolest readers" went one recent masthead) is for one specific page—okay, *and* the "Cyber Surfer" columnist, who's a funny read and a really active-in-the-community dude*—by

* That is the one and only time the necessary word "dude" will be used in this series—promise.

Christina Mulhke called "A to Z" which actually lists the coolest, weirdest, and wisest things to do. It has no rhyme or reason and anyone who reads this book, or their brothers, knows it's the most "righteous" way to think. Plus, the "Staying Alive" column on people with AIDS and AIDS-related topics is missing these days but a helpful note to the editors that it is informative and noncondescending. (CyberSurfer is Jason, who publishes the new *Silicon Alley Reporter:* for a free issue of *SAR,* the New York cyber trend magazine, e-mail csurfer@interport.net.)

Also: Newish magazines like *Manhattan File, Resident* magazines, and *Flatiron,* one of the lamest reads but best-looking magazines around, and the refurbished pages of *Interview . . .* But you must read the dailies regularly or forget the above, filled with inside jokes and New York-ese.

Flatiron, meanwhile, is the only free regularly-scheduled magazine (not *New York Press,* which is a newspaper whose columnists' ideas are a flock-of-seagulls to me) meant for the neighborhood but geared for the city (Flatiron is the area known as Ladies Mile, around Chelsea), and has loads of necessary info! A snobby magazine put out by nonjournalists is *Manhattan User's Guide*—subscription only—for whitebread New Yorkers. It tells you about what shirt to wear with what scarf. Lotsa lists of things if you're into that. . . .

City Family, also free and very ambitious, available at libraries and social service agencies—and hospitals—gives all sorts of tips for people who really "live" this city: the immigrant population. It gives hints on gardening, lawyer's advice, and info on celebs, inoculation, even good cooking. Also produced in Spanish.

One thing: *Paper,* which I mentioned above, used to be at one time the only thing that really cared about New York—that is until now. (*Paper* does a better job of covering the city on the Web—see the "Cyber Situation.") Today there's *Time Out New York,* which is hipper than thou (or at least portends as such).

TONY is the magazine that costs you two bucks and tells you, in list form, all the things to do in New York . . . using tiny descriptive paragraphs. A bargain, indeed. Not to mention the fact it, like *Native's Guide,* doesn't take the city too seriously. Bravo! (Their little sidebars on all things New York really work. I learned from these folks, for instance, how much you get beaned for a typical misdemeanor.)

That having been said, I've not been a fan of its many books, with its funny and unneeded British witticisms, but yet again I've always been a fan of *TOL.* That's the British acclaimed version and *TONY*'s brother. Therefore I was amazed to see the people at *TONY* take the British idea of "lists are everything" and turn it into a magazine that is so well researched, I may have to say, "It's been really okay" that they steal ideas and entries from me every few weeks. But they printed my letter on the club scene, after all! (What'd I say? That "24 million people annually could not have possibly been in the clubs," as a reporter reported—see "La Club" for proof of how few night spots there truly are.)

Meanwhile, *Time Out New York* tries to inform and may be our best bet yet. Check out the "Byte Me" column for the latest and strangest in a newly essential cyber world.

Time Out (self-dubbed "OBSESSIVE GUIDE TO IMPULSIVE ENTERTAINMENT") taught me about The Law recently in a spectacular CRIME issue:

• Spitting is a violation of city ordinance, maximum penalty 10 days, $50.
• Speeding is a moving violation, maximum penalty $55.
• Unhygenic use of fountains and pools is an unclassified misdemeanor, maximum penalty 90 days, $1,000.
• Running over a traffic cone is a moving violation, maximum penalty $65.
• Making graffiti is a Class A misdemeanor, maximum penalty 1 year, $1,000.

SOURCES TO HAVE AND TO HOLD

- Public lewdness is an unclassified misdemeanor, maximum penalty 90 days, $250.
- Trespassing is an unclassified misdemeanor, maximum penalty 90 days, $250.

Then lastly, *Project X*. Not a weekly, not a monthly, not even a quarterly, I like to think of this as the magazine for know-it-alls, put out by same. Recently put out of business, then somehow brought back from the dead, this self-proclaimed "Inside Guide to N.Y.C.'s Trendiest Scene!" is a good source for dirt on clubs, and where to buy fur-lined pumps. Which we need.

Lots of fashion spreads and club-life gossip. Published occasionally and available at bookstores, some independent bookstores, some friendly business. However, it is being produced by people who refuse to offer their phone number, so none of my information about *Project X* can be proven accurate. (Read the periodical for fun, not for details! And of course read the magazine *Details* for the latest dish on New York City fashion, even if they say downtown is dead . . .) *Project X* was once supported by club maven Peter Gatien, who went to jail for his alleged illegal drug-related activities and stopped supporting magazines. Perhaps he needed money.

INFORMATION PLEASE

Take notes and be sure to write down on (and keep) scraps of paper so you can go back to the places you happen upon, even when you're going to the laundry and see a brand new restaurant.

More than any other city, if you're not informed, you are left out. Here are some last tips for keeping active and informed

First, use your phone. When you read about a company, establishment, or organization that appeals to you, call them up and get on their mailing list. Or fax them! Almost everyone uses mailers now. It's a cheap way to advertise and it's effective.

You may receive more bushels of mail, but many of it will be helpful because you'll get information on events that are often unadvertised and always worthwhile. (If the topic but not the place intrigues you, call anyway: They are likely to swap with groups of similar interest, and you'll end up with tons of good stuff.)

Then, use your mailbox. Use it for membership details as well. When you give even a small parcel of cash to a group or society that sponsors a museum, a private home, or a monument, you are sent regular bits of information relevant to that organization. Sort of a modern pen-pal's club! You will also feel good about supporting a worthy and usually tax-deductible venture. (Oh, and let's not forget about those incredible parties they throw! GMHC, the AIDS health charitable group, throws fêtes on a Chelsea rooftop herb garden.)

And use your newsstand. Your best bet for information is the neighborhood kiosk. In this sidebar I have only touched upon a few of the many magazines and newspapers available to you in New York. Go to the newsstand at the end of the month to buy new editions or magazines that relate to the city, such as *Cover Arts New York,* a bizarre paper with some good writers; or *Cups,* a magazine about the all important coffee culture. ("Coffee is my religion," said the author.)

But it's not just New York! There are other topics in those magazines: Try *Garbage* for information on those recyclable items in your blue bags, or *Prison Life,* with stories that pertain to those in jail. Read. Magazines and papers act as guides to what's happening culturally, and as mirrors to society. You are never more informed than when you know what people are into. Knowledge is indeed power.

Finally, use your notebook. Don't have one? Buy a spiral. Make a list of subjects, then make calls to find out about them. Technology can help. If you have a PC or a Mac, you can get a program (there are a few on the market) that acts as a "virtual

Rolodex" where you record phone numbers on pages of notes for you to refer to when you need them. Typically, when you call someone you will at first talk to the company's answering machine. They will call back. It's too simple.

All of this information-gathering takes very little time, and it's well worth it.

After you get into the habit of collecting data on the things that interest you, never again will you have to answer the oddly worded question: Hey, how do I become better informed?

MEDIA FOR JUNKIES

In a nutshell the newspapers that come out daily in the city are not at their peak. Something has happened that has forced them to dumb-down, the *New York Times* and the *Wall Street Journal* included. Often I find more intelligent reporting in (gasp!) the *USA Today* Life section. And it has to do with what Cliff Robertson said in *Charly* about thirty years ago, when the formerly mentally challenged young man was surgically turned into a genius, and as he stood before scientists, he called for a "brave new war . . . [to find] a TV in every room," something about TV becoming the most important thing on earth to the world at large.

Now that I've gotten that off my chest, where's the INFORMATION? This is the answer: The informed news-seeker is in a bad state today.

In order to report on the state of the papers, first I must point out a shocking factoid: The *New York Post* is now the only paper in so-termed Silicon Alley to contain a daily coverage of the bigtime neighborhood that now employs 105,771 little people in New York City and surrounding suburbs, and has annual revenues of $5.7 billion. Cyberspace may not yet be crucial in the city, but to businesses, it's the only new way to go.

In addition to cyber and general media coverage, this erstwhile junky (sic) paper (I'm talking junk = crap) is the only thing "of record" to care about the companies making this industry the fastest-growing sector of New York industry.

The *New York Times'* much-bally-hyped modernity seems a little uncalled for, but then again, so is all this talk about color. The *Times* gets color, and we're supposed to stop the presses. The only change I noticed besides a front page that looked like an *Arizona Gazette* is that each section (there are now umpteen) is smaller. An arts section a day. Gee, *USA Today* started that in 1983. The *Washington Post* runs a much better written and much more beloved Style section every day. But the *Times,* well, they waited until late 1997 to start something up to make the Arts something special.

And then there's all this TV coverage. I love TV. I try to watch A & E's "Law & Order" three times a day like most do. But don't you find it odd that TV coverage is the only thing that has truly improved in all these papers? It's a pull-out in the gorgeous Sunday *Post*—it, too, is in color (red and black ink)—and it's a page-plus in the *Wall Street Journal* (kid you not). The *Journal* covers CNBC and the dirty shows on Cinemax.

TV is the big issue. This medium is humongous news. *Entertainment Weekly* now spends almost a quarter of its pages idolizing the TV devil.

It is, however, too often a cover story in the newly launched Arts section in the *Times.* It creeps too much into the news section on most days in *USA Today.* It's the *Daily News'* and *USA Today*'s raisons d'être. (How shocking—the front page: what happened on "ER," to Ellen, with Kirstie, after Murphy!)

Not the least of which, the newspaper that makes media into news, the *New York Observer,* runs a not-ironically titled "NYTV" page, devised with strenuous alacrity. Yet I want to slap them for having TV on the brain.

In a single leap of faith, their editor-at-large wrote a several page summary of new TV shows while the "Edgy Enthusiast" talked endlessly about "new" "Melrose Place," as the real estate column got itself into a tizzy over Michael "Spin City" J. Fox's new pad?

This sophisticated media-wet paper surely held a staff meeting, where editors said let's can the piece on Leonard Stern and do a soggy TV season exposé.

Speaking of the *Times*—and I was—the new format simply makes it difficult to find anything. And this is where I end my rant. The *Times,* that bastion of color papers (explanation of sarcasm: *New York Newsday* was in color in 1985) now contains a section called Arts. In my house, we call that the Daily Newsletter . . . It is a smattering of stories and a listing of the "ratings overnight" of TV shows. Outside of you people, who the hell gives a rat's behind about "overnights" besides our own?

The arts section is about money. Since it's come down to just covering money, I vote for the paper covering all the money, all the time. If I get a choice, me, a media-watcher, a guy who writes for a living and runs a media relations company, a man who's read "Dear Ann" in the *Daily News* since boyhood . . . go for the *Post.* At least they're honest about what they are going after.

The *Daily News* wants to be a "paper for the people," so they hired scribe Pete Hamill, who fired the crappy gossip columns. Soon after, the *DN* fired Hamill, and they went hogwire back to gossip. (*DN* covers the media industry, but only the local stars.) Still, the *News* calls itself New York's serious tabloid.

The *Post,* a paper mocked for sport, has the wherewithall to call themselves gossipy and more. Read this recent *Post* ad—brackets mine: GOSSIP [seven pages], SPORTS [eight pages], BUSINESS [loads o' pages, countless, at times so much you think it never ends], SAVVY SHOPPER [restaurants, 'bahgains,' listings, places-to-go, shops and boutiques and malls and department stores], COMMENTARY [true, right of Goldwater but I have my own opinions], CROSSWORD [British and Noo

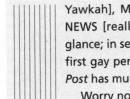

Yawkah], MOVIES [and a theater column] and my favorite, NEWS [really—covering New York and the world, not at a glance; in serious detail: They "broke" the story of the world's first gay perfume!]. I rest the case. By the way, the *New York Post* has multiple pages of TV listings.

Worry not, brave new world.

CONSUMER INFORMATION

BETTER BUSINESS BUREAU
533-6200; fax 477-4912; http://www.newyork.bbb.org

DEPARTMENT OF CONSUMER AFFAIRS
487-4444

GAS EMERGENCY FROM CON EDISON
Hotline: 683-8830

DOMESTIC ABUSE AWARENESS
Hotline: 353-1755

EMERGENCY TREATMENT
Bellevue Hospital, 462 First Avenue at East 27th Street, 562-4347

EMPIRE STATE BUILDING
736-3100; fax 967-6167
It's tall and it's there for the viewing, seven days from 9:30 A.M. to midnight, when it closes, even if your date hasn't shown.

GAMBLERS ANONYMOUS
Hotline: 903-4400

GAY AND LESBIAN ANTI-VIOLENCE PROJECT NUMBER
807-0197; fax 807-1044; http://www.avp.org

SOURCES TO HAVE AND TO HOLD

HEAT COMPLAINTS FROM LANDLORD NEGLECT

960-4800 (strictly recordings)

MAIL FRAUD

330-3844; fax 330-2720

Processing System 201-324-3720

MAIL II

800-725-2161

Twenty-four-hour computerized information. (An ironic service is available at 800-STAMP24: Stamps-by-mail, with a fee. Yes, it takes a while.)

MAPS AND GUIDES NEW YORK

Citybooks, 669-8245, near City Hall

This is the place you can go to buy the Green Book which lists all the city "players." GB is a helpful resource for New York "buffs."

NEW YORK CITY RENT GUIDELINES BOARD

http://www.nycrgb.com

This Web site is geared to help tenants who can't find answers to housing questions. Just some basic, good information available at this site: Tenant/Landlord Guide, Division of Housing "Fact Sheets," lead paint rules and forms, and stabilization lease renewal rules.

PARKS DEPARTMENT

800-201-PARK; fax 718-383-7477

PHONE BOOKS LITTLE PAGES

The Little Pages is handy and free, offering system numbers from Wall Street quotes to sex lines, and other info about the new Ma Bell. Call your Bell Atlantic representative to get one. Get to know the Blue Pages in the back of the Bell Atlantic Yellow Pages: coupons, events, seat locations at concert halls and stadia, basic city information, maps, and Consumer Affairs Information Guide, in addition to pages produced by *Crain's* New York business magazine.

POLICE

374-5000

For precinct location and general information. In an emergency, dial 911.

POTHOLES

POT-HOLE (768-4653); fax 442-7347

Pot Holes, Sidewalk Holes, Broken Street Lamps, Trash Problems, Waste Not (Recycling), and City/State Agencies That Can Help You Out

788-4636

This is a number for repairs and other agencies. It's an automated system that really works. A host of other agencies are listed, and listen carefully for instructions on how to get to them and their incredibly helpful information.

STREETLIGHTS

(Department Of Transportation) 442-7070; fax 442-7127

 **TAXI COMPLAINTS**

212-NYC-TAXI

See sidebar on Taxi "Do's."

U.S. GOVERNMENT HANDY INFORMATION

Free booklets from the Feds (26 Federal Plaza) from 8:00 A.M. to 4:00 P.M. ALSO: You can hear about the President's day (202-456-1414; it's the press office of the President; in town press information!). OR find out the status of a certain bill by dialing 202-225-1772. What a government!

Visitors Bureau (New York City Conventions and Visitors Bureau) Well, not the GREATEST resource for NEW information, but they have literature and facts on things like the Circle Line and are now putting out a brochure for city dwellers each season. I like their fact sheet on what Big Apple means. See them at 2 Columbus Circle, call 397-8222, or visit the Web site: http://www.nycvisit.com. NYCCVB is about to be changed by Mayor Giuliani, who is instating a new "regime."

SOURCES TO HAVE AND TO HOLD

The Grand Central Partnership provides tourist information in several languages. Write to them at 6 East 43rd Street, Suite 2100, New York, NY 10017; call 818-1777, or fax to 661-4384.

 LIBRARY REFERENCE SERVICE
340-0849

I once was asked a trivia question I simply couldn't find the answer to; the reference librarians helped. Note: If you call to ask a question on your homework, they won't help you. Always make up some excuse for why you want to know the answer.

LOTTO (TO FIND OUT WINNING NUMBERS)
976-2020

NARCOTICS ANONYMOUS
Hotline: 929-6262

DRUG AND ALCOHOL HELPLINE
800-821-4357; fax 801-272-9857

PLANT HOTLINE
718-817-8705; fax 718-220-6504; http://www.nybcl.org

POISON CONTROL LINE
764-7667; fax 447-8223

RUNAWAY HOTLINE
800-231-6946 (recordings for counselors)

SEX CRIMES
267-7273; fax 374-6762

SKY REPORTER
769-5917 (recorded information line)

TAX HELP
718-935-6736 (recorded information line)

TENANT PROBLEMS FROM THE DEPARTMENT OF HOUSING
960-4800

VICTIMS SERVICES
577-7777

VOTING
886-3800; fax 886-3820

GAY AND LESBIAN HELP LINES

BI-WAYS NEW YORK
459-4784 (recorded information line)
Monthly social events for the bisexual community. An important group that can help people, both young and old, who are confused about their sexuality.

LESBIAN AND GAY SWITCHBOARD OF NEW YORK
777-1800
Usually called the Switchboard, and a very important part of gay life in New York and many other American cities. Rap, referral, information: free and confidential and TTY-equipped for hearing-impaired users. Open noon to midnight. They will answer the most bizarre questions ("What do I do if I meet someone and they say, 'Be back here at twelve-thirty,' and I'm not sure if they meant A.M. or P.M.?"), and those about serious issues, such as alcoholism, disease, and safer sex. Since 1972, the board has been a friendly listener. Everyone who answers is a volunteer, so be nice.

Good to note: When you call the switchboard after hours you will be able to access an information retrieval system. Push 1 for info on volunteering; 2 for making a donation; 3 for AIDS information; 4 for emergency and suicide hotlines you can call; 5 for bars and clubs; 7 for comments and feedback or to suggest ideas or changes for them to make on this line. This is a new service set up during those moments when no volunteers can make it to the switchboard.

Also good to note: the Samaritans Suicide emergency phone number is 673-3000.

AIDS-RELATED HELP

AIDS HOTLINE

from Gay Men's Health Crisis (GMHC): 807-6655

AIDS HOTLINE

from New York City Health Department: 447-8200; fax 788-4749

PEOPLE WITH AIDS COALITION

Hotline: 800-828-3280

The PWA Coalition is a clearinghouse for information useful to people with AIDS. The hotline is staffed entirely by people living with AIDS (PWAs). The PWA Coalition helps PWAs with urgent needs: food, clothing, shelter, and medicine. The coalition also runs an underground drug-buying program to provide drugs to people who need them.
AIDS Coalition to Unleash Power (ACT UP)
966-4873

AIDS DISCRIMINATION PROJECT

961-8624; fax 961-4126; 800-523-AIDS; 961-8999 (TTD)

The AIDS Discrimination Division of the New York City Human Rights Commission handles complaints from people who have suffered discrimination in housing, employment, and public accommodations. Call to file a complaint about discrimination.

GAY MEN'S HEALTH CRISIS (GMHC) HOTLINE

807-6655; fax 367-1220; 645-7470 TTD; http://www.gmhc.org

For information about safe sex and HIV-related health services, and for one-time, walk-in AIDS counseling services. GMHC's hours are 10:30 A.M. to 9 P.M., Monday through Friday at 119 West 24th Street, sixth floor.

GAY AND LESBIAN NUMBERS

MAYOR'S OFFICE FOR THE LESBIAN AND GAY COMMUNITY
788-9600
This is the place to call when you have a serious complaint about a city-sponsored group or politician. This line is getting busier all the time.

NEW YORK CITY GAY AND LESBIAN ANTI-VIOLENCE PROJECT RAPE INTERVENTION HOTLINE
807-0197; fax 807-1044; http://www.avp.org
The Anti-Violence Project offers services to assist lesbians who have been raped, including a 24-hour intervention hotline; in-person counseling; support groups; advocacy with police, legal, medical, and social service agencies; court monitoring; assistance with crime victim compensation; and information and referrals.

GAY AND LESBIAN SWITCHBOARD OF NEW YORK
777-1800
The Switchboard is the number for New York, just like all other major cities and some towns, when you want to find out what's up: rap, referral, information, free, confidential, TTY-equipped. They answer all, from the bizarre to the banal.

NEW YORK STATE HIV COUNSELING HOT LINE
800-872-2777
Hours are Monday–Friday, 2:00 P.M.–8:00 P.M.; Saturday–Sunday 10:00 A.M.– 6 P.M.

ASSOCIATION OF GAY SQUARE DANCE CLUBS
800-835-6462

EXTRAS!

BASEBALL

Mets: 718-507-8499; fax 718-507-6395 (ticket office)

Yankees: 718-293-6000; fax 718-293-4841; http://www.yankees.com

THEATER, CINEMA, ETC:

New number for TKTS half-, third-, and quarter-off tickets for theater (47th & Broadway): 768-1818 New York City On Stage

Also in Spanish. Their Web site is http://www.tdf.org. For theater and performance events; dance and music; on TKTS booth; for Newsday events line in the borough; and for pure family entertainment information.

Also, for free movie information, 777-FILM (good way to find out about movie-oriented events and to buy tix by phone) or try them online at http://www.moviephone.com.

Lastly, you should know that all arts exhibition and auction information can be found at 777-ARTS, sponsored by the New York Observer.

DIAL A DINNER

779-1222; fax 653-1585

Delivers meals from ritzy restaurants; steep but classy. Hint: A 20 percent surcharge is added—so drivers are well-paid and tip is included.

Food information including connection to restaurants (and most crucially, who delivers in your area), try http://www.nycdelivery.com, our favorite site.

CELLULAR/HELP IF YOU'RE STUCK IN TRAFFIC

*JAM

For most mobile customers. Note: Also note that for now Bell Atlantic Mobile's "Info-assist"—information—offers movie listings. Just ask!

 **POLLUTION CHECK**
643-2111

VINE

For toll-free information on who in your neighborhood is a killer or sex offender. Call VINE or "victim information and notification, every day," at 888-VINE-4. Who is that masked man at your nabe's bodega? Well go and find out. Anonymous. So much so, that it has touch tones for help.

MORE EXTRAS!

- 24-hour Ice: 397-1500
- Passport Services: 800-987-2826 (they do the dirty work)
- Notary Public—24-hours-a-day: 473-8480
- Delivery of Milk/Donuts/Papers/Bread: 987-3001 (on "doorstep" by sun-up)
- "Free Time": 545-8900 (call for events under $5)

Easy Address Chart of Manhattan

To figure out cross-streets in Manhattan: Take the number of the address, cancel the last figure, divide by 2 and *add* or *subtract* the number below.

Avenue A: Add 3
Avenue B: Add 3
Avenue C: Add 3
Avenue D: Add 3
First Avenue: Add 3
Second Avenue: Add 3
Third Avenue: Add 10
Fourth Avenue: Add 4
Fifth Avenue
    Up to #200: Add 13
    Up to #400: Add 16
    Up to #775 to #1286: Cancel the last figure and subtract 18
    Up to #1500: Add 45
    Above #1800: Add 20
Sixth Avenue: Subtract 12
Seventh Avenue
    Up to #1800: Add 12
    Above #1800: Add 20

Eighth Avenue: Add 10
Ninth Avenue: Add 13
Tenth Avenue: Add 14
Amsterdam Avenue: Add 60
Audubon Avenue: Add 165
Broadway (#750 is 8th Street)
    From #756 to #846: Subtract 29
    From #847 to #953: Subtract 25
    Above #953: Subtract 31
Columbus Avenue: Add 60
Convent Avenue: Add 127
Central Park West: Divide address by 10 and add 60
Edgecombe Avenue: Add 134
Fort Washington Avenue: Add 158
Lenox Avenue: Add 110
Lexington Avenue: Add 22
Madison Avenue: Add 100
Manhattan Avenue: Add 100
Park Avenue: Add 35
Pleasant Avenue: Add 101
Riverside Drive to 165th Street: Divide address by 10 and add 72
Nicholas Avenue: Add 110
Wadsworth Avenue: Add 173
West End Avenue: Add 60
York Avenue: Add 4

SIDEBAR SPECIAL Taxi "Do's"

Say you're riding in this crazy town, in a taxi, where the driver has no seat belts and has no memory of Diana's dying. . . . Say that driver is too bizzzzy to pay attention to the road. After all, this is a town with road signs as nutty as its inhabitants, true, with monikers for stores like AND BOB'S YOUR UNCLE or DOES YOUR MOTHER KNOW? It's a place you want to see as you whiz by it, for sure.

Now there's a way to fight back against those drivers . Here's how. Our newish taxi commish, Diane McGrath-McKechnie, she of the "do something" dual-name commissioners, is the woman who followed Christopher Lynn, our first openly gay taxi commissioner (yes, there's a first for everything, kids). Lynn, whom I have never met, was a little bit over the top when he passed a law during his reign that made drivers DRESS better. No, Chris. SPEAK better. DRIVE better. *Not* DRESS better.

So Diane decides this is the time to remind people to wear seat belts and I couldn't agree more—those barricades are hard, man, and if you careen into them you will break a nose or two! So she got Joe Torre and Judd Hirsch and Joan—you know, those famous old geezers—to record a greeting when you open a cab door. This is very difficult to hear sometimes, particularly when you are sure Joan will never shut up (they also talk when the cab stops at your destination). According to a rumor, "Could you imagine listening to that all day?" is what the taxi drivers hear more often than the Hirsch/Rivers recordings.

Diane says this is good. *I* say escape the obnoxious one you hate by using the code. And we are going to give it to you in easy clip-out style, so you can carry this around with you everywhere.

Here is how it works. Each taxi is given a three numbers/one letter license number. This is now much easier to see because Diane has told taxi owners they must place these on the back seat in white easy-to-read characters, along with the brand new number she has introduced for calling in: (212) NYCTAXI.

Now, thanks to this ONE letter discovery, Diane pins the letters with those inimitable voices, so you can choose to hear, or not to hear, a voice when you enter the cab.

The chart, as released by commissioner Diane:

g, p, or y   Eartha Kitt ("Cat Thing")
a or h   Placido Domingo ("The One Tenor")

EASY ADDRESS CHART OF MANHATTAN

b or j	Joan Rivers ("No, Don't Talk")
c or k	Ruth Westheimer ("Dr. Ruth")
d or l	Jackie Mason ("Oy Gevalt in Triplicate")
e or m	Joe Torre ("Mr. Torre, Where Have You Gone")
f, n, or w	Judd Hirsch ("Yeah, Hm")

Note: The city was reportedly changing some voices as we went to press; Dan Ingram, legendary jock for WCBS-FM, was being installed as seatbelt-warner—whom he replaced, nobody knew. The city is also considering dropping the "backseat celebrity" program.

However, there's *more*. Diane has also finagled funding for a new, brighter, more organized system for reporting (see above) a horrible or just plain yucky cabbie. You call (212) NYC-TAXI and tell them your sad tale. After you fill out a *faxed* complaint and send it in, they then set up an appointment for you to complain at a time that is convenient for you! And then the driver will be fined, or worse, if he is truly guilty.

Not that I want to start trouble, mind you, but I think the driver who said, "Oh really, now," when I pointed out his lack of seatbelts, deserved the hot water my NYCTAXI call got him. Oh, and while I'm on about taxis, make careful note about this three-numbers-and-one-letter notion. How great for lazy people: If you (like me) are totally disinterested in small scraps of paper ("receipts"), then just jot down the four digits on a notepad and if you forget something in the cab, call it in! That, my friends, is another fine gift from Diane: tracking down lost stuff.

END NOTE: The property clerk's office is 374-5084. Of course, the Taxi and Limousine Commission also recommends you report the stolen or lost property to the police precinct closest to the place the driver dropped you off. And hope your cabbie has good eyesight, eh?

General Index

Abigail Adams Smith Museum, 76
Abraham & Strauss (A&S) Plaza, 53
Accurate Distribution Network, 47
Acme's, 264
Adventure on a Shoestring, 90
Afghanistan Kebab House, 138
African-American Wax Museum, 101–2
Aggie's, 121
Algonquin Hotel, 32–33, 88, 119
Alice Austen House, 35
Alice Tully Hall, 210
All-Craft Community Center, 217
Alley's End, 293
Alliance for Downtown New York, 90
Alliance Française/French Institute, 207
Alternative Museum, 68
American Academy of Arts and Letters, 102
American Golf Reservation Line, 29
American Museum of Natural History, 32, 75–76, 204, 310
American Museum of the Moving Image, 203–4
American Place Theater, 239–40

American Restaurant, 130
Amsterdam Avenue Festival, 175–76
Amsterdam Billiard Club, 114
Andrade Shoe Repair, 175
Angelo & Maxies, 137
Annie Moores Bar & Restaurant, 265–66
Ansonia Democrats, 103–4
Anthology Film Archive, 197–98
Apollo Theater, 88, 99
arcades, 270
Arizona, 153, 206
Arlene's Grocery, 245
Art Bar, 270
Art Deco Society of New York, 88
Art Directors Club, 83, 103
Arthur's Tavern, 270
Artificial Intelligence, 232
Artmakers, 95–96
Art of Shaving, 25
Arts at St. Ann's, 210, 240
Asian-American Festival Day, 176
Asian-American Film Festival, 204
Asian-American Video Festival, 204
Asphalt Green, 40, 306

Brotherhood Synagogue, 56
Brownstone Billiards, 114
Bryant Park, 213
Bubble Lounge, The, 271–72
Burger King, 165
Butterfly Zone, 194

Cacique Jamaican Restaurant, 143–44
Café Aubette, 136–37
Café Croissant, 124
Café des Artistes, 33
Café Inferno, 280
Café Luxembourg, 167
Café Nicole, 139
Cajun, 128
Cal's Restaurant, 295
Cammareri Brothers, 202
Canal Street, 45
Cancer Care Shop, 55
Captain Tilly Memorial Park, 106
Carbon, 255
Caribe, 131
Carmine's, 130
Carnegie Hall, 88, 211
Carnegie Mansion, 211
carousels, 106–7
Castle Clinton, 98
Catch-N-Fetch Tournament, 104
Cathedral of St. John the Divine, 56–57
Cedar Hill, 113
Cedar Tavern, 264
cemeteries, 100
Center 54, 306–7
Center for Adult Learning at the 92nd
    Street YM-YWHA, 88
Center for the Study of the Presidency,
    77–78
Central Synagogue, 65
Century 21, 50
Chambers Street, 51
Chaos, 255, 275
Charas After-School Program, 307
Charas Teatro La Terrazza, 206–7
Chase Manhattan, 233

Cheetah, 255
Chelsea Billiards, 115
Chelsea Hotel, 96–97
Chelsea Piers, 23
Chelsea Piers Bowling Alley, 115
Chelsea Piers Studios, 184
Cherry Lane Theater, 134
chess, 268
Chez 2020, 165
Chicago B.L.U.E.S., 281
children's activities, 71, 179–80, 194,
    195, 211, 243, 299–310
Children's Museum of Manhattan, 303–4
Children's Museum of the Arts, 302
China Club, 254
China Institute, 78
Chinatown History Museum, 77
Chinese Museum, 270
Christine's Polish-American Restaurant,
    142
Christmas festivities, 82, 211
Chumley's, 264, 272
Church of St. Ann, 196, 210, 240
Church of the Transfiguration, 62
Church Street, 52
Cinema Village, 197
Cine-Vision, 204
Circa, 256
Circular Track, 111
City Hall Park Sculptures, 93
Claremont Riding Academy, 23, 108
Classic Stage Company (CSC) Repertory,
    225–26
Clayton Hats, 54–55
Clearview, 29
Cleo's Ninth Avenue Saloon, 272
Cloisters, The, 57
clothing history, 103
Clubhouse, 259
Coffee Shop, 171
Cola's, 128
Colden Center for Performing Arts, 211
Columbia University, 206, 207
Columbia University Dances, 252–53, 293

Neighborhood Index

NEIGHBORHOOD INDEX

NEIGHBORHOOD INDEX